Obscenity and Public Morality

Harry M. Clor

Obscenity
and Public Morality

CENSORSHIP IN A LIBERAL SOCIETY

The University of Chicago Press

Chicago & London

ISBN: 0-226-11033-8 (Clothbound): 0-226-11034-6 (Paperbound)

Library of Congress Catalog Card Number: 69–16772

The University of Chicago Press, Chicago 60637
The University of Chicago Press, Ltd., London

To my mother
and to the memory of my father

Contents

Foreword

One of the unanticipated consequences of the sexual revolution of our times has been to make the Supreme Court our national authority on obscenity. During recent terms the distinguished members of the court have incongruously been attending private showings of allegedly dirty movies and reading lurid paperbacks to see whether the legal tests of obscenity have been met in proceedings against them. By all accounts the justices have not relished these assignments. During the oral argument on the *Fanny Hill* case in 1965, Chief Justice Earl Warren wondered aloud whether the Supreme Court was going to be "the final censor to read all the prurient material in the country." Only Justice Hugo Black has escaped this chore. Since he believes the First Amendment is an absolute protection for printed material and oral expression, all prosecutions for obscenity are unconstitutional and so the content of the particular book or movie is irrelevant.

In its first decade of struggle with the obscenity issue, the Court succeeded in creating what C. Peter Magrath has called a "disaster area." But in justification of the Court, it can be argued that the justices have simply been reflecting the ambivalence of our society in this field. The foundation opinion in *Roth* v. *United States* (1957) faced both ways. In support of traditional morality, the Court held that obscenity was a socially worthless type of communication not protected by the First Amendment. At the same time, the Court removed the dead hand of the nineteenth-century Anthony Comstocks and established that contemporary community standards must be given effect in legal definitions of obscenity.

The contemporary standards of an increasing component in American communities now approve stage and film nudity, four-letter words have moved from the walls of public rest rooms into novels and college newspapers, and filthy speech has become an inseparable part of social and political protest movements. A two hundred-year-old pornographic classic, *Fanny Hill,* circulates freely for the first time because of its "redeeming social importance." In an odd turnabout, books are published in the United States which are banned as obscene in France.

The current flooding of bookstalls, mails, and movie theaters with pornography or near-pornography raises major problems of public policy. Opinion polls show that a considerable majority of the American people want censorship of some kind to be applied against obscenity. The Supreme Court, stung by publicist Ralph Ginzburg's open attribution of the new sexual freedom to the Court's permissive decisions, in 1966 reversed its field and upheld Ginzburg's conviction for pandering, though the magazine involved was relatively innocuous by judicial obscenity tests. In its most recent decisions the court appears to take still a different tack; it will leave adults free to read what they like, but guarantee to the states the right to protect children from obscenity and to control the open and offensive flaunting of obscene materials in public.

The intellectual debate over the handling of obscenity has been a highly unequal combat. Since Freud, the public image of the censor has been that of an insecure person with a twisted mind, bent on imposing his emotional hangups upon his less inhibited fellows. Censorship is big brotherism and 1984. It is equated with dictatorships, temporal and spiritual.

On the other hand, the libertarian case for freedom of expression has been given classic statements of eloquence and force. In an open society there is an obvious appeal in the argument that people must be trusted to decide for themselves what they shall read or see. Low motives join high motives in the defense of freedom, as the self-interest of publishers and other enterprisers guarantees that restraints on free circulation will be continually challenged.

It is the unique value of this volume that it seeks to redress the balance by challenging both the extreme libertarians and the extreme moralists. Clor disputes the moral relativism of Morris Ernst and William O. Douglas. The traditional libertarian position on obscenity he finds to be a complex combination of truths, partial truths, fallacies, and unexamined assumptions. At the same time he has no sympathy for the bluenoses. What he does believe is that an intelligent and restrained use of controls can promote public standards of civility essential to our democracy, and he makes a thoughtful case for such restraints.

Is it true, Clor asks, that the state has no business seeking to enforce moral norms? Then what about the laws against prostitution, adultery, polygamy, incest, euthanasia, gambling, or cruelty to animals? Is it true that there is no evidence that exposure to obscenity affects character? Clor cites some reasons for believing that obscenity is sometimes a factor in the promotion of anti-social behavior and can have subtle and long-term influence contributing to the debasement of moral standards.

For Clor the crucial question is, What is the public interest in moral norms and moral character, and how is that interest best served? He argues that society must have some model of approved and unapproved, esteemed and unesteemed sexual behavior reflecting ends other than those of individual satisfaction. He believes that censorship can promote public morality by preventing or reducing the most corrupt influences, and by holding up an authoritative standard for the guidance of opinions and judgment.

As a moderate democrat, Clor does not "delight" in censorship, and he is concerned to demonstrate that the restrained controls he advocates would not interfere with the essential freedom of artistic expression. He uses quotations from various works which might be considered pornographic to demonstrate how broadly he would interpret artistic freedom.

One of the most valuable features of the book is Clor's liberation of obscenity from a sex-centered obsession. The essence of obscenity for him consists in making public that which is private, intruding on intimate physical processes and acts or physical-emotional states and thereby degrading the human dimensions of life to a subhuman or merely physical level. Not only the sex organs and sexual activities, but all bodily functions, physical suffering, and death, can be treated obscenely. In Europe, motion-picture censorship has been concerned more with violence than with sex. Televised scenes of the suffering of wounded soldiers in Vietnam, or television interviews which seek to exploit the reactions of victims of emotional crises for public titillation—these are obscenities as gross as any sexual display.

Clor grants that obscenity is ineradicable and serves as an escape mechanism which may do some good. But he finds it on balance to be an evil of sufficient magnitude to require the attention of organized society. He believes it is possible to draft standards which will provide a barrier against the worst intrusions upon intimacies of the body and against some of the most obscene portrayals of sex, brute violence, and death.

A character in Christopher Morley's *Thunder on the Left* encountered a friend, whom he knew to be an unbeliever, reading the Bible. When he was asked why, the friend replied: "To strengthen my unbelief." Clor recognizes that in our libertarian culture the policies he advocates are unlikely to be adopted in the near future, but he does hope that moderate men—both liberals and conservatives—may be brought to agreement on certain principles and values. The experience of grappling with the thoughtful case for a modest assumption of moral responsibility by the state which he presents should be healthy for both libertarian and moralist.

C. HERMAN PRITCHETT

Obscenity
and Public Morality

Introduction
The Law and the Obscene

In recent decades the controversy over censorship of obscenity in the United States has been growing in intensity. It has assumed the proportions of a major social issue—a stubborn one which persists in spite of the efforts of so many judges, authors, and scholars to resolve it.

Why, it may be asked, in an age which is not lacking in life-and-death issues, must we continue to wrestle with this one? It can hardly be said that this is our most urgent public problem; it does not compare in urgency with international crises, for example, or dilemmas of urban strife, racial justice, or increasing lawlessness. Yet this problem of obscenity manifests a strange capacity to arouse the interest, engage the passions, and enlist the efforts of large numbers of Americans. Perhaps this pervasive interest in the subject reflects an awareness (however unarticulated) that vital questions, ultimate questions, lie beneath the surface of what may appear to be a relatively insignificant matter of social policy.

Laws against obscenity are often made or defended in the name of public morality; such laws seem to presuppose that there is such a thing as public morality that has some claim on the individual member of the community. Obscenity has some connection with sex, and sex is related to love—an intimate private concern of all men. Thus the problem of obscenity involves far-reaching questions about the nature of our community—the ends and values by which this civil society should be governed—and it also involves the most delicate and personal interests of individual human beings. The way of life of "We, the People" and the relation between the public and private spheres of life are, ultimately, at issue. The obscenity problem points to considerations of purpose and principle which transcend that specific problem and which are quite relevant to many of the issues confronting liberal democracy. But appropriate inquiry does not begin with these large matters; it begins with more immediate concerns.

Since the early 1950's there have been several congressional committee investigations and numerous state legislative investigations concerning the circulation of obscene and pornographic publications in this country. In Congress, the Gathings, Kefauver, and Granahan committees[1] have conducted extensive hearings and issued reports embodying, among others, the following conclusions:

1. The circulation of salacious "literature" (including books, magazines, and motion pictures) is widespread and is steadily increasing.

2. The commercial exploitation of obscenity has become a highly efficient large-scale business enterprise realizing enormous profits.

3. Most of this material is designed wholly to arouse sexual passions, and much of it appeals to extreme, abnormal, or perverted interests in sex and violence.

4. In their form and in their contents, these materials violate and depreciate fundamental standards of morality or decency.

In 1956 the Kefauver Committee estimated that the gross mail order traffic in pornography amounted to $500 million a year.[2] In 1959 the Granahan Committee of the House published estimates that the total commerce in salacious materials may have reached one billion dollars a year. This committee heard informed testimony on the extensive operations of the "pornography business," it methods of advertising, its channels of distribution, and its acquisition and use of mailing lists—some of these compiled from the responses of children to apparently innocent advertisements. The committee's report quotes a statement of the Postal Inspection Service that "possibly one million children this year will receive solicitations for lewd and obscene materials through the mails."[3] The congressmen found that obscenity, in addition to its accessibility through the mails, is often easily obtainable, by both children and adults, at local newsstands, magazine shops, and bookstores. Subsequent investigations have continued to report these and similar findings.

The Granahan Report distinguishes between two types of obscenity. It states:

> This material takes various forms. It may be classified into two categories, however, according to the degree of vulgarity. The first is "hard-core pornography." This consists of depictions of acts of sexual intercourse or perversion. . . .
>
> The second type is described as "borderline material." It includes photographs, movies, slides, magazines and articles which, though unfit for the undiscriminating mind of a child, cannot meet the definition of "hard-core pornography."
>
> The great problem existing today is with the borderline material. More specifically, it concerns the flood of so-called girly magazines and others of the for-men-only variety that have been introduced on the news-stands which are devoted exclusively to erotic writings and portraying the human body in wholly nude or semi-nude form.[4]

The committee was also particularly concerned about the increasing publication and consumption of prurient fiction, largely in paperback editions, dwelling upon themes of sex, brutality, and perversion, and embodying "false moral standards."[5] A large part of the hearings consisted of testimony concerning the values and attitudes prevailing in these writings, in both the "pornographic" and "borderline" varieties. The 1959 report includes, and endorses, this statement by the Board for Christian Social Action of the American Lutheran Church:

> FALSE VIEWS ABOUND. The attitudes toward life, its pleasures and satisfactions, and the standards of conduct espoused in materials of this type reflect a moral depravity. . . . Among others, one may observe the following thoughts recurring with considerable frequency: . . . A flippant, lewd, low tone toward marital fidelity, glorifying infidelity, makes light of marriage vows and monogamy. Sexual immorality is "smart," not sinful; sex is for personal enjoyment, a biological necessity like eating and drinking, a woman is a means for gaining sexual satisfaction, . . . and love is a passion which cannot be restrained, only surrendered to. Homosexuality is enticingly presented; . . . Basic moral principles of honesty, integrity, forthrightness, purity, respect for authority, and regard for person, life, property and good name are ridiculed as antiquated relics of a simple era. Male and fe-

male characteristics are exaggerated and exploited in photographs and sketches toward the end of stimulating lust. The body, not human personality, is made dominant, even idolized. . . .[6]

To summarize, numerous congressional and state legislative inquiries have found that publications embodying these views of life and appealing to these interests abound in our society. Such materials enjoy an expanding market and encounter multitudes of willing customers.

What is the political and social significance of these findings, and what, if anything, should the law undertake to do about them? Does the prevalence of such interests and attitudes constitute a social problem and one to which secular government should address itself? Should the law endeavor to control written and visual materials which "stimulate lust," teach that "sex is for personal enjoyment," and "ridicule basic moral principles"?

On these matters Americans are deeply, and often passionately, divided. Those who tend to be "moralists" and those who tend to be "libertarians" differ in their perception of facts, in their definition of terms, and in their interpretation of basic principles: political, ethical, and legal. The moralists are inclined to see the committees' findings as further evidence of moral laxity, if not moral decay, in our society and to insist upon action by both public and private agencies to defend fundamental values. The libertarians are inclined to regard the newer and more permissive attitudes toward sex as change rather than decay and to welcome some of this change, or all of it, as a liberation from oppressive constraints. Furthermore, the libertarian insists that it is no function of government to defend the moral standards of the day or to control the reading and the artistic tastes of free citizens. The moralist replies that liberty is not license, and that government can certainly act against material which promotes juvenile delinquency, crime, and perversion. The libertarian asserts that there is no evidence demonstrating a causal connection between exposure to obscenity and antisocial conduct and that, furthermore, the term "obscenity" has never been adequately defined and may even be meaningless. The moralist answers that the teachings of common sense and the practical experiences of mankind must not be abandoned in these matters, and he accuses the libertarians of having abandoned them. The libertarian replies that it is on just such terms that great literature has been suppressed in the past, and he accuses the moralist of insensitivity to both literature and constitutional guarantees.

Much of this controversy centers on the meaning and proper interpretation of the First Amendment command that "Congress shall make no law abridging the freedom of speech or of the press." The libertarian and the moralist approach the First Amendment with differing and sometimes sharply conflicting presuppositions. The libertarian will often bring to his interpretation of the First Amendment a conception (implicit or explicit) of the primacy of individual freedom in our constitutional and political order. Hence he is inclined to regard censorship, in any form, as more destructive or more dangerous than anything that could result from obscenity. According to Morris Ernst, "every attempt to throttle free expression, no matter what the source or purported reason, must be stubbornly and aggressively resisted in the courts. A default to the censor is not individual surrender, it is a betrayal of the public."[7] The American Civil Liberties Union asserts that "since any kind of censorship infringes the principle of that constitutionally guaranteed freedom of the press which protects the free exchange of ideas in our country, it is imperative that the American people be warned of the danger in which their freedom stands."[8] The moralist will sometimes deny the doctrine of the primacy of freedom;[9] more often he will insist that it is not just the freedom to do as we please, but "rational freedom" or "true freedom" which is the end of our political order. Monsignor Thomas J. Fitzgerald says: "Human freedoms are essentially subordinated to good morals and are safeguarded by them. A campaign for good morals is not an infringement upon freedom, but a preparation for the enjoyment of true freedom."[10] The moralist is likely to approach the First Amendment with the presupposition that some forms of censorship are simply inherent in the exigencies of social life. Finally, to his opponent's concept of individual liberty, the moralist will frequently oppose the concept of majority rule—the majority wants laws to suppress obscenity.*

Thus, the debate over the nature and effects of obscenity and

---

* Terrence J. Murphy says: "The majoritarians are alarmed at what appears to them to be an anti-democratic strain in the libertarian position, namely, the unwillingness to allow the citizenry at large to use the legislative process to cope with a social problem." Terrence J. Murphy, *Censorship: Government and Obscenity,* pp. 120–21. Murphy's defense of censorship is based, in part, on the "majoritarian" argument.

the meaning of constitutional guarantees is part of a larger conflict of views involving opposing political and social philosophies. Moralists and libertarians disagree about the proper functions of government in a free society and, perhaps, about the nature of civil society itself—the relative social importance of moral standards, freedom of expression, and literature.

This is, of course, a simplified version of the controversy. There are differences of opinion among moralists and among libertarians; there are different degrees of libertarianism and moralism, and there are viewpoints which transcend this distinction altogether. Nonetheless, the issues raised in the conflict between these two schools of opinion are fundamental ones, confronting the citizen, the courts, and the scholar with the most perplexing questions concerning the relation of law to morality in a liberal society.

This problem—the proper posture of the law toward moral standards and opinions—is the central and underlying issue in the obscenity debate. The problem has, essentially, two dimensions: a philosophic or theoretical dimension and a practical or operational dimension. On the level of political and social theory, what is required is reflection on the ends of liberal democracy and the needs of civil society. On the level of practice the problem consists largely in arriving at definitions of the obscene which will be appropriate to the circumstances of present-day American society.

Why, and to what extent, should the liberal state concern itself with the moral life of citizens, with sex, and with literature? A distinguished British scholar, Norman St. John-Stevas, provides one kind of answer. He says:

> Undoubtedly, the general moral standards and social customs prevailing in a community are frequently formed or changed by the influence of books. . . . The law, however, cannot be invoked to protect prevailing moral standards, first because this assumes a finality which such standards do not possess, since much of what passes for morality is merely convention, and secondly, because in a country such as England there is no common agreement on ultimate moral attitudes.[11]

St. John-Stevas draws from these premises the conclusion that the only legitimate aim of censorship is to control that kind of literature which has "a directly undesirable effect on sexual *behavior*" (italics mine).

This argument and its conclusion pose a number of questions concerning the nature of law, morality, and society. If "much of what passes for morality is merely convention," does the political community have an interest in the protection of that aspect of morality which is not merely conventional? Can there be a public interest in the maintenance of certain ethical norms which may not have the finality of absolutes or about which there may not be complete agreement among all citizens? Should legislation and adjudication take their bearings from whatever moral attitudes may happen to exist in society, or do they have an educative role to play in the formation of "common agreement" on moral standards? If, contrary to the views of St. John-Stevas, the political community is legitimately interested, not only in the conduct of its members, but also in the values and opinions which affect conduct, then what is the nature and what are the limits of this public interest? What can or should be done by law in a liberal democracy to influence moral opinion or to control those influences (such as literature and other media of communication) which shape opinion? These and similar issues, constituting the philosophic side of the obscenity problem, require examination of human society in its relation to thought and art.*

But the task facing the citizen, the courts, and the scholar is not simply that of reflection upon first principles and purposes. How should we define the obscene and apply the definition under the circumstances of present-day American society—a society in which values concerning sex and allied subjects are diverse, changing, and often uncertain? It is a commonplace of the debate over obscenity that socially approved conceptions of what is decent and indecent have undergone continuous change in the twentieth century. In large sections of our community the norms governing what language should or should not be used, by whom, and where, and what parts of the body may or may not be exposed in public have been steadily liberalized. Indeed, among some groups in our society there appears to be taking place a "sexual revolution" which, according to its proponents, promises the destruction of all traditional morality in a new era of beneficent sexual freedom. Yet practically all citizens still maintain some conception of limits im-

---

* Thus the problem of censorship provides one of the most revealing vantage points from which to look at human society—that of its relation to things of the mind.

posed by decency and some notion of a boundary line beyond which lies the impermissible. Those involved in a realistic effort to determine what is obscene in our time and place must strive to take adequate account of what is changing and what is unchanging in the beliefs of our people. They must strive to distinguish ephemeral fashion from fundamental conviction. And, beyond this, they must probe beneath opinion for whatever knowledge may be attainable about the nature of the obscene and its effect upon human beings.

When these tasks reach the courts they are compounded by the need to arrive at tests of obscenity which can be the basis for reasonable legal prohibition and fair criminal procedure. This requires a certain degree of precision in determining the scope, the contents, and the objects of the legal term "obscenity." Should it encompass only material dealing with sex? What kind of materials dealing with sex (or other subjects) are obscene? Should obscenity be defined with a view to the protection of children, or certain categories of adults, or all citizens? In the definition and identification of obscenity what cognizance should be taken of literary values and literary purpose?

In the most practical terms, defining the obscene means drawing a line somewhere between obviously good literature, on one extreme, and obviously pornographic trash, on the other. Practically all Americans would probably agree that *Hamlet* is great literature and is not obscene, though in Act III Ophelia says: "You are keen, my Lord, you are keen" and Hamlet replies: " 'Twill cost you a groaning to take off mine edge."[12] A large majority of Americans would probably agree that the novelette *Passion-Psycho,* dwelling in graphic detail upon brutality, sodomy, sadism, and necrophilia, is pornographic trash.[13] The vast majority of literature (including books, plays, magazines, motion pictures) falls between these two extremes. Most literary critics would regard D. H. Lawrence's *Lady Chatterley's Lover* as a serious and good, if not great, work. But there would be some argument among citizens concerning its obscenity. The literary status of Henry Miller's *Tropic of Cancer* would be somewhat more debatable among critics, and its language more offensive to many persons. As we move along the spectrum from works which can lay some claim to artistic distinction and seriousness of purpose toward unmitigated pornography, a number of intermediate forms will appear. In the novels of Mickey Spillane sex and brutality are intertwined and often identified,[14] but this is done without the use of four-letter words and without the kind, or degree, of physical detail which is found in pornography. Next, we find sensationalist or exposé "newspapers," such as the *National Enquirer* and the *National Insider* which have often featured accounts of violent deaths, adultery, rape, incest, matricide, and extreme physical disfigurement, and which appeal generally to an interest in the horrible, the morbid, and the scatological. The men's adventure magazines and "girly" magazines appeal more directly to lewd sensuality without claiming to report the "news."[15] Finally, next door to hard-core pornography itself are pocket book novels which describe, with vivid specificity, acts of sexual intercourse, torture, masochism, and lesbianism. Some motion pictures intended for the general public might belong in this category, though these have usually avoided any *direct* portrayal of sexual perversion.*

Where should the law draw the line? Should the line be drawn as close as possible to hard-core pornography in order to insure that no serious work of literature will ever come within the cognizance of the law? Or, should we be willing to tolerate some restraints on some forms of serious literature in order to restrain sensuality and indecency which falls short of the worst extremes?

If the circulation of obscenity is to be controlled at all, then drawing the line requires the exercise of political judgment in the broadest and deepest sense. It is always hard to determine "in what the law is to bid restraint and punishment, and in what things persuasion only is to work."[16] It is never an easy matter to acquire, and to combine, theoretical and practical wisdom, to reason rightly about fundamental principles, *and* to apply principles with intelligent sensitivity to changing circumstances. But the problem of obscenity and its regulation confronts the decision maker with more than the ordinary difficulties of judgment. This is due, in large part, to the variety and complexity of the factors which must be taken account of: moral, legal, social, psychological, and literary. Serious judgment on this subject requires consideration of

---

* This statement may not continue to be true for very long. Since it was first written, this author has noted the movement of the "exploitation film" toward more and more direct portrayal, not only of sexual acts, but of the perversions as well.

the status of the moral values involved, the meaning of the First Amendment, the nature and effects of obscenity, the views prevailing among our citizens, and the nature and role of literary values. And these things must be considered in the light of long-range ends *and* present circumstances. In the making of such judgments there are many ways to err, to disagree, and to fall short of certitude. Hence, obscenity remains the subject of unresolved controversy among us.

The purpose of the study undertaken here is threefold:

1. To analyze and evaluate the arguments, evidence, and assumptions employed in the controversy over obscenity.

2. To explore the difficulties encountered by the law when it seeks to define public morality in a constitutional democracy and in a society characterized by pluralism and rapid change.

3. To contribute to the development of a philosophy of censorship and a test of obscenity which will do justice to the public interests in morality, in free expression, and in literature.

The first two chapters will be devoted primarily to examination of the contemporary legal situation and the legal developments which have contributed to it. Chapter 3 will evaluate libertarian approaches to the First Amendment and the doctrines from which they derive. Subsequent chapters will explore the major considerations which must be involved in any valid endeavor to resolve the problem which obscenity poses for liberal society. These chapters embody an argument or rationale for a certain kind of legal control, but their author is as much concerned with making clear what are the underlying issues as he is with making a case for legal control. Thus the analysis begins with the problems of the law and of judges, and it moves from these to broader considerations of public policy and political theory. Ultimately, the dilemmas of the law cannot be adequately understood or resolved without inquiry which at least enters the domain of moral and social philosophy.

Since this study cannot aim at an exhaustive coverage of the whole field, it may be desirable to call attention here to two important aspects of the subject which will not be treated—or not treated adequately. Much of the present controversy centers on problems of administrative and judicial procedure in obscenity cases. Should the Post Office have any censorship powers, and, if so, under what restraints? Should obscenity be controlled by means of criminal or civil proceedings? Do injuctions against the sale of a book constitute "prior restraint"? Another subject of debate is the activities of private groups, such as the Citizens for Decent Literature and the National Office for Decent Literature, which seek to rid their local newsstands and bookstores of obscenity. What should be the public's attitude toward the aims of these associations and the means used to achieve them? What kind of cooperation between these groups and public officials (such as the police) constitutes unlawful coercion of a bookseller? Though these matters are of great importance, they will be treated here as tangential to the discussion of the prior issues: What should the political community censor? Why should the political community censor? Since these questions are primary, clarity about them is a precondition for clarity about procedures and about the censorship activities of private citizens.

1

The Evolution of Standards and the *Roth* Case

In 1957 the Supreme Court decided the case of *Roth* v. *United States* and laid down what is, up to the present time, the leading decision in this field.[1] In the *Roth* case and its companion case, *Alberts* v. *California,* the Court was directly confronted, for the first time in this century, with the question of the constitutionality of federal and state obscenity statutes under the First Amendment.[2]

The majority opinion, delivered by Justice Brennan, declared that "obscenity is not within the area of constitutionally protected speech or press," but that "sex and obscenity are not synonymous. Obscene material is material which deals with sex in a manner appealing to prurient interest."[3] Justice Brennan analyzed the history and aims of the First Amendment in order to determine what is included and what is not included therein. Then, having established the broad scope and limits of its protection, he turned his attention to the legal test of obscenity. In the effort to insure a legal test of obscenity which would meet the requirements of the First Amendment, he definitely rejected the old "*Hicklin* rule" and sanctioned the "modern rule" which had been evolving in federal and state courts for several decades.

Thus two fundamental considerations underlie the reasoning and the conclusions in *Roth:* what the First Amendment protects, and what is legally obscene. Some discussion of the history of these two considerations is a necessary prelude to the analysis of *Roth.*

The federal obscenity statute was first upheld, though indirectly and without interpretation, in *Ex parte Jackson* in 1878.[4] In *United States* v. *Bennett* (1879) a court of appeals briefly considered the question of First Amendment freedoms in their bearing upon the application of the statute.[5] Judge Blatchford sanctioned the following distinction, made by the trial judge, between what is and what is not freedom of speech and press:

> All men in this country, so far as this statute is concerned, have a right to their opinions. . . . Freelovers and freethinkers have a right to their views, and they may express them and they may publish them; but they cannot publish them in connection with obscene matter and then send that matter through the mails. . . . Freedom of the press does not include freedom to use the mails for the purpose of distributing obscene literature.[6]

In *United States* v. *Harmon* (1891) the statute was directly and vigorously assailed on First Amendment grounds.[7] The district court, though resting on *Ex parte Jackson,* found it necessary to meet and to discuss at some length an objection "urged with such force and vigor of reasoning."[8] Judge Phillips argued that, while our institutions afford the widest latitude to expression of opinions "touching questions of social ethics, political and domestic economy and the like," it is for the lawmaking power to draw the boundary line between liberty and license.[9] The court, however, did not locate this "boundary line," except to indicate that the newspaper in question had crossed it.

These two cases may stand here as typical of the early approach to the freedom of expression considerations. The courts uphold the liberty of public discussion and debate on political, social, and ethical questions, but this does not include the liberty to publish obscene materials. Expressions of opinion shall be free. Obscenity either is not expression of opinion or it is a licentious form of expression. This distinction was presumed to be clear enough to enable courts to make it on a case-by-case basis without reference to more explicit principles.

The other side of the problem—the legal definition of obscenity—requires a more extended treatment here. The term received its first authoritative definition in *United States* v. *Bennett.* In the trial court Bennett's counsel had asked for a charge to jury that words and sentences which are used in "good faith" and not "wantonly, or for the purpose of exciting lust or disgust" are not within the law, and that the true character of these words must be determined by "the whole scope of the essay and the purposes and intent of the author."[10] The trial judge had directed the jury to apply the *Hicklin* test laid down by Lord Chief Justice Cockburn in 1868: "I think the test of obscenity is this, whether the tendency of the matter charged as obscenity is to deprave and corrupt those whose minds are open to such immoral influences, and into whose hands a publication of this sort may fall."[11]

Chief Justice Cockburn did not define "deprave and corrupt," but he did remark that the pamphlet in question in the *Hicklin* case "would suggest to the minds of the young of either sex or even to persons of more advanced years, thoughts of a most impure and libidinous character."[12] Judge Blatchford ruled that it is the suggestion of "impure and libidinous thoughts" which "depraves and corrupts," and that, on the basis of this test, the trial judge was correct in rejecting as irrelevant the defendant's contentions concerning his good faith and the general character of the whole book. He also held that a work is within the statute if it excites impure thoughts and desires "in the young and inexperienced."[13]

Thus the *Hicklin* rule enters American law, and authority is provided for later application of the "isolated passages" and "most susceptible persons" tests. Under such standards a book can be found legally obscene if it contains some passages which would tend to have a libidinous effect upon children or some other particularly susceptible persons. It is open to question, however, whether the most stringent applications of these tests could find sanction in either *Bennett* or *Hicklin*. The *Bennett* ruling was that the defendant is guilty if the book is obscene in "any substantial part,"[14] and defendant's counsel was permitted to read and comment upon the immediate contexts of the passages marked by the prosecution. And in the *Hicklin* case it was admitted on all sides that approximately one-half of the work was obscene, and that the undesirable thoughts would be suggested "even to persons of more advanced years."

The central issue in the *Hicklin* case was presented by the defendant's contention that the pamphlet *The Confessional Unmasked: Showing the Depravity of the Romish Priesthood: The Iniquity of the Confessional, and the Questions Put to Females in Confession* could not be legally obscene, because the motive of its author was not obscenity but, rather, religious and political education. Therefore, the real significance of Justice Cockburn's ruling is to be found in the words "tendency to deprave and corrupt." Obscenity is to be judged by the objective tendency of the material, its most likely effect, and not by the motives or intentions of the author.

It is also open to some question whether the Supreme Court has ever itself adopted the *Hicklin* rule. But, whether adopted by the Court or not, and whether distorted or not, *Hicklin* became the predominant test of obscenity in the American courts.*

The general adoption of the *Hicklin* test did not settle all issues concerning the meaning of "deprave and corrupt." In this regard, two lines of cases are of particular interest: one involving a steady restriction of meaning and the other involving an elaboration and, perhaps, an extension of meaning.

In *Swearingen* v. *United States* (1896) the Supreme Court held that "the words 'obscene,' 'lewd' and 'lascivious' as used in the statute, signify that form of immorality which has relation to sexual impurity."[15] Language which is merely "exceedingly coarse and vulgar" but does not relate to sexual impurity does not fall within the law. There were four dissenting Justices. In *People* v. *Eastman* (1907) the New York Court of Appeals held that a "scurrilous and vile" attack on the Catholic church is not "indecency" within the meaning of the New York statute.[16] The decision was rendered by a majority of four against three dissents.

The other class of cases involves what is sometimes called "critical" or "ideological" obscenity. In 1924 the New York Supreme Court held that Arthur Schnitzler's *Casanova's Homecoming* was obscene under the state's penal law.[17] Counsel for the

---

* In *Commonwealth* v. *Friede*, 271 Mass. 318 (1930), the Massachusetts high court upheld a trial judge's refusal to allow counsel to read Theodore Dreiser's *An American Tragedy* to the jury in its entirety. The trial judge had permitted the reading of only those chapters in which allegedly obscene passages appeared. The court concluded that "the seller of a book which contains passages offensive to the statute has no right to assume that children to whom the book might come would not read the obscene passages, or having read them, would continue to read on until the evil effects of the obscene passages were weakened or dissipated with the tragic denouement of the tale" (at pp. 322–23). At late as 1951, *Hicklin* was applied in the first "Henry Miller case," *U.S.* v. *Two Obscene Books,* 99 F. Supp. 760 (ND Cal. 1950).

publisher had argued that the statutory term "obscene" applies only to publications which tend to incite "lustful and lecherous desires." Judge (later U.S. Senator) Robert Wagner rejected this definition as too narrow and restrictive to serve the purpose which the legislature had in view and as likely, if adopted as the only test, to render the statute inoperative. The judge asserted: "As it is the duty of our law-enforcing branches of government to enforce with vigor these laws, so it is the co-relative function of the courts not to narrow the law's application by accepting tests restrictive of the commonly accepted meaning of the words."[18] Although Judge Wagner quoted *Hicklin* as the "important but not sole test," the extent to which his opinion was actually based upon it is uncertain.

In 1929 the City Magistrates' Court of New York, relying upon Judge Wagner's ruling and upon *Hicklin,* declared Radclyffe Hall's *The Well of Loneliness* obscene under the state statute. The magistrate granted that the work is "a well written, carefully constructed piece of fiction and contains no unclean words."[19] But he maintained that the moral tone and thesis of the novel brought it within the statute. This court held, in effect, that *The Well of Loneliness* depraves and corrupts by means of its teachings: its idealization of lesbian love; its argument that this love is as worthy as normal love; and its implication that lesbians have a right to contract relationships with normal persons, married or unmarried. In summary of its position the court concluded:

> The theme of the novel is not only anti-social and offensive to public morals and decency, but the method in which it is developed, in its highly emotional way attracting and focusing upon perverted ideas and unnatural vices, and seeking to justify and idealize them, is strongly calculated to corrupt and debase those members of the community who would be susceptible to its immoral influences.[20]

It is difficult to determine whether this is the *Hicklin* rule applied as Chief Justice Cockburn or Judge Blatchford would have applied it. Judgment on this matter will turn upon one's understanding of "deprave and corrupt." Do these words apply *only* to the stimulation of impure and libidinous thoughts? And, if so, what kind of thoughts are these? The terminology may have been intended to cover only thoughts characterized by lust—"thoughts" more akin to a passion than to an idea. Or, "impure thoughts" may also mean "immoral thoughts"—morally base attitudes toward sexual and other human relations.

It appears that this problem was never explored very thoroughly in the cases decided under *Hicklin*. In *People* v. *Berg* (1934) the New York Supreme Court adopted the rule that an obscene work is one which "tends to lower the standards of right and wrong, specifically as to the sexual relation."[21] But it adopted this criterion as one among several, including a requirement that, to be deemed obscene, a publication must "tend to stir sex impulses." In 1944 a New York City judge concluded that "the ban is against the publication of a book which contravenes the moral law and which tends to subvert respect for decency and morality."[22] Under this standard *Lady Chatterley's Lover* was brought within the prohibition.

These rulings did not go unchallenged. Alongside of the developments referred to above, there emerged a series of cases questioning the *Hicklin* rule, undermining it, and finally, giving rise in the 1930's and 1940's to the modern rule.

This development originated with the opinion of Judge Learned Hand in *United States* v. *Kennerley* in 1913.[23] Judge Hand felt obliged to apply *Hicklin* to the case before him, but in the process of doing so he cast doubt upon its applicability to "the morality of the present time" and, in effect, asked for a searching reconsideration of it. He looked forward to a time when men would no longer regard as obscene any language which is "honestly relevant to the adequate expression of innocent ideas." The following is probably the most influential paragraph in the history of the subject between *Kennerley* and *Roth:*

> Yet if the time is not yet when men will think innocent all that which is honestly germane to a pure subject, however little it may mince its words, still I scarcely think that they would forbid all which might corrupt the most corruptible or that society is prepared to accept for its own limitations those which may perhaps be necessary to the weakest of its members. If there be no abstract definition, such as I have suggested, should not the word "obscene" be allowed to indicate the present critical point in the compromise between candor and shame at which the community may have arrived here and now. . . . To put thought in leash to the average conscience of the time is perhaps tolerable, but to fetter it by the necessities of the lowest and least capable seems a fatal policy.[24]

The immediate practical import of this opinion lies in its condemnation of a system which, in order to protect the young and the infirm, denies to the mature community its rightful share of serious literature and new insights. But the "philosophy" of the opinion is equally important. Judge Hand has put the problem into a historical perspective, a perspective of changing or evolving morals. His opinion designates three moralities and three legal standards relative to them. The old morality is passing away, and the old legality should pass away with it. The new morality has not yet arrived. We should adopt a legal standard which is in accord with the intermediate stage in which we live, and which is flexible enough to accommodate the coming of the new.

But Judge Hand was not advocating the adjustment of the law to a mere process of change. It is clear from the whole text of his opinion that he expects the new morality to be a serious and valid one, one which will embody and impose standards of decency. He also expects that the new latitude will be abused; that many will make use of it "as a cover for lewdness" and for attacks on decency; but he suggests that when such abuses arise the courts will recognize them and deal with them.[25]

The effect of Judge Hand's opinion was not immediate. Subsequent decisions reflect its influence in varying ways and degrees. In 1930 the United States Court of Appeals for the Second Circuit held that Mary Dennett's *The Sex Side of Life* could not be barred from the mails.[26] Judge Augustus Hand discussed the importance of sex instruction for children and the merits of the particular volume under consideration and concluded: "We hold that an accurate exposition of the relevant facts of the sex side of life in decent language and in manifestly serious and disinterested spirit cannot ordinarily be regarded as obscene."[27]

Although such a work may incidentally arouse the sexual desires of some persons, the statute does not "bar from the mails everything which *might* stimulate sex impulses" (italics in original). This is the origin of the "dominant theme" requirement adopted in later cases.

The court took into account the "sincerity of feeling" with which the author had treated the phenomena of sex, but it disclaimed any intention of making personal motive a significant factor in the determining of obscenity. It appears that the court was endeavoring to make something like the following distinction:

If an author has written a book which is in fact obscene, it is no mitigation that he does not think so or that he sincerely believes that obscene books should be published. But if seriousness of purpose, as distinguished from obscenity, is reflected in the writing itself, this is a factor which weighs in its favor.

Some propositions implicit in the *Dennett* case were made explicit by Federal Judge Woolsey in the *Ulysses* case.[28] According to Judge Woolsey the judicial task is two-sided. First, one must determine whether the book was written with "pornographic intent" (i.e., written for the sake of exploiting obscenity). If so, then the inquiry is at an end and forfeiture follows. If not, or if there is some doubt about this, then the judge proceeds to apply a "more objective standard." He seeks to determine the effect of the books on readers—whether it "tends to stir the sex impulses or lead to sexually impure and lustful thoughts."[29]

In pursuance of the first task Judge Woolsey examined Joyce's use of offensive language and descriptions of physiological processes with a view to determining the literary function of this language and description. He concluded that these are an integral part of the author's honest and skillful effort to portray his character's "stream of consciousness." The judge recognized that this is a new and significant literary mode, with its own appropriate techniques, and, therefore, it is not "dirt for dirt's sake."

This independent literary analysis is one of the two distinguishing features of Judge Woolsey's approach to the problem. The other distinguishing feature of his approach is his insistence that, in determining the objective effect of a work, the test must be "its effect on a person with average sexual instincts . . . what the French would call *l'homme moyen sensuel.*"[30] The "average man" concept should perform the same function in this branch of the law as does the "reasonable man" in other areas of law. By this test it was found that the book does not act as an "aphrodisiac."

It may be of some value to indicate what Judge Woolsey did *not* say. He did not say that a book must be "dirt for dirt's sake" in order to be legally obscene. Although we do not know with certainty what Judge Woolsey would have done with a work of literary integrity which does act as an aphrodisiac, his ruling leaves untouched previous determinations that this effect constitutes obscenity.

Judge Woolsey's reasoning was upheld by a two-to-one majority in the Court of Appeals. Judge Augustus Hand took explicit notice of the "originality" and the "excellent craftsmanship" of the book, and, going somewhat beyond Judge Woolsey, he made it the central question of the case whether a work of such artistic value and insight could be regarded as obscene.[31] In addition, Judge Hand spelled out and emphasized the requirement that a book's obscenity must be judged by its "dominant effect." He suggested that for evidence of dominant effect one might consider the relevance of the offending parts to the theme of the work and the status of the work among literary critics.

The *Ulysses* Court explicitly rejected the "rigorous doctrines" of *Bennett* and *Hicklin* and, insofar as it was able, overruled them.[32] But this observation should be qualified by two others. One important tenet of *Hicklin* is left standing—it is "libidinous effect" which constitutes obscenity. And the books involved in the *Ulysses* case and in the cases it relies upon were unquestionably serious works.

In *United States* v. *Levine* (1936) this same court heard a case involving books of a very different sort.[33] Judge Learned Hand brushed aside the artistic and scientific pretensions of *Crossways of Sex* and *Secret Museum of Anthropology,* but, since the trial judge had applied the *Hicklin* rule, he ordered a new trial under a new standard: "The standard must be the likelihood that the work will so much arouse the salacity of the reader to whom it is sent as to outweigh any literary, scientific or other merits it may have in that reader's hands."[34]

This "balancing test," like the *Kennerley* "compromise between candor and shame," is designed to effect a compromise between divergent social valuations. But the philosophy of the *Levine* opinion is something more than a restatement of *Kennerley.* According to Judge Hand, the trouble with the old *Hicklin* rule is that it "necessarily presupposed that the evil against which the statute is directed so much outweighs all interests of art, letters or science, that these must yield to the mere possibility that some prurient person may get a sensual gratification from reading."[35] But, contrary to this old proposition, "the problem is to find a passable compromise between opposing interests whose relative importance, like that of all social or personal values, is incommensurable."

Now, the "evil against which the statute is directed" is the corruption (however that may be understood) of minds and morals. Judge Hand's opinion suggests that the real defect of the old rule is that it weighs the scales too heavily in favor of moral considerations—as against literary and scientific ones. The new test will restore the balance by requiring that equal weight, or at least significant weight, be given to both kinds of social interests. How the balancing is to be done, or how much weight is to be given to each in a particular case, would depend upon how one is to interpret the implication that these social interests are "opposed" and "incommensurable." At any rate, the weighing must be done with a view to effects upon a particular reader or type of reader. It may be unlawful to distribute a certain publication to youth and quite lawful to distribute it to adults.

In *Parmelee* v. *United States* (1940) the Court of Appeals for the District of Columbia adopted the *Kennerley* "contemporary standards" test and vigorously applied it to the Customs Bureau's censorship of nudism in art.[36] In this important decision Judge Learned Hand's conception of variable and evolving morals was finally ratified and incorporated into the law of obscenity.

But the liberalization of standards from *Kennerley* to *Parmelee* had taken place without explicit reference to First Amendment considerations. In 1948, in *Doubleday* v. *New York*,[37] the Supreme Court heard arguments relying exclusively on the First Amendment and addressed exclusively to freedom of expression issues. Counsel for Doubleday insisted that Edmund Wilson's *Memoirs of Hecate County* could not be suppressed without a showing that it poses a "clear and present danger" to substantial interests in order and morality. The Court divided in a four-to-four vote, without publishing an opinion. We may reasonably assume that controversy over the application of the "clear and present danger" test was a major cause of the division.

In its October 1956 term the Supreme Court took the *Roth-Alberts* case under a grant of certiorari limited to the constitutional issues. Roth's conviction for mailing obscene advertising and an obscene book had been upheld in the Court of Appeals. He challenged the constitutionality of the federal obscenity statute as a violation of the First Amendment, of due process of law, and of the reserved rights of the states and the people under the Ninth and Tenth Amendments. Alberts challenged the obscenity provisions of the California penal code as a violation of the freedom of speech and press protected from state action by the Fourteenth Amendment.

In its consideration of the overriding freedom of speech and press issues the Court was confronted with two interpretations of the First Amendment and two formulas for rendering decisions under it. Counsel for Roth and several briefs *amicus curiae* argued for an application of the clear and present danger test. The government argued for a "balancing" test, involving the weighing of competing interests. Some aspects of the case are, perhaps, best understood in the light of these arguments presented to the Court.*

The petitioners' briefs contended that the government must meet the clear and present danger test as modified in *Dennis* v. *United States*. The government has the burden of showing a "probability" that publications alleged to be obscene will bring about a "substantive evil" that Congress has a right to prevent. The substantive evil must be defined in terms of criminal or anti-social conduct. Since the argument in support of the statute cannot establish a probability that such publications incite such conduct, the statute is invalid.[38] This position is most succinctly stated in the brief filed by the American Book Publishers Council: "Neither the statute itself, nor any authoritative interpretations thereof, informs us whether it is designed to prevent in the normal reader: (1) the arousing of lewd thoughts and desires or (2) incitement to crimes and other anti-social conduct."[39]

If, the argument continues, the former be the aim of the statute, then this is clearly not a substantive evil which Congress can reach. If the latter be the aim of the statute, then there is no evidence of either clear and present or probable danger that such conduct will result from exposure to obscenity.

The government replied that the prevention of harmful conduct incited by speech is not the only public interest which may justify restriction of speech. What the First Amendment requires is: "The weighing of these basic factors: the value of the kind of speech involved, the public interest served by the restriction, and the extent and form of the restriction imposed."[40]

* This chapter considers the *Roth* case on its own terms, without reference to such interpretations or elaborations of it as may be found in later cases.

The government's brief urged that the value of obscene speech be judged in the light of a comparative scale of First Amendment values based on the purpose of the amendment as interpreted in Supreme Court decisions. This scale of values was tendered as illustrative:

Political speech
Religious
Economic
Scientific
General news and information
Social and historical commentary
Literature
Art
Entertainment
Music
Humor
Commercial advertisements
Gossip
Comic books
Epithets
Libel
Obscenity
Profanity
Commercial pornography[41]

The public interest required to justify restraint would diminish as one moves down the scale and increase as one moves up. The brief then proceeds to the "weighing." Expression characterized by obscenity has extremely low value in the light of basic First Amendment purposes. Arrayed against this expression are social interests in the preservation of moral standards. The brief argues at considerable length that these are important interests committed to the care of both state and federal governments and that these interests may be harmed by the free circulation of obscenity in a number of ways. Some kinds of obscenity may incite some readers to harmful conduct. Continuous circulation of obscenity is likely to debase moral standards, weakening their influence upon conduct, and thus promote, in the long run, an increase in immoral conduct. Finally, the corruption of sexual morality is likely to affect ethical standards in other areas, thus weakening the whole moral and legal fabric. The government concluded with a showing that the restraint imposed by the statute is legitimate, involving neither discretion nor prior restraint.

In its holding that obscenity is not protected speech, the Court rejected both the petitioner's and the government's First Amendment standards. But it rejected them in different degrees. The majority opinion offers, essentially, four arguments in support of its position.

First, the states which ratified the First Amendment did not regard it as extending protection to every kind of utterance. In support of this view the Court cites state statutes, in operation at the time the Constitution was ratified, providing for the prosecution of libel, blasphemy, and profanity, and a Massachusetts statute of 1712 making publication of obscenity a crime. Justice Brennan's reasoning seems to be that, since most of these states had free speech or press provisions in their constitutions, they must have understood these freedoms in terms less than absolute. This would presuppose that the states which ratified the First Amendment regarded it as embodying provisions essentially the same as those embodied in their own constitutions. The Court's opinion contains no argument against petitioner's contention, and that of Morris Ernst, *amicus curiae,* that the framers designed the First Amendment to deny to the national government any power whatsoever over the press, while they intended that the states would retain ample powers to restrain licentious and defamatory newspapers.[42] Justice Brennan appears to have rejected this view in favor of the government's argument that the strong disfavor in which the states held these forms of speech is conclusive evidence that the First Amendment could not have been designed to protect them.

The second argument offered by the Court is based upon its interpretation of First Amendment purposes. The aim of the First Amendment is "to assure unfettered interchange of ideas for the bringing about of political and social changes desired by the people."[43] Thus, the scope of First Amendment protection, as determined by this purpose, is very broad, but it is not all-inclusive. It includes "all ideas having even the slightest redeeming social importance" and excludes obscenity, which is "utterly without redeeming social importance."[44] This concept of "redeeming social importance" is the core of Justice Brennan's argument, since his other arguments rest, to a large extent, upon it.

Justice Brennan's third reason for excluding obscenity involves an appeal to history and to "the universal judgment that obscenity ought to be restrained reflected in the international agreement of over fifty nations, in the obscenity laws of the forty-eight states and in the twenty obscenity laws enacted by the Congress from 1842 to 1956."

Finally, the Court relies upon its own recent precedents in *Chaplinsky* v. *New Hampshire* and *Beauharnais* v. *Illinois*. The *Chaplinsky* decision had included the lewd and the obscene in "certain well-defined and narrowly limited classes of speech, the prevention and punishment of which have never been thought to raise any constitutional problems."[45] And the *Beauharnais* decision asserted that "libelous utterances not being within the area of constitutionally protected speech, it is unnecessary to consider the issues behind the phrase 'clear and present danger.' Certainly no one would contend that obscene speech, for example, may be punished only upon showing of such circumstances."[46]

The *Chaplinsky* opinion contains the original version of the "redeeming social importance" concept and relies upon it as a basis for exclusion of "fighting words" and obscenity from First Amendment protection. These forms of speech are excluded because they are "no essential part of any exposition of ideas, and are of such slight social value as a step to truth that any benefit that may be derived from them is clearly outweighed by the social interest in order and morality."[47] Further, the Court's third argument for exclusion is also dependent upon the doctrine of redeeming social importance. Justice Brennan's reference to the "universal judgment" of mankind can be read as a reference to the judgment that obscenity is without social importance, and not simply to the judgment that obscenity should be restrained.

Thus, the Court has found a way to decide obscenity cases without applying either the clear and present danger test or the "balancing of interests" test. The Court need not determine clear and present danger because it has found that obscenity is not entitled to any First Amendment protection whatever. But of equal importance is the rejection of major features of the proposed alternative. Justice Brennan did not adopt the government's proposed scale of values. Or, rather, he adopted only the very bottom part of the scale. In holding that obscenity is worthless, he did not necessarily hold that political speech occupies a position higher than religious and economic speech and that these stand higher on our list of priorities than literature and art. Further, he did not respond to the government's invitation to weigh the public interests standing against obscene speech. Justice Brennan did not explore the public interest in moral standards, the threats to morality posed by circulation of obscenity, or the role of government (except to the extent that these are explored in his brief reference to the "universal judgment" on the matter and in the *Chaplinsky* reference to "the social interest in order and morality"). It is not too much to say that the "redeeming social importance" formula was the Court's way of avoiding what it must have regarded as highly undesirable or dangerous alternatives.

But what, in a positive sense, is the meaning of "redeeming social importance"? It is of the greatest significance that this formulation was derived from interpretation of the ultimate purpose of the First Amendment. It might be generally admitted that any analysis of what the First Amendment means which is based upon consideration of its ends must encounter, at one point or another, the limits of its protection. Purpose inevitably implies and entails limits. The Court had in the briefs before it an argument which would have rendered unnecessary any consideration of purposes and, hence, any statement of limits. The American Book Publishers Council had strongly urged upon the Court the doctrine of *Winters* v. *New York*. In *Winters,* Justice Reed asserted for the majority:

> We do not accede to appellee's suggestion that the Constitutional protection for a free press applies only to the exposition of ideas. The line between informing and entertaining is too elusive for the protection of that basic right. . . . What is one man's amusement teaches another's doctrine. Though we can see nothing of any possible value to society in these magazines they are as much entitled to the protection of free speech as the best of literature.[48]

This doctrine would require of the courts, and of the law (both constitutional and statutory), a double neutrality: neutrality toward the distinction between public discussion and entertainment, and neutrality toward the distinction between socially valuable and socially worthless literature. The law shall look with equal benevolence upon the worthy and the worthless, protect them equally, and subject them equally to whatever restraints can be legitimately imposed. Does the *Roth* standard of redeeming social importance indicate a rejection of, or at least a movement away from, the judicial relativism of *Winters* v. *New York?* I think it does—insofar as the Court has rested its argument on considerations of First Amendment purpose and, in some sense, on consideration of social value. But it is difficult to determine how far the Court intended to go in this direction, because it is difficult to determine just what the Court's standard of social importance is.

Justice Brennan did not define "redeeming social importance," but he did indicate what, *at least,* is included therein. The government's brief invited the Court to adopt a view of the First Amendment which places heavy emphasis upon its political function. The government implied (though it did not wholly commit itself to this view) that the overriding concern of the amendment is with political speech, broadly conceived—speech about public matters or speech related in some way to citizenship. It is evident that Justice Brennan wished to go substantially beyond this. His opinion quotes a letter of the Continental Congress explaining to the inhabitants of Quebec that freedom of speech and press aims at "the advancement of truth, science, morality and art in general" as well as "diffusion of liberal sentiments on administration of government" and popular control of office holders. And *Thornhill* v. *Alabama,* also cited by the Court, asserts that freedom of discussion "embodies at least the liberty to discuss publicly and truthfully *all matters of public concern*" and "all issues about which information is needed or appropriate to enable the members of society to cope with the exigencies of their period."[49]

Justice Brennan has made it clear that social importance shall be attributed, at least, to any serious "exposition of ideas" or "discussion" about significant issues confronting the public, whether these issues be political or not. But it is not so clear whether this is the outer limit of the "socially important," and, if not, how far beyond this the concept extends and what kind of materials it embraces. With regard to the scope of this principle a number of questions remain.

Do novels, short stories, and poems contain an "exposition of ideas" about "matters of public concern"? While it is certain that Justice Brennan intends that such literature be protected (the letter from the Continental Congress mentions the arts), it is difficult to find in his opinion a solid rationale for the protection of imaginative literature. That is to say, it is difficult to find in it a rationale which would do justice to the stated purpose of the First Amendment *and* to the nature of imaginative literature.

Is redeeming social importance to be attributed to any idea whatsoever, or only to ideas seriously and responsibly addressed to genuine social problems? What about expressions of opinion which do not advance "truth, science, morality and the arts" but, rather, retard them, and which do not provide "information and education" about the issues of the times but, rather, obscure these issues by means of falsehood, sensationalism, or invective?

Perhaps Justice Brennan would be loath to commit the courts to the making of such distinctions and would prefer to extend protection to expressions or communications of ideas as such. But problems lurk in the very term "idea," unless this term be explained or related to some context. Shall redeeming social importance attach to any words which have ideational content or which reflect a process of thought? Shall any words suffice which are, in the opinion of the user, designed to convey some point of view? It will not be contested that all language has ideational content and is intended to convey something. Such a minimal conception of what constitutes an idea, if meaningful at all, would be perfectly useless for Justice Brennan's purpose. It could not distinguish between an idea and anything else that occurs in the mind of a human being, or between a discussion and anything else that may occur between human beings.

One may confidently infer that, if the protection of ideas was his aim, Justice Brennan must have had something more in mind than the very minimal definition of what constitutes an idea or an exchange of ideas. It may also be inferred that "ideas having the slightest redeeming social importance" are so designated because they meet some social standard of worth. But the social standard of worth may be a minimal (or lowest-common-denominator) standard or a maximal (or high) standard. According to the former, the redeeming quality of a work may be nothing more than the appearance in it of some recognizable opinions or arguments which some people think are important. According to the latter, the redeeming quality of a work would lie in the seriousness of its approach to vital issues or in the value of its contribution to the public, even though the approach and the contribution be in terms "hateful to prevailing opinion."

It is evident that the *Roth* majority intended to make some distinction between socially worthy and socially worthless literature and that it regarded such a distinction as compatible with the First Amendment and obligatory upon any constitutionally valid obscenity law. But Justice Brennan did not indicate whether he had in mind a minimal or a maximal standard of worth, or something lying between these. His opinion does not point clearly in one direction or the other.

It may be felt that the Court declined to spell out its criteria of social worth because it did not wish to commit the judicial system prematurely to the making of delicate literary judgments. For if the social importance of a work turns on the value of its contribution to the public or its literary virtue, then judges may be required to make subtle determinations concerning aesthetic values and ideational content. But there is no reason to conclude that, because of its awareness of these difficulties, the Court must have meant the expression "redeeming social importance" to be so broad and all-encompassing as to include any words which can lay claim to being an idea. There is no reason to conclude that Justice Brennan used the expression in such as way as to render it almost meaningless.

We now turn to the other half of the *Roth* decision—its definition of obscenity. The legal test must establish standards of judgment which will protect socially important literature. Sex is declared to be a "vital problem of human interest" and a matter of "public concern." Therefore, literature dealing with sex in a manner not appealing to prurient interest is socially important literature.[50] Since such literature is endangered by *Hicklin*'s "isolated passages" and "most susceptible persons" tests, *Hicklin* must be rejected. The authoritative test shall now be: "Whether to the average person, applying contemporary community standards, the dominant theme of the material taken as a whole appeals to prurient interests."[51]

For its precedents the Court refers to the *Parmelee, Levine, Ulysses,* and *Dennett* cases, among others. Thus, the "average man" and "dominant theme" concepts are taken from the work of Judge Woolsey and Judge Augustus Hand. The "contemporary community standards" concept is derived, by way of *Parmelee,* from the work of Judge Learned Hand. The precise meaning of the reference to the *Levine* case is somewhat obscure. It is not clear whether Justice Brennan intended to adopt the particular balancing test set forth in that decision or only its argument against *Hicklin.*

It can also be questioned whether, or to what extent, the Court intended to adopt the *Ulysses* approach to literary and aesthetic considerations. The wording of the new definition directs one's attention primarily to the "appeal" of the work, its most likely appeal to the average man, and not primarily to its intrinsic merits. But the requirement that the appeal be that of "the dominant theme of the material taken as a whole" opens the way for the consideration of literary and other qualities intrinsic to the work. Indeed, it is hard to see how a trial judge or jury could really consider the dominant theme of a literary work without taking into account aesthetic aspects of the work or without asking what the author is seeking to achieve in it.

In spite of the labors of the *Roth* Court's predecessors in this field, this aspect of the definition it not free of complications. To identify the dominant theme of some works requires a judgment of some subtlety, as does an understanding of the work as a whole. The judicial decisions upon which the Court relies reflect differing interpretations of the requirement that a work be considered as a whole.* And these decisions differ somewhat in their application of the "average man" requirement.

These, however, are problems of a secondary order. Some of them may be unavoidable and tolerable. Others may be resolvable as the new test is refined and elaborated in the federal courts. Difficulties of a more serious kind arise from the concept of "prurient interest" and that of "contemporary community standards."

Justice Brennan's opinion contains two explanations of what is meant by the term "prurient interest." These two explanations appear to conflict. The tension between them poses an acute problem in the definition of terms which seem to elude definition. And

---

* See *Commonwealth* v. *Isenstadt,* 318 Mass. 543 (1945). This court ruled that a book may be obscene "as a whole" if it contains a comparatively few salacious passages strong enough and important enough to "flavor the whole" (at p. 549).

behind the problem of definition lie significant issues of public policy.

Justice Brennan defines "material appealing to prurient interest" as "material having a tendency to excite lustful thoughts." He upholds, as consonant with this standard, the trial judge's instructions to the jury that material is obscene which tends to "arouse sexual desires or sexually impure thoughts." From this it would appear that the Court intended to leave intact one important aspect of the *Hicklin* formula—that aspect of it which designates the effect or consequences which the law seeks to control. That is, it would seem that the Court intended to remain in harmony with the liberalizing decisions it cites, all of which had identified the essence of obscenity in terms of tendency to "stir sex impulses" or "arouse libidinous thoughts."

But the Court also cites with approval the definition offered in the American Law Institute's Model Penal Code: "A thing is obscene if, considered as a whole, its predominant appeal is to prurient interests; i.e., a shameful or morbid interest in sex, nudity or excretion, and if it goes substantially beyond customary limits of candor in description or representation of such matter."[52]

In explanation of the emphasis on a *shameful* or *morbid* interest the ALI asserts: "We reject the prevailing test of tendency to arouse lustful thoughts or desires because it is unrealistically broad for a society that plainly tolerates a great deal of erotic interest in literature, advertising and art, and because regulation of thought or desire unconnected with overt misbehavior raises the most acute constitutional as well as practical difficulties."[53]

The ALI is at great pains to distinguish "a normal interest in sexual matters" from a "prurient interest" which is "an exacerbated, morbid or perverted interest."[54] Justice Brennan could not have been unaware of the significance of this distinction in the ALI formulation, since his opinion explicitly refers to the pages wherein the distinction is made and the prevailing test rejected. The problem of interpretation here is insoluble on the basis of anything one may read in the *Roth* case and supporting materials. Did Justice Brennan intend the concept of "prurient interest" to incorporate what, in the case law, is traditionally meant by "arousing sexual desires and impure thoughts"—or did he intend to adopt the ALI's explicit departure from that meaning? Does the authoritative test of obscenity refer to sexual desires and thoughts as such—or only to such desires and thoughts in an extreme and perverted form? However this question might be answered, there is justification for Justice Harlan's assertion that the Court could not reasonably uphold both the ALI formulation and the standard applied in the lower court.

The *Roth* Court has, indeed taken an ambiguous position on a crucial matter. But some of the difficulty may be traceable to the subject matter itself and the terminology relevant to it. A degree of ambiguity inheres in the very term "lust"—the term which this court employed, and which is frequently employed, to designate the obscene effect.

When used in ordinary discourse and in a sexual context the word can convey a wide range of meanings. It can mean desire, immoderate desire, corrupt desire, or immoral desire. A popular dictionary definition includes "pleasure," "sensuous desire," "a degrading passion," "an inordinate or sinful desire."[55] In religious discourse the term is often used to designate sexual activity outside of marriage. Also, it frequently indicates sexual activity in the absence of love or strong affection. Finally, "lustful thoughts" can mean thoughts dwelling upon and fixated upon sexual considerations and sexual objects, as distinguished from thoughts accompanying ordinary spontaneous sexual desire.

The term "lust" is not the only term employed by the law in this area and in others which is characterized by a high degree of semantic elasticity. Terms like "prurience" and "sexually impure thoughts" are elastic in the same way. Justice Brennan cites a dictionary definition of prurience: "Itching; longing; uneasy with desire or longing; of persons having itching, morbid or lascivious longings; of desire, curiosity or propensity, lewd."

It will be observed that this definition also denotes meanings ranging from that of ordinary desire (which is always an "itching" and a "longing") to that of perverted desire. It may be that Justice Brennan intended that the word "lust" should stand for approximately what the ALI meant by "prurience." Or he may have deemed it the wisest course to let the word stand for its variety of meanings, thus leaving the matter open to common sense applications and adjudications.* The wording of the opinion does not point conclusively in one direction or another.

* The semantic problem will be further explored in chapter 6.

These complications might be avoided if one could accept the suggestion offered by Lockhart and McClure that the *Roth* Court's test of obscenity was really constructed with hard-core pornography in view.[56] These authors point to that part of the government's brief which emphasizes hard-core pornography as the "main objective and major catch" of the obscenity statute. The Solicitor General pointed out that such pornography constitutes 90 percent of the material caught by the statute.[57] He did not contend, however, that Roth's publications were hard-core pornography; in fact, he explicitly excluded Roth's materials from that category. Furthermore, Justice Harlan's dissent in the *Roth* case is premised on the Justice's understanding that the publications judged obscene were not hard-core pornography and that the Court was upholding the statute in its application to materials outside of that category.

Thus, the legal concept of obscenity emerges from the *Roth* case with its essential element somewhat unclear and its boundary lines obscure. Behind this terminological obscurity lie unresolved questions of public policy and constitutional law. Contained in the Court's definition of obscenity are two alternative censorship policies based upon two alternative views of what ought to be prohibited, and why. And, as the dissenting opinions indicate, these policies raise constitutional issues of a high order.

The "contemporary community standards" element of the new definition is as perplexing as the "prurient interests" element. It is settled that obscenity is to be judged by *contemporary* community standards, not by the standards of some previous generation. But, what contemporary "community" shall be used as the touchstone for judgment? What "standards" of that community shall be applied? How shall these be ascertained? And how shall they be applied?

The community in question could be the local community in which the material is sold, the state, or the entire nation. The choice of one or the other of these communities would involve considerations of federalism among others. It might be thought desirable that the standards applied be those of the state in which the publication is sold. In this way the diversity of customs and attitudes prevailing in various sections of the country would be accommodated. Or, perhaps, the rural population and the urban population of a state should each have an opportunity to apply its own criteria. Finally, it could be argued that a uniform nation-wide standard is necessary in the interest of First Amendment freedoms, or in the interest of the ends to be served by the regulation. The *Roth* majority does not address itself to these considerations.

Neither does the *Roth* majority address itself to the nature of the standards to be applied. That there is a problem here can be illustrated by reference to one of the cases cited by the Court as a precedent for its position. In *Commonwealth* v. *Isenstadt* (1945) the Massachusetts high court stated:

> Although in their broadest meaning the statutory words "ob-scene, indecent, or impure" might signify offensive to refinement, propriety and good taste, we are convinced that the legislature did not intend by these words to set up any standard merely of taste, even if under the Constitution it could do so. Taste depends. upon convention, and sometimes upon irrational taboo. It varies with the period, the place, and the training, environment, and the character of persons.[58]

Here the *Isenstadt* court seems to reject changeable community conventions as a source of criteria for obscenity regulation. But later in its opinion the court rules that "a book is to be judged in the light of customs and habits of thought of the time and place of the alleged offense," even though these "do vary with time and place."

If this court was endeavoring to distinguish between mere standards of "taste" and standards embodied in "customs and habits of thought," what is the basis of such a distinction? It could be that the former are arbitrary and irrational while the latter are grounded in rational, or at least serious, considerations. It could be that, while both kinds of norms are variable, the customs and habits of thought are more deep-rooted and change more slowly.

Whatever the *Isenstadt* judges had in mind, their reasoning reflects a distinction between (at least) two kinds of community standards: one kind which can be deemed ephemeral and another which is to be considered more substantial and taken seriously. There are different sorts of community standards, existing on different levels of significance. Some are more important or more permanent than others; some are rooted more deeply in the public mind than others. Terms such as "fashion," "custom," and "conviction" suggest a hierarchical scale of significance and degrees of public commitment.

Justice Brennan did not discuss the character of the standards to be sought, though he did cite the trial judge's reference to the "common conscience of the community." This implies that the standards to be employed shall be something more than tastes and fashions. But "community conscience" does not mean the same thing to all men. Some men will look for it in the conduct of the members of the community; others will look to the beliefs and convictions of the community, even though conduct may fall short of conviction. It would make some difference whether Justice Brennan's "contemporary community standards" are to be identified with community conduct or community ideals.

These considerations bear heavily on the problem of how community standards are to be determined. Shall the members of a jury be the exclusive judges of the "common conscience," or shall they weigh evidence offered to them on this matter? Shall book reviews and box office receipts be considered as evidence of community standards, or do we require the testimony of men experienced in the study of American society? If community conduct is the test, then newspaper reports and sociological studies may provide appropriate evidence. If community conviction is the test, then insights of a different sort may be required, depending, of course, on the nature of the convictions to be ascertained.

But the most perplexing questions are those which arise in connection with the application of this rule. The *Roth* decision quotes with approval from the trial judge's instructions:

> The test is not whether it [the publication] would arouse sexual desire or sexually impure thoughts in those comprising a particular segment of the community. . . . In other words, you are to determine its impact upon the average person in the community. . . . You judge the circulars, pictures and publications which have been put in evidence by the present day standards of the community. You may ask yourselves does it offend the common conscience of the community by present day standards.[59]

On the basis of this passage it is hard to determine how the "community standards" test is supposed to function. Is an obscene publication one which violates the community's current standards of right? Or which offends the average person in the community? Or which arouses the sexual desires of the average person?

Of course, a publication may violate community morals in a number of ways, without arousing sexual desire. It is inconceivable that this Court would leave in operation a test resembling that employed in *People* v. *Berg*.[60] It is not inconceivable, however, that it would leave in operation one resembling that suggested in *Kennerley*. But the test also refers to the effect or "impact" of a work. This could mean that the work must have some actual emotional impact on readers. If so, what sort of impact is required: a strong feeling of moral disapproval? a feeling of revulsion? or sexual desire? Did the Court mean to make "offensiveness" (in addition to arousal of desire) in some sense a test of obscenity? If so, this could not be easily reconciled with the heavy emphasis on "prurient interest" as the essence of the test. If not, if it was intended that a "prurient impact" be the sole test, then why should a jury take account of the common conscience and present-day standards?

The relation between the "community standards" and "prurient interest" elements of the Court's definition is unclear. It is evident that community moral values shall play some role in judgments about obscenity. But it is not evident whether, or how, repugnance to prevailing values is to be considered along with prurient appeal. And, if we now have two standards, it would be a matter of some importance to determine which shall take precedence.[61]

The Court, however, may simply have meant to indicate that a judgment about contemporary moral attitudes is an intrinsic part of any genuine judgment about prurient appeal. A work which would have appealed to the prurient interests of a Victorian man may well leave a contemporary man unmoved. If this is what Justice Brennan had in mind, then his "contemporary community standards" requirement is nothing more than an adjunct of his "average man" requirement. Under this interpretation an injunction to take account of community conscience would amount to this: In judging the impact of this book you must keep in mind that your average man is living now, under the climate of opinion prevailing now, and not in some previous time, under the climate of opinion prevailing then.

In this area, as in others, the text of the *Roth* decision does not provide a conclusive answer. And in this area, as in others, questions of policy and of principle lie behind verbal imprecision.

Thus far I have considered the two parts of the *Roth* case separately, without exploring the relation between them. The Court's definition of what the First Amendment protects is designed to exclude obscenity, and its definition of obscenity is designed to exclude works of redeeming social importance. But the formulations employed fall short of this objective. Exploration of this problem should bring to view the central dilemmas of the *Roth* decision.

The Court's formulations provide no guarantee that works found to be obscene under the new test will not also be found to possess redeeming social importance. Indeed, conflicting determinations under these two standards are quite likely. This is due, in part, to the ambiguities discussed in this chapter. Let us suppose a jury which understands "prurience" as ordinary sexual desire, and "offensiveness to the common conscience" in the ordinary sense of these words. Let us also suppose a federal judge who understands "redeeming social importance" as embracing any work which expresses a point of view on any social matter, or which contains any traces of artistry. One would not have to look far for publications about which this jury and this judge would reach opposite conclusions. Now, let us suppose that the judge understands "redeeming social importance" as requiring something more than the mere presence in a book of *some* social opinions or *some* literary skill. He requires that the work contain serious arguments on important subjects, or genuine aesthetic merit. It is still quite possible that a jury of average Americans would find that a work meeting the judge's requirements nonetheless appeals to prurient interests by contemporary standards. If the jury would adopt the ALI formulation the probability of conflicting determinations would be reduced but not obliterated.

The tension between these two sets of standards is rooted in the diversity of the judgments required under them. A judgment under the *Roth* test of obscenity is primarily a judgment about the effects of a work on the majority of the public, involving a consideration of the attitudes and propensities of the public. A judgment under the *Roth* definition of what the First Amendment protects is primarily a judgment about the merits or qualities of a work. The potentialities for conflict are greater where the former judgment is to be made by the average man himself and the latter is to be made by a judge under the guidance of sophisticated intellectual or literary considerations. But even if both determinations are to be made by a judge, the tension remains, for the two sets of judgments involve disparate considerations. It is true that, under the obscenity test, intellectual and literary qualities would receive some attention, since presumably it would have to be determined that the prurient appeal predominates over other appeals the work may have. Nonetheless, the test is primarily concerned with how a work will affect the average person in the community and only secondarily with its literary and intellectual qualities. Thus, it will often come about that works found to be of redeeming social value because of their intellectual and aesthetic attributes will also be found to entail the obscene effect because of prevailing inclinations, attitudes, and values. When this occurs, which shall take precedence, and why?

The *Roth* decision can be read as a struggle to find formulations which would accommodate the public interest in free expression and the public interest in the control of obscenity. It may be that the tension between the two standards established by the Court reflects an inevitable tension between these two public interests. But even if this tension be ultimately unresolvable, the problems arising from it can be more or less manageable, more or less amenable to rational solution. The extent to which rational resolution is possible would depend largely on the extent to which the social interests involved have been adequately stated and adequately embodied in law.

But Justice Brennan's opinion does not address itself to the public interest involved in obscenity regulations. Not only does the *Roth* decision fail to signify what that public interest is, it also fails to provide any insight into the importance of that public interest and, hence, its weight in the legal scales. The *Roth* majority does not indicate whether its definition of obscenity is designed to protect certain vital standards of morality or to accommodate prevailing popular feelings and moral attitudes. And it does not indicate why either of these should be supported by law.

As a result, it is most difficult, on the basis of the *Roth* concepts, to resolve the problem of conflicting determinations. We do not know when, or whether, the prurient effect of a work would outweigh its possible contribution to literature, because we do not know what is wrong with a prurient effect and why the law seeks to prevent it. We do not know how to weigh the intrinsic merits of a work against its repugnance to the common conscience, because we do not know how these two factors are related to the legitimate ends of the law. We do not even know whether these factors can or should be weighed against each other.

The Court's failure or refusal to concern itself with the rationale for legal regulation of obscenity is the source of most of the deficiencies and ambiguities which can be found in the *Roth* decision. Without some attention to the nature of the evil at which the regulation aims it is impossible to decide between the alternative censorship policies implicit in the Court's definition of "prurience." In order to determine whether the law should control materials which stimulate libidinousness *or* materials which stimulate extreme and perverted libidinousness, it is necessary to consider what social values are implicated and how these can be endangered. In order to determine what kind of community standards are to be applied and how they are to be applied it is necessary to consider the nature of the public interest served by the regulation. Are citizens to be protected from expressions offensive to their sense of decency, whatever that may be? Or are moral standards essential to the functioning of liberal democracy to be preserved from decay? If the former, then conduct prevalent in the local community may be an appropriate touchstone, and a test based on it could be reasonably set up in addition to that of prurient interest. If the latter, then some other standard may be requisite; indeed, the entire test may require further elaboration. Finally, the concept of "redeeming social importance" must remain somewhat vague as long as one does not know what it is that requires redemption.

It has been noted that the *Roth* Court rejected the government's formula for the decision of obscenity cases, a formula which would have involved it in judgments concerning the importance of public morality and the role of government, as well as judgments concerning the effects of obscenity and the relative value of different forms of speech. The Court preferred to decide the case on the narrow and negative grounds that obscenity is without redeeming social importance. The Justices might have valid reasons for declining to adopt the government's balancing test in its entirety. They could reasonably deem it unwise to commit themselves to the government's position on the effects of obscenity and to a complete scale of First Amendment values. But the failure to provide any rationale at all for government regulation of obscenity leaves many questions unanswered, including those raised by the dissenters.

The dissenting opinions touch upon (but touch lightly upon) the fundamental issues which the majority opinion evaded or postponed. Justice Harlan argues that state governments do have a legitimate interest in the protection of society's moral fabric, but that the interest of the federal government in sexual morality is "attenuated" and "indirect."[62] The only answer to this which can be derived from the *Roth* decision is that the federal government can do what it chooses about obscenity because obscenity is not protected. This is not an answer to the disturbing questions about federal activity per se in the area of morality.

Justice Douglas contends that neither the federal government nor state governments may control expression with a view to protecting moral standards, or on the grounds that the expression instills undesirable thoughts. He finds the "community conscience" standard equally repugnant to constitutional principle: "Certainly that standard would not be an acceptable one if religion, economics, politics or philosophy were involved. How does it become a constitutional standard when literature treating with sex is concerned?"[63]

The majority opinion cannot provide a real answer to these arguments. It is not a satisfactory answer that, because obscenity is not protected, courts have no cognizance of the matter. Justice Douglas' objection to regulation concerned with "thoughts" carries with it the grave charge that, in its censorship of obscenity, government oversteps its outer limits and invades the realm of privacy. His objection to community standards as a test of censorable expression contains the charge that the Court has made a groundless and unexplained exception to established rules of First Amendment adjudication. Such charges as these are not met by the merely negative argument that certain materials are socially unimportant and that control of them raises no questions for judicial determination. While the idea of redeeming social importance can be valuable as a definition of what should be protected, it cannot serve as a defense of regulation. Justices Harlan and Douglas can be answered only by a course of reasoning which provides some grounds for government activity in the area of morality, showing that the ends are legitimate and important, which provides some justification for the claims of community conscience, and which explores, more thoroughly than does the Court, the character of the "thoughts" with which the law is here concerned.

It is not suggested that Justice Brennan should have set forth such reasoning in the form of a complete philosophy of censorship, or that in his judicial capacity he could do so. But his failure to provide any basis for a rationale renders the *Roth* decision ambiguous, and his avoidance of underlying issues renders it vulnerable to its judicial critics.

It was not to be expected that the *Roth* Court would be able to resolve all the problems bequeathed to it by the liberalizing movement of the twentieth century. The *Roth* decision did settle some questions, and it did wrestle with others. It definitely established at least that works of real value to society shall not be censored as obscenity; that a book shall not be judged by the impact of a few of its passages upon a special class of persons, and that the standards of judgment shall be those of our time. But it left open basic questions of principle and of purpose, without providing the guidelines for their future resolution.

2

Aftermath of *Roth*

In 1959 the Supreme Court decided the *Kingsley Pictures* case, ruling unanimously that New York could not ban the showing of the motion picture *Lady Chatterley's Lover*.[1] But the Justices disagreed sharply in their reasons for reaching this conclusion. And their disagreement, far more significant than their agreement, revealed the depth and scope of the issues remaining to be resolved.

The New York motion picture licensing statute provided, in part, that a license shall not be issued for a film which is "obscene" or "immoral." In 1954 the legislature, in the effort to avoid the defect of vagueness, defined an "immoral film" as: "A motion picture film or part thereof the dominant purpose or effect thereof is erotic or pornographic, or which portrays acts of sexual immorality, perversion or lewdness, or which expressly or impliedly presents such acts as desirable, acceptable or proper patterns of behavior."[2]

In 1958 the New York Board of Regents held the *Lady Chatterley* film immoral for its presentation of adultery as a "desirable, acceptable and proper pattern of behavior." The New York Court of Appeals, relying solely on this clause of the statute, upheld the Regents' ruling. Chief Judge Conway interpreted this clause as aiming at motion pictures which "alluringly portray sexually immoral acts as proper behavior."[3] It is around this formula that the major issues of the case revolve.

Justice Stewart's majority opinion holds that the New York statute, as construed by the state's Court of Appeals, strikes directly at the advocacy of ideas. According to Justice Stewart, New York has prevented the exhibition of a film because that film advocates the idea that adultery may be proper behavior. Thus "the state, quite simply, has struck at the very heart of constitutionally protected liberty."[4]

But Chief Judge Conway had emphasized the "alluring portrayal" of conduct contrary to public morality and the legal code of the state. The Court brushed aside these factors on two grounds. With regard to the immorality and illegality of the conduct advocated the Court says: "Its [the First Amendment] guarantee is not confined to the expression of ideas that are conventional or shared by a majority. It protects advocacy of the opinion that adultery may sometimes be proper no less than advocacy of Socialism or the single tax." An advocacy of conduct proscribed by law may not be restrained where that advocacy falls short of incitement. As for the "alluring portrayal" of such conduct, the First Amendment protects "expression which is eloquent no less than that which is unconvincing."[5]

To a large extent, the Court's conclusions rest upon the premise that motion picture censorship must be confined to obscenity as defined in recent cases and that the test must be applied to motion pictures in the same manner as it is applied to other forms of expression. As the Court interprets the statute and the state court's opinion, New York is attempting to extend the scope of censorship beyond obscenity. Justice Stewart quotes, as conclusive of the matter, the following statement from Judge Conway's opinion: "Precedent, just as sound principle, will not support a statement that motion pictures must be 'out and out' obscene before they may be censored."

Justices Frankfurter and Harlan concur in the result but strongly disapprove of the majority's way of handling the issues. Justice Frankfurther would decide the case on the narrow grounds that this particular film cannot constitutionally be banned. He regards this as a "due process" case, to be decided on the basis of careful examination of the particular facts. Instead, the Court has sought to avoid the difficulties of particular judgment by "sounding abstract and unqualified dogmas about freedom."[6] According to the Justice, this "dogmatic" approach fails to allow for legitimate state action against a recognized evil. The "due process" approach would require one to face the difficult task of recognizing both the evil and the claims of free expression as they arise from the specific facts of the case.

Justice Harlan also insists upon the need for particular adjudication, and he criticizes the Court for interpreting the statute in such a way that it must necessarily be voided. As the Justice reads the New York opinion, that court construes the statute as being aimed at obscenity and not at advocacy of ideas. He finds passages in that opinion to support his contention, among them the statement: "It should first be emphasized that the scope of section 122-A [the relevant part of the statute] is not mere expression of opinion in the form, for example, of a filmed lecture whose subject is the espousal of adultery. We reiterate that this case involves the espousal of sexually immoral acts *plus* actual scenes of a suggestive and obscene nature."[7]

According to Justice Harlan, what the statute outlaws is advocacy of immoral acts accompanied by obscenity and incitement. Justice Clark replies that the statute as construed must fall because it "place[s] more emphasis on what the film teaches than on what it depicts."[8]

The Justices diverge considerably in their interpretation of what the New York court was trying to do. Reflected in this disagreement are perplexing problems concerning the meaning of "advocacy" and "ideas" in the context of motion pictures and their regulation. A brief exposition of Chief Judge Conway's opinion should serve to bring these problems to view and to demonstrate their importance.

There is material in Chief Judge Conway's opinion to support the interpretation given it by both Justice Stewart and Justice Harlan. The Chief Judge begins with an explication of the applicable clause of the statute.

> It embraces not only films which are visually suggestive and obscene, nor only those which are sexually suggestive and immoral in theme, but those which combine the two. The statutory rejection is aimed at those films which, not being satisfied with portraying scenes of rank obscenity, go further and recommend sexually immoral acts, thus portrayed in a manner appealing to prurient interests, as proper conduct for the people of our state.[9]

Here the Judge is obviously endeavoring to bring the statutory prohibition squarely within the *Roth* definition of obscenity. But this section of the statute is not primarily concerned with "rank obscenity." Other parts of the act are designed to reach such material.[10] Also, if the film in question clearly appeals to prurient interests (in the *Roth* sense), there would be no reason to go further and consider what it "recommends." It is evident that the statute aims at a kind of "recommendation" which is not in itself strictly obscene. Chief Judge Conway admits as much toward the end of his opinion when he asserts that "to lay hold of obscenity as the *only* proper basis for motion picture censorship is to ignore substance in favor of form."

The text of Chief Judge Conway's opinion bears all the signs of an intellectual struggle. It is a struggle to accommodate diverse public purposes, principles, and considerations. If the Judge has not quite succeeded in this endeavor, at least the endeavor is instructive. He strives to accommodate the principles of the First Amendment and the intentions of the legislature (with perhaps some modification of the latter) and to reconcile the standards of the *Roth* case with the aims of motion picture regulation (with perhaps some modification of the former). He labors to find a formulation which, while having a foothold in the strict definition of obscenity, will reach an evil which lies beyond that strict definition. The formulation at which Chief Judge Conway arrives is that of the "alluring portrayal" of immoral conduct as proper conduct. He reads the terms "alluringly portray" into the statutory phrase, "presents such acts as . . . proper patterns of behavior." Thus the statute will not condemn mere advocacy of adultery. It will condemn such advocacy when presented in a certain manner —in the context of an "alluring portrayal." What the Chief Judge means by such a portrayal is evident from some of the scenes he refers to, among them the scene in which "Mellors assisted Lady Chatterley in her preparations for the sexual act by unbuttoning her blouse and unzipping her dress; during which Mellors expressed his passion by caressing her buttocks, after reaching with his hand under her dress, noting that she had obligingly come to him clad only in a dress, without undergarments."[11]

Now this scene may not be in itself out-and-out obscenity. It may not meet the *Roth* test—especially if that test be applied to it in exactly the same manner as it would be applied to the same scene appearing in a book. Therefore, a number of such scenes appearing in a film would probably be insufficient to render it obscene. The "alluring portrayal" would fall short of clear-cut obscenity, though it would have some of the appeals and effects of obscenity. The appeals and effects would be intensified if—and to the extent that—the film is also immoral in theme and tone. What the statute, under the guidance of Chief Judge Conway, prohibits is a dominant theme characterized by recommendation of immoral conduct set in a context of sexual allurement such that the recommendation and the allurement, taken together, achieve the same effects that obscenity achieves.

Chief Judge Conway's approach to motion picture censorship relies for its justification upon two considerations: (1) the special problems posed by motion pictures and (2) the aims of obscenity regulation. The special problems posed by motion pictures result from the nature of their "communications" and their audiences.

> This is not a case of a book on a shelf or in a home—it is a case of mass dissemination of approved illicit sex by the spoken word and a visual act. It is a case not of one showing but of hundreds of showings. It is a case not of an audience of one but audiences of hundreds—in some cases thousands—at each showing. It is a case not merely of a theme of words but of a theme woven about scenes clearly portraying and suggesting acts of adultery.[12]

The film *Lady Chatterley's Lover* does not quite "clearly portray acts of adultery," but this passage directs attention to the fact that films such as this can scarcely be regarded as mere rational arguments in favor of one course of action or another. The "argument" of a motion picture is not simply verbal and intellectual—it is also visual and emotional. The "argument" for adultery is presented in a context of visual representations which arouse the passions. The effect is accomplished in a mass audience and in public.

Chief Judge Conway contends that such presentations achieve the result that obscenity regulation aims to prevent:

> There is no difference in substance between motion pictures which are corruptive of public morals, and sexually suggestive, because of a predominance of suggestive scenes, and those which achieve precisely the same effect by presenting only several such scenes in a clearly approbatory manner throughout the course of

the film. *The law is concerned with effect, not merely with but one means of producing it. We do not believe that a film which is rank pornography is objectionable simply because it excites a human appetite. Rather the objection lies in the corrosive effect upon the public sense of sexual morality* [italics in the original].[13]

Thus Chief Judge Conway endeavors to address himself to the real objective of obscenity regulation. He asks that the peculiar characteristics of motion pictures be considered in relation to the essential evil with which censorship is concerned. That evil cannot simply be the arousal of human desire—it must be, rather, the "corrosion" of "the public sense of sexual morality." The Chief Judge's opinion contains no definition of this expression. The language of his opinion suggests, however, a process of moral desensitizing, the deterioration of sensitivity to decency and indecency. This result, according to the Judge, can be brought about in more ways than one. It can be brought about by films which blatantly portray sexual acts and thus arouse lust in scene after scene. It can be brought about by films which present a few such scenes combined with immorality of theme and tone, thus arousing similar lust. Or it can be brought about by films which stimulate sexual desires to a lesser extent—because the sexual scenes are less blatant or because there are fewer of them—while extolling immoral conduct and depreciating moral standards throughout. In Chief Judge Conway's opinion, it would be absurd to say that public morality shall not be corrupted by the first device but that it may be corrupted by the last two. The absurdity would consist in regulating a factor conducive to an evil while leaving the evil itself alone. Films which are designed solely to arouse lust are to be condemned *because* they corrupt and corrode the public sense of what is decent. The same consequence results from films which approvingly portray immoral acts in scenes which arouse and stimulate the senses.*

Pornographic motion pictures seldom reach the general public. Of the films designed for the general public, those falling squarely within the strict definition of obscenity are few. Producers and directors will know how to make films which escape the precise terms of the definition. Therefore the greatest danger

---

* Chief Judge Conway's approach to the problem of *ends* raises the most difficult questions concerning censorship of obscenity in a liberal society. These questions will be considered in later chapters.

is to be expected from the "immoral" films in which corrupted forms of life are made appealing and in which depreciation of virtue and appeals to the senses are inextricably intertwined.

It is on the basis of premises and reasonings such as these that Chief Judge Conway has endeavored to frame a constitutional standard to meet the problems posed by motion pictures in recent times. His standard does not reach advocacy of ideas as such. Nor is it confined to obscenity as such. It reaches that intermediate area wherein advocacy and obscenity blend into an "alluring portrayal." It aims at that intermediate form of expression (characteristic of a certain kind of contemporary motion picture) in which advocacy, suggestiveness, incitement, and obscenity are combined.

The United States Supreme Court has struck down the New York effort to control material of this kind. Chief Judge Conway's formulations are not without difficulties, and it can certainly be argued that they are misapplied to this particular film. But, if the Chief Judge's reasoning be taken seriously, it is not simply the case that "the state, quite simply, has thus struck at the heart of constitutionally protected liberty."[14] At most, the state has struck at a mixed and ambiguous form of advocacy. Further, Chief Judge Conway does not, as the Court asserts, uphold "the denial of a license to any motion picture which approvingly portrays an adulterous relationship, quite without reference to the manner of its portrayal."[15] He upholds the denial of a license to motion pictures in which approval and a certain manner of portrayal are combined in a certain way. Finally, the Court accuses New York and the Chief Judge of banning a film because it argues "eloquently" for adultery. According to Justice Stewart, New York is willing to extend constitutional protection only to arguments which are unconvincing. This view overlooks the more subtle considerations which entered into the construction of the concept—"alluring portrayal." In Justice Stewart's opinion an appeal to sensuality is confused with an eloquent argument.

Chief Judge Conway's opinion leaves the impression of a judge wrestling with a problem. Justice Stewart's opinion does not leave this impression. If, as Justice Frankfurter asserts, the Court has disposed of the case by "sounding abstract and unqualified dogmas," the fault is in its failure to confront the two central considerations upon which the New York decision was based. Justice Stewart did not address himself to the issues involved in Chief

Judge Conway's interpretation of the ends of obscenity regulation, and he did not address himself to the arguments concerning the special character of motion picture "expression." The Court was ill-equipped to deal with the problem of ends on the basis of *Roth,* which had itself evaded the problem of ends. With regard to the problem of motion picture "advocacy," the Court was in a dilemma arising from the decision in 1952 of *Joseph Burstyn, Inc.* v. *Wilson.*[16]

The *Burstyn* decision declared that motion pictures are within the protection of the freedom of speech and press provisions of the First Amendment. This ruling rests upon the affirmation that motion pictures are "a significant medium for the communication of ideas" and "an organ of public opinion." Justice Clark asserted: "They may affect public attitudes and behavior in a variety of ways, ranging from direct espousal of a political or social doctrine to the subtle shaping of thought which characterizes all artistic expression."[17]

Burstyn rejected and overruled the doctrine established in the *Mutual Film* case (1915) that "the exhibition of moving pictures is a business pure and simple . . . not to be regarded . . . as a part of the press of the country or as organs of public opinion."[18] The *Mutual* doctrine rested upon three propositions: (1) motion pictures are products of a business enterprise conducted for profit; (2) their predominant concern is with entertainment; and (3) they have an inherent "capacity for evil" resulting from their large and mixed audiences and the attractions involved in their mode of presentation. According to the Court, "There are some things which should not have pictorial representation in public places and to all audiences."[19]

To these arguments Justice Clark's opinion replies: (1) the publication of books, magazines and newspapers is also a business enterprise conducted for profit, but it is not, for that reason, denied protection; (2) the fact that motion pictures are designed to entertain as well as to inform does not detract from their importance as organs of public opinion; and (3) if this form of expression has a special capacity for evil, such fact may be "relevant in determining the permissible scope of community control," but it cannot be grounds for denial of First Amendment protection.

These propositions do not answer all of the arguments which might be made on the basis of the *Mutual* position. Motion pictures, designed for mass audiences, must cater primarily to the public's desires for entertainment of various sorts. It can be reasonably predicted that that part of the public which goes to the movies for learning, for insights, or for art will remain numerically negligible. One cannot reasonably deny that the overwhelming majority of films—and particularly those which reach the largest audiences—are and must be vehicles of amusement. It will be argued that many books and magazines are also designed as vehicles for amusement. But these receive constitutional protection because of the character of the medium to which they belong, which in our society is an essential means for the communication of ideas and information. This cannot be said of motion pictures as it cannot be said of television.

But the Court, no doubt, is influenced by the changes which have taken place in the motion picture industry since 1915 and by the significance which motion pictures have assumed in American society in recent decades. It is quite true that motion pictures have become an influential factor in American life. They do "affect public attitudes and behavior," and they do contribute to "the subtle shaping of thought." But does this necessarily render them "organs of public opinion"? Some films "communicate ideas"—they address the mind (e.g., *Man's Fate,* based on the novel by André Malraux). But there are very few of this type compared to the number of those whose effect upon attitudes and whose shaping of thought is only a by-product of their effect upon emotions and their appeal to senses or desires. Such films may influence men's thoughts, but they do not, in any significant degree, address the faculties of thought. They may alter the opinions of a community, but they do not espouse or discuss opinions. If they affect behavior, it is probably not because they have stimulated the public to think about behavior or promoted insight into behavior. It is more likely that such effect upon conduct as most films may have is the result of their influence upon inclinations or psychic dispositions.

There are, of course, differences of degree, and the problem is complicated by the fact that genuine art engages the whole mind and not merely the intellect. Nevertheless, there is an essential distinction to be made between two radically different ways in which "the subtle shaping of thought" may take place. It is one thing to have one's thought and conduct concerning sexual morality shaped by the reading of Bertrand Russell's arguments in a book like *Marriage and Morals* and quite another to have them shaped by the viewing of films designed to present the most emotionally exciting scenes. In the former case the higher faculties are active; in the latter they are passive. In the former case one is invited to think about social or personal problems; in the latter, one is invited to experience sensations or desires.

Some of the earlier judicial decisions reflected cognizance of this distinction. In 1922 the New York Supreme Court said that a motion picture is "clearly distinguishable" from a newspaper because it "creates and purveys a mental atmosphere which is absorbed by the viewer without conscious mental effort. It requires neither literacy nor interpreter to understand it."[20] The older courts may have underestimated the potentialities of the film and they may have been insensitive to the complexities of artistic expression, but they kept in view the difference between addressing the mind and conditioning it. By declaring films "organs of public opinion" have the courts now begun to blur distinctions which ought to be kept clear?

This question is of practical import to subsequent courts which must wrestle with the implications of the *Burstyn* decision. That decision declares that films are communicators of ideas; but, nonetheless, it recognizes that they are not "necessarily subject to the precise rules governing any other particular method of expression."[21] Courts must now attempt to weigh these two factors. It is not quite clear what are the "peculiar problems" posed by motion pictures that *Burstyn* recognizes, and therefore it is not clear how these are to be weighed when an idea is present in a film. Whatever these problems (or dangers) are, presumably they may justify "prior restraint."[22] But do they justify the application of standards of obscenity designed with a view to the peculiar characteristics of a visual and public performance? The most obvious of these peculiar characteristics is that a film might reach multitudes of people before subsequent punishment could take effect. But did the Court also intend to recognize the differential effects of reading in private and viewing in public? A prurient appeal experienced in private and a prurient appeal experienced in public may constitute two different experiences. And it could often be the case that an event described in a book would not promote the lust of the average reader, while that same event presented on the screen would promote the lust of the average viewer. Likewise, the experience resulting from exposure to some particularly "suggestive" scenes in a film might well be similar to that resulting from the reading of pornography. And it is not unreasonable to suggest that one long sequence in a film could produce effects the equivalent of those produced by a novel whose "dominant theme, taken as a whole, appeals to prurient interests."

If legislators and courts are permitted to take account of such factors, they must now also take account of ideas and opinions expressed in motion pictures. Thus the *Burstyn* decision points, seemingly, in two directions. The dilemma posed by this duality is evident in the *Kingsley* case. The New York Court, relying on *Burstyn,* attempted to fashion a rule appropriate to motion pictures. Justice Stewart, relying on *Burstyn,* protected the advocacy of an idea.*

The *Kingsley Pictures* decision established rules which may be read as further definition of the *Roth* concept of "redeeming social importance." Advocacy of opinions or values concerning personal relations is to be included within the concept and may not be restrained. Advocacy of conduct contrary to community morals is included within the concept and may not be restrained. Such advocacy is protected whether or not it is presented visually or whether or not it is set in a context of emotional allurement.

The Court might well have protected the *Lady Chatterley* film without making freedom to advocate ideas the central issue of the case. Censorship of the novel on which it is based raises that issue more directly. The novel conveys, far more than does the film, a serious teaching about human affairs. Thus, in *Grove Press* v. *Christenberry*[23] Judge Frederick van Pelt Bryan relies in part upon *Kingsley*'s approach to "advocacy" to free the novel from Post Office censorship. But his primary reliance is upon the *Ulysses* decision and upon his interpretation of "contemporary community standards."

---

* The effects of this "duality" are also evident in cases concerning the constitutional validity of motion picture licensing systems. The Court, having upheld the constitutionality of motion picture licensing as such (on the grounds of the "peculiar problems" posed by motion pictures), then proceeds to impose increasingly strict limitations upon the operation of the licensing systems. See *Freedman* v. *Maryland,* 380 U.S. 51 (1965).

According to Judge Bryan, the *Ulysses* case provides the standards which, under *Roth,* ought to be applied to works of recognized literary merit. Thus, like Judge Woolsey, Judge Bryan makes his own literary analysis of the work. He concludes: "The book is replete with fine writing and with descriptive passages of rare beauty. There is no doubt of its literary merit."[24] And, like Judge Augustus Hand, he makes the artistic status of the work a decisive consideration. He offers as ingredients of the test a number of criteria: the author's literary status, the opinions of literary critics, the reputation of the publisher, and the character of his advertising and publicity for the book. D. H. Lawrence is an author of recognized literary stature. Most critics regard this book as an important one; its publication is a "major literary event." Grove Press is a reputable publisher and has not employed sensualism in its promotion of the book. This last consideration—concerning the promotion and advertising of a work—is emphasized in Judge Bryan's analysis. He emphasizes the fact that the publisher's advertising has focused on the serious literary qualities of the work and not on such appeals as it may have to sensuality. He observes that "there is no suggestion of any attempt to pander to the lewd and lascivious-minded for profit." These factors militate against the obscenity of the work.

Judge Bryan's use of the *Ulysses* decision is open to question on two points. He lays great stress upon the *Ulysses* criteria of "literary merit" and "honesty and seriousness of purpose," but he devotes little attention to the *Ulysses* tests of "libidinous effect." As a result, Judge Bryan's opinion leaves the impression that *Ulysses* has declared literary skill, or honesty, and obscenity to be mutually exclusive categories. Considerably more questionable is the judge's apparent identification of the *Ulysses* test and the American Law Institute definition of obscenity. According to Judge Bryan, the *Ulysses* judges meant by an "obscene" work one which appeals to "shameful or morbid interest in sex." This formula comes close to expressing what those judges meant by *pornography*—not obscenity.[25]

Judge Bryan's definition of "contemporary community standards" is the most important feature of his decision and its major contribution to the evolving case law. The Postmaster General had declared the work obscene in the light of contemporary community standards. Judge Bryan replies with what is, in effect, a list of forbidden definitions of this legal concept:

> The tests of obscenity are not whether the book or passages from it are in bad taste or shock or offend the sensibilities . . . of a substantial segment of the community. Nor are we concerned with whether the community would approve of Constance Chatterley's morals. The statute does not purport to regulate the morals portrayed or the ideas expressed in a novel, whether or not they are contrary to the accepted moral code, nor could it constitutionally do so.[26]

Of course, *Kingsley Pictures* would clearly forbid (and *Roth* would probably forbid) censorship of a work on the grounds that its explicit ideas are contrary to the prevailing moral code. But Judge Bryan's injunction also forbids censorship on the grounds that the "morals portrayed" are contrary to community standards. Further, offensiveness—of language and description—to the community's moral sense seems also to be ruled out as a test. If Judge Bryan's declarations on this subject are to be taken literally, one may ask what is left of the "contemporary community standards" test. This question can be broken down into two parts: (1) What are the community standards which may be applied? (2) What is the subject matter to which they may be applied?

Judge Bryan's opinion provides an answer to the first question. He points to the fact that "in one best-selling novel after another frank descriptions of the sex act and 'four-letter words' appear with frequency." This trend toward "frankness" appears in the mass media, in advertising, and in other areas of modern life. Judge Bryan asserts that "today such things are tolerated whether we approve or not." From these considerations he concludes that *Lady Chatterley's Lover* "does not exceed the outer limits of tolerance which the community as a whole gives to writing about sex and sex relations."

Thus the contemporary community standards to which the law may have recourse are not the community's present moral standards; they are its "outer limits of tolerance." The test is not what the community approves—what it regards as right—but what it is willing to tolerate. And, of course, the community may tolerate many things of which it disapproves. According to Judge Bryan, it is not enough that material be offensive to the members of the community or that it be in violation of their moral codes—it must be unendurable. For evidence of where these "outer limits" are, Judge Bryan recommends that one look to newspaper articles and reviews, to the kinds of materials which circulate in the medium of expression to which the work belongs, and to trends in the various media and in the general climate of opinion.

Presumably, the criteria, when discovered, cannot be applied to the idea content of a work. To what aspects of a work may they be applied, and how shall they be applied? This matter is left open and ambiguous. If the statute may not regulate the "morals portrayed," the only thing left for it to regulate is the manner of portrayal. These two aspects of portrayal are not easily separated in some literary works.

The Court of Appeals upheld Judge Bryan. In his "reluctant concurrence," Judge Leonard Moore was highly critical of Judge Bryan's application of contemporary community standards. He asserted:

> The fallacy of the "changing climate of opinion" argument is that it rotates in a circle. During recent years authors of the so-called school of realism have vied with each other to depict with accuracy all that could be observed by peeking through hypothetical keyholes and hiding under beds. . . . Each book contributed a few additional degrees to the temperature and by its unchallenged existence created the "contemporary community standards" which are used to justify its acceptance as consonant with such standards.[27]

Here Judge Moore argues that changes in community moral values are not entirely spontaneous and ungovernable developments. They are fostered by authors and judges. Authors venture into new fields of salacity on the assumption that a section of the public will be receptive and that judges will be permissive. The judges are permissive; noting an increase in the publication and consumption of such material, they conclude that community opinion is changing. Under the influence of these publications, plus their legal sanction, the climate of opinion does change. On the basis of this new opinion, authors venture farther beyond the earlier standards, carrying their publics with them. The judges, noting these changes, once again revised their conception of community standards. This is followed by increasingly sordid materials and further changes of opinion.

Judge Moore contends that judges have been substituting their understanding of community standards for the communities' understanding of their own standards and that courts are now caught up in an endless effort to discover "some vague and ever-retreating boundary line." He asserts that this will continue unless the various communities can manage to speak through their legislatures and make known their standards. In the meantime, "this case must be decided in accordance with contemporary judicial standards, and therefore I reluctantly concur."[28]

Judge Moore's objections to the novel *Lady Chatterley's Lover* are questionable. He does not sufficiently distinguish between serious and sordid literature dealing with sex. Yet, Judge Bryan is open to similar criticism. In order to protect an evidently serious work, he has formulated standards which indiscriminately protect the serious and the sordid. Judge Bryan's formula excludes from the definition of obscenity expression of a very different sort from that of D. H. Lawrence, thus blurring the distinction between, for example, a work like *Lady Chatterley* and a work like *Candy*.[29] Both are tolerated; neither is obscene.

Was it necessary to defend *Lady Chatterley* by recourse to the "outer limits of tolerance" formula? Is there any reason to conclude that this work could not be adequately defended on the basis of its redeeming social importance as a serious and powerful statement about modern life and human happiness? Such an argument could be supplemented by the *Ulysses* opinion (properly interpreted and applied) and by an application of contemporary community standards which recognizes changes in public attitudes toward literature.

The worth of this novel need not be argued solely on the basis of the author's "sincerity" and the "fine writing" it contains—as Judge Bryan's opinion tends to argue. The aesthetic virtues of the work are not equally acclaimed by all critics. Judge Bryan might have relied more upon that part of the *Ulysses* opinion which emphasized the depth of the author's insights into the life and times of his characters. While such evaluations are difficult for judges to make, they could be applied to *Lady Chatterley's Lover* in the same manner as they were applied to *Ulysses*.

Considering both the book as a whole and its nature, it could also be argued that *Lady Chatterley's Lover* would not appeal to the prurience of the average man in the contemporary community. Community standards concerning literary expression *have* changed to an extent that would render the prurient appeal of this work subordinate to its other—redemptive—appeals. In support of this contention one could point, as Judge Bryan points, to reviews appearing in newspapers with circulations of millions.

Such arguments, though not flawless in all respects, should be sufficient to decide the case and save this work.* But Judge Bryan has gone much further than this. The "outer limits of tolerance" concept covers more ground than is necessary. And it is susceptible to the charge directed to it by Judge Moore that it imposes upon the community standards and attitudes which the community does not really hold.

Judge Bryan's interpretation of community tolerance appears to be derived from observation of the latest trends. It may be that "frank descriptions of the sex act" which now appear in novels represent "trends appearing in all media of public expression."[30] But it is only Judge Bryan's formulation which requires him to take his bearings from the most "advanced" forms of expression and conduct. As Judge Moore's argument implies, Judge Bryan appears to derive his judicial criteria from anticipation of the community standards of the near future.

In this manner the tendencies and standards of the most permissive sections of society are applied to the whole community. Large sections of the community may disapprove of those tendencies and standards but they "tolerate" forms of expression flowing from them. This concept of tolerance is ambiguous. Many members of the community do not tolerate *Candy*. The National Organization for Decent Literature campaigns against it. Many citizens are deeply concerned about those very trends in the mass media and in advertising which Judge Bryan says they tolerate. How are citizens to indicate that they find a certain form of expression or a certain publication unendurable? How are they, in a liberal society, to express the difference between that which they strongly disapprove of but will tolerate and that which they will not endure? Some seek to express their conception of "outer limits" by pressing for legal action against obscenity, by picketing

* Here I consider the case for *Lady Chatterley's Lover* solely in the context of present-day constitutional law. For a discussion of the novel in a broader literary and political context, see chapter 6, pp. 236–38, and chapter 7, pp. 250–51.

theaters, and by "clean-up" campaigns in local neighborhoods. But if they fail to achieve their objectives, they, like most citizens of liberal society, will tolerate the continuation of the evils they object to.

How, then, are judges to determine when society's outer limits of tolerance have been reached and exceeded? This concept is evidently more serviceable for the purpose of relaxing restraints than it is for the purpose of enforcing them. It is not difficult to determine that a motion picture or paperback novel does not exceed the outer limits. Applying some of Judge Bryan's criteria, one can note that the motion picture is shown in many theaters to large audiences and that many thousands of copies of the novel have been sold. One can also note that similar films and novels enjoy similar circulation. These forms of expression are, therefore, within the outer limits of community toleration and cannot be obscene. This, however, would be a perplexing conclusion. The widespread circulation of obscenity is supposed to be the very evil against which the statutes are directed. It would be an anomaly if such circulation, tolerated by the public, were to become a sufficient condition for a publication to lose the character of obscenity.

Judge Bryan inherited the "community standards" problem from the *Roth* case. He resolved it by defining "community standards" in such a way that this criterion is least likely to conflict with the other criteria laid down in that case. It is unlikely that findings under the "outer limits of tolerance" standard would result in condemnation of a work of "redeeming social importance" *or* a work which does not arouse perverted lust. This process of reconciliation is continued in *Manual Enterprises* v. *Day*.[31]

Manual Enterprises, Inc., was engaged in the publication of magazines designed for homosexuals. They consisted largely of photographs of nude or nearly-nude male models in various provocative poses, presented with the name of each model and photographer and the address of the photographer. They also contained advertisements by independent studios offering sensually provocative photographs of nude men.

The distinguishing features of this case arise from the fact that the prurience of the magazines was not contested and was indeed acknowledged by all parties. The publisher avowed that he had designed them to appeal to the prurient interests of homosexuals.

He did not seriously claim that they possessed educational, literary, or scientific value. In the administrative hearings psychologists called by the government had testified in considerable detail concerning the symbolic significance and prurient appeal to homosexuals of the various poses and objects portrayed in these magazines.* The publisher and the government agreed that "the magazines are read almost entirely by homosexuals, and possibly a few adolescent males," and that they would not appeal to the average adult.[32]

The judicial officer of the Post Office held that, since prurient appeal is evident and admitted, the determination of obscenity must depend upon interpretation of the "average man" requirement of *Roth*. He held that publications aimed at a special audience must be judged by their effect upon that audience. Since the magazines have a prurient appeal to the average homosexual, they fall within the statute. Further, since some of the advertisers were found in possession of hard-core pornography, the publications fall under the advertising provisions of the statute which forbid "giving information" on where obscene materials can be obtained. The judicial officer's findings and rulings were upheld by the District Court and the Court of Appeals.

The Supreme Court reversed these rulings, holding that the judicial officer and the lower courts had addressed themselves to the wrong issue. They had erroneously assumed that, once they had established prurient appeal, the dispositive question before them was that of the relevant audience in terms of which such

---

* The following is an extract from the government's description of the magazines: "The magazine contained little textual material, with pictures of male models dominating almost every page. . . . Many of the photographs were nude male models, usually posed with some object in front of their genitals. . . . A number were of nude or partially nude males with emphasis on their bare buttocks, . . . although none of the pictures directly exposed the model's genitals, some showed his pubic hair and others suggested what appeared to be a semi-erect penis, . . . others showed male models reclining with their legs (and sometimes their arms as well) spread wide apart. . . . Two of the magazines had pictures of pairs of models posed together suggestively. . . . Each of the magazines contained photographs of models with swords or other long objects. The magazines also contained photographs of virtually nude models wearing only shoes, boots, helmets or leather jackets. . . . There were also pictures of models posed with chains or of one model beating another while a third held his face in his hands as if weeping." See 370 U.S. 478 (1961) at 489–90, n. 13.

appeal shall be tested. But, according to Justice Harlan,* the *Roth* case did not establish prurient interest appeal as the sole test of obscenity. In adition, it established a test of "patent offensiveness." Said the Court:

> We do not reach the question thus thought below to be dispositive on this aspect of the case. For we find lacking in these magazines an element which, no less than "prurient interest," is essential to a valid determination of obscenity under S 1461, and to which neither the Post Office Department nor the Court of Appeals addressed themselves at all. These magazines cannot be deemed so offensive on their face as to affront current community standards of decency—a quality that we shall hereafter refer to as "patent offensiveness" or "indecency."[33]

Thus a finding of obscenity must now involve two distinct findings and meet two separate tests. The findings of the Post Office meet the "prurient interest" test but fail the "patent offensiveness" test. Justice Harlan grants that these homosexual magazines are "dismally unpleasant, uncouth and tawdry," but he concludes: "Divorced from their 'prurient interest' appeal (a separate issue), these portrayals of the male nude cannot fairly be regarded as more objectionable than many portrayals of the female nude that *society tolerates*"[34] (italics mine).

Such definitions of patent offensiveness as appear in the opinion point to an "outer limits of tolerance" standard or a "hard-core pornography" standard. An "outer limits of tolerance" standard is implicit in the sentence just quoted. It is also implicit in the Court's assertion that the magazines under consideration "cannot . . . be deemed to be beyond the pale of contemporary notions of *rudimentary decency*" (italics mine). Evidently, the Court now reads the "community standards" criterion to mean "beyond the pale" of the community's most minimal moral demands. A hard-core pornography standard is implied in Justice Harlan's identification of patent offensiveness with "obnoxiously debasing portrayals of sex" and with "material whose indecency is self-demonstrating."

---

* This decision was announced by Justice Harlan, in an opinion in which Justice Stewart joined. The Chief Justice and Justices Brennan, Douglas, and Black concurred in the result. In the discussion which follows I refer to Justice Harlan's opinion as that of "the Court" because the doctrine of that opinion has been adopted by a majority of the present Court and incorporated into the constitutional law of this subject.

Yet, he neither affirms nor denies this implication. He does not commit the Court to a hard-core pornography standard, but he reads the federal obscenity statute and *Roth* in such a way that they become susceptible to interpretations moving in that direction.

The opinion also considered two other problems: the relevant "community" by whose standards of decency the materials shall be judged, and a publisher's liability for materials advertised in his publication. Justice Harlan concluded that the relevant community must be the nation, and the standards of decency a national standard. With regard to the advertising, he held that, while some of the advertisers were purveying "what undoubtedly may be regarded as 'hard-core' photographs," there was no proof that petitioners had knowledge of this. The requirements of *scienter* must be applied to the Post Office's civil proceedings in the same way and with the same rigor as they are applied in criminal proceedings.[35] Justice Clark, in dissent, charges the Court with requiring the Post Office to be "the world's largest disseminator of smut and grand informer of the names and places where obscene material may be obtained."*

Thus in *Manual Enterprises* v. *Day* the Supreme Court extends the protection of the First Amendment to materials falling squarely within the *Roth* definition of "prurience" (whether that definition be understood in terms of ordinary lust or perverted lust), even when such materials are unredeemed by any intellectual or literary values. The record shows that the Manual Enterprises magazines contained very little textual material and no material with any redeeming qualities. *Manual Enterprises* v. *Day* involves a radical extension of First Amendment protection. In support of the doctrine of "patent offensiveness," Justice Harlan presents an argument based on *Roth* and an argument about the consequences to be expected from failure to apply the doctrine.

The Justice asserts that the *Roth* decision established the "patent offensiveness" concept no less than the "prurient interest" concept. But his opinion does not succeed in revealing just where

---

* 370 U.S. 478 (1961) at 519. Justice Brennan, joined by the Chief Justice and Justice Douglas, would decide the case on the grounds that the Post Office is without power to remove matter from the mails prior to judicial determination of obscenity. His concurring opinion contains a long argument against the constitutionality of "administrative censorship."

in the *Roth* case this concept is to be found. Its endeavors to do so are ambiguous. Justice Harlan maintains that the expression "prurient interest" was "but a compendious way" of embracing both tests.[36] But it is most difficult to discover "patent offensiveness" in the *Roth* terminology which sets forth "prurient interests." Justice Harlan refers to the American Law Institute definition of obscenity (cited in *Roth* in a footnote): "A thing is obscene if, considered as a whole, its predominant appeal is to prurient interests . . . *and* if it goes substantially beyond contemporary limits of candor in description or representation of such matters." Admittedly, the ALI definition contains two tests. But Justice Brennan had spoken of "prurient interests" as a single test, defined in terms of "lust" or "lustful thoughts." Furthermore, it is by no means clear that the second ALI test is coextensive with "patent offensiveness." A representation may well go substantially beyond customary limits of candor without having the character of "self-demonstrating indecency," and without being, or bordering on, hard-core pornography. The ALI clearly rejects a hard-core pornography standard.[37]

As is suggested in the preceding chapter, it is open to question whether or not the *Roth* Justices intended to establish a separate community standards test. But, whatever they intended in this regard, they said nothing to indicate that their community conscience standard would reach only such material as the Court now calls "patently offensive." Neither the trial judge nor the text of *Roth* nor any passage in any opinion therein gives indication of such a major departure from the ordinary case law understanding of such terms as "community standards" and "community conscience." Indeed, considering the language of *Roth*—the majority as well as the concurring and dissenting opinions—and the precedents cited therein, the indications are to the contrary.*

The *Roth* decision did not establish a "patent offensiveness" test. But this new test does enable the Court to extricate itself from some of the dilemmas of *Roth*. As indicated in chapter 1, "pru-

---

* The observation is relevant that Justice Harlan (the formulator of "patent offensiveness") dissented from the *Roth* majority on the grounds that its obscenity test was too broad and inclusive (see 354 U.S. 476 [1957] at 507), while Justice Brennan (the formulator of "prurient interests") does not refer to "patent offensiveness" in his *Manual Enterprises* opinion and concurs "for a reason different from my Brother Harlan's." 370 U.S. 478 (1961) at 495.

rient interests" could be defined as sexual desires *or* as extreme or perverted sexual desires, and community standards could be applied in more ways than one. The *Manual Enterprises* Court could have sought to resolve the problem by settling for one or the other definition of prurience. Instead, it adopted the concept of outer limits of tolerence and set this up as a separate community standards test which confines the operation of the obscenity statute at least as much as would the second definition of prurience referred to above. The patent offensiveness test insures that the statute can reach only such material (and probably not all such material) as would be reached by the ALI concept of prurient interests. Thus the *Roth* tension between obscenity and redeeming social importance is greatly reduced. The potential conflict between determinations of redeeming social importance and determinations of prurient appeal is reduced by the addition of the new test.

Justice Harlan's case for patent offensiveness does not rest solely on such tenuous support as may be found for it in *Roth*. His second line of argument concerns the protection of worthwhile literature. He contends that to dispense with the requisite of patently offensive portrayal would be to "put the American public in jeopardy of being denied access to many worthwhile works in literature, science or art." But the *Roth* decision established a number of criteria designed to minimize this danger, among them its "redeeming social importance" criterion and its "average person," "dominant theme," and "prurient interests" criteria. If Justice Harlan does not regard these concepts as sufficient to serve the purpose, it must be because of his view that "one would not have to travel far even among the acknowledged masterpieces in any of these fields to find works whose 'dominant theme' might, not beyond reasonable doubt, be said to appeal to the 'prurient interest' of the reader or observer."[38]

The Justice does not name any masterpieces which can reasonably be said to fall within this category. Nor does he defend the assumption (implicit in his assertion) that a substantial portion of the world's great literature is calculated to appeal to prurience as that term is used in *Roth*. It might well be argued that one would have to travel quite far to find any genuine literature the dominant theme of which is designed to arouse lust and does arouse lust in the average reader. Perhaps Justice Harlan had in mind the works of such authors as Boccaccio, Rabelais, and D. H. Lawrence. It is evident that the objective of these authors, as discoverable in their works, is not to arouse sexual desire, but to teach a view of life or to entertain by means of satire or, as in the case of Rabelais, to expose the follies of men by means of ridicule. To say that great literature treating of sex often appeals to prurient interests is to ignore the crucial differences between an aesthetic (or intellectual) and a pornographic purpose, and between an aesthetic experience and an experience of lust.* If the protection of good literature was its aim, *Manual Enterprises* may be said to have achieved its aim by blurring the distinction between what is genuine literature and what is not.

It may be contended that a great work may incidentally—contrary to its purpose and its nature—have a prurient effect on certain persons. But it would require more discussion of the matter than *Manual Enterprises* contains to show that works like those of Boccaccio, Rabelais, and Lawrence have a tendency to affect the average modern reader in this way. And even where such effects could be demonstrated, *Roth* has provided protection for works of redeeming social importance. It is difficult to understand why Justice Harlan does not regard this standard as adequate for the protection of acknowledged masterpieces.

If the Court's arguments in support of patent offensiveness are highly questionable, so also is its concept of community standards. Patent offensiveness is designed to function as a contemporary community standards test indicating society's outer limits of tolerance. The Court finds that these homosexual magazines do not transcend the outer limits because their contents are not "more objectionable than many portrayals of the female nude that society tolerates." The question of whether society does indeed tolerate such portrayals has already been discussed. But even if society can be said to tolerate lust-inciting portrayals of female nudity, it would require some argument to show that society does not make the distinction between normal (heterosexual) and abnormal (homosexual) lust. The Court offers no defense of its refusal to differentiate between appeals to perverted prurience and appeals to normal prurience.

Furthermore, the majority opinion fails to deal with certain evidence presented in the case which could well be significant. It does not consider, or mention, the psychiatric testimony concern-

---

* These distinctions will be explored in chapter 6.

ing the psychological meaning and impact of the various poses and instruments portrayed. This evidence would certainly be relevant to any determination of the effects of these materials upon readers. And the Court does not concern itself with the possible import of testimony in the record before it that these magazines may appeal to "a few adolescent males." The ends of the statute would surely require that these factors receive some attention.

The reasoning employed in *Manual Enterprises* v. *Day* is at best inadequate. It ignores significant aspects of the case and fails to establish the validity of the conclusions reached. But the consequences of the defective arguments employed in this decision extend beyond the case. These defective arguments contribute to the distortion of basic issues and concepts in this field, and, further, they may contribute to the confusion of the public. The nature of great literature is obscured when such literature is rendered indistinguishable from prurient appeals. The concept of community standards is distorted when the normal and the perverted are confounded and when materials openly appealing to prurience and nothing else are held to be within "the prevailing bounds of decency."[39] Finally, the arguments of *Manual Enterprises* do not clarify, but, rather, they obscure the purposes of obscenity regulation.

The Court grants that these magazines aim at the commercial exploitation of unfortunate persons by means of blatant appeals to their weaknesses and, further, that they are utterly lacking in any redeeming qualities which might be balanced against this exploitation. The Court asserts, in effect, that it is not, and never was, the purpose of the statute to reach such material and prevent such exploitation. What, then, is the purpose of the statute? The *Manual Enterprises* Court never addresses itself to this question directly. What emerges from the case is its conclusion that the operation of the statute is confined to materials which appeal to prurient interests in a manner extremely offensive to the members of the community. But why should mere "offensiveness" be the decisive criterion? Why is "offensiveness" more obnoxious to the purpose of the statute than are invitations to sexual perversion or the exploitation of psychologically sick persons? If the statute is designed to prevent the occurrence of something harmful, it would seem that the latter effects are more obviously harmful than the former. None of the major judicial decisions of the past, either liberal or conservative, have rested the case for obscenity regulation simply on a need to protect citizens from materials which offend them. Nor does Justice Harlan endeavor to make a case for such protection as a legitimate aim of regulation. But the effect of his decision is to impose this purpose upon obscenity statutes. Thus *Manual Enterprises* further confuses the problem of the rationale for obscenity regulation.

These confusions and distortions are the result of the Court's one-sided approach to its problem. The text of *Manual Enterprises* does not reflect any concern with the rationale for obscenity regulation. It does not consider the ends of the statute in relation to the principles of the First Amendment. Rather, to the extent that the opinion concerns itself with the purpose of the statute at all, it does so only with a view to extending and securing the categories of materials protected from it. Thus the *Manual Enterprises* decision reads as if its sole concern were to effect the maximum restriction of censorship by the most effective means. It is difficult to avoid the conclusion that the doctrine of patent offensiveness, the arguments brought to its support, and the manner of its application to this case are but devices to reach this predetermined end.

Was it necessary to adopt this means of protecting First Amendment values? If the Court's aim was to extricate works of acknowledged excellence or importance from the tensions of the *Roth* decision, it could have done that by declaring that, where such works are concerned, redeeming social importance shall be the decisive criterion. Works of disputable social importance would still remain subject, somewhat, to the *Roth* tensions. Their social value would have to be weighed against such prurient appeal as they may be found to have under the liberalized obscenity test. The *Roth* concepts were designed to create a strong presumption in favor of works which can claim artistic or intellectual merit and to place a heavy burden of proof upon people who would charge them with obscenity. The Court could have emphasized this aspect of *Roth,* thus clarifying some of the ambiguities, by elaborating and refining its redeeming social importance doctrine. This would mean that materials in the borderline area (and an occasional good work) would remain open to charges of obscenity, and the courts would have the task of deciding upon their social importance.

The *Manual Enterprises* Court has chosen the other way out of *Roth*'s problems—it has further restricted the legal definition of obscenity. The new definition releases from any taint of obscenity all materials except those wholly, self-evidently, and extremely obnoxious to the great majority. Since, under present attitudes, works of acknowledged excellence can never fall within the latter category, they are utterly secure. Works of less than acknowledged excellence which, however, evidence some merit of some kind are almost completely secure; it would require a rare set of circumstances to bring them legitimately within the new definition. The price of this additional protection is the exposure of the community to a great mass of materials conspicuously appealing to prurience, much of it verging on pornography. This kind of material was hitherto believed to be obscene. Under its new conception of community standards, the Court authoritatively declares that such material is not obscene. The possible effects of this declaration upon community decency, though difficult to determine with precision, may also be weighed as a cost.

Justice Harlan's opinion does not devote any attention to the possible cost. It does not consider whether the gains in terms of additional protection for valuable materials justify the losses in terms of the ends of obscenity regulation. It could be argued that the additional protection which *Manual Enterprises* provides for works of great merit or of some social value is small compared to the protection it provides for materials of great prurience and no value. The former could have been protected almost, but not quite, as adequately under a redeeming social importance doctrine which would have permitted the law to operate upon worthless prurient material. This solution would have involved the refinement of criteria which would enable the law to distinguish more effectively between the worthy and the worthless, between art and obscenity. And it would have required the Court to confront some cases in which the distinction is difficult to make. In such cases it would have to weigh the virtues and vices of the materials before it. Instead, under the doctrine of patent offensiveness, the Court has chosen a course of action which relieves it of the task of making these distinctions and greatly reduces the number of occasions on which it may be required to weigh diverse values. This approach to the problems of obscenity regulation, begun in *Kingsley Pictures* and developed in *Grove Press* v. *Christenberry* and in *Manual Enterprises* is carried to its conclusion in *Jacobellis* v. *Ohio*.[40]

The *Jacobellis* decision was announced by Justice Brennan in an opinion which was joined by Justice Goldberg. The core of the opinion is contained in the following passage:

> The question of the proper standard . . . has been the subject of much of the discussion and controversy since our decision in *Roth* seven years ago. Recognizing that the test for obscenity enunciated there—"whether to the average person, applying contemporary community standards, the dominant theme of the material taken as a whole appeals to prurient interest" . . . is not perfect, we think any substitute would raise equally difficult problems, and we therefore adhere to that standard. We would reiterate, however, our recognition in *Roth* that obscenity is excluded from constitutional protection only because it is "utterly without redeeming social importance." . . . It follows that material dealing with sex in a manner that advocates ideas . . . or has literary or scientific or artistic value or any other forms of social importance may not be branded as obscenity and denied the constitutional protection. Nor may the constitutional status of the material be made to turn on a "weighing" of its social importance against its prurient appeal, for a work cannot be proscribed unless it is "utterly" without social importance. . . . It should also be recognized that the *Roth* standard requires in the first instance a finding that the material "goes substantially beyond customary limits of candor in description or representation of such matter." . . . In the absence of such a deviation from society's standards of decency, we do not see how official inquiry into allegedly prurient appeal of a work of expression can be squared with the guarantees of the First and Fourteenth Amendments. See *Manual Enterprises, Inc.* v. *Day* . . . (Opinion of Harlan, J.).[41]

This passage represents an effort to resolve, as definitively as possible, the major judicial dilemmas arising out of *Roth*. It is apparent that the concept of redeeming social importance is to be defined in minimal terms. Materials shall be held to possess the redeeming qualities whenever they are found to contain *any* "advocacy" of any "ideas" or *any* kind or degree of literary merit. Presumably, the Court will apply only the most minimal standards for the determination of intellectual or aesthetic worth. Further, if a work embodying some intellectual or artistic content be also prurient and patently offensive, there shall be no weighing of the degree or amount of its social value against the degree or amount of the prurience and offensiveness. Its social importance (as here defined) shall suffice to save it from the operation of obscenity statutes. Likewise, the absence of patent offensiveness shall suffice to save a work characterized by prurience (in any degree) and utter lack of social value. Finally, if a work be found patently offensive and totally worthless, it can receive constitutional protection on the grounds that it does not meet the prurience test. Thus, enforcement of obscenity law is required to run the gauntlet of three separate tests, failure to meet any of which shall be a sufficient condition for judicial protection of any written or visual expression.

The above interpretation of *Jacobellis* finds confirmation in the Court's citation of *Attorney General* v. *Tropic of Cancer*[42] as a decision in accord with its opinion. A brief explication of the reasoning of the Massachusetts high court in that case will throw some additional light on the nature and application of the minimal standards sanctioned by *Jacobellis*.

The Massachusetts court finds it irrelevant that *Tropic of Cancer* "at many places is repulsive, vulgar and grossly offensive" or that "the result is as dull, dreary and offensive as the writer of this opinion finds almost all of 'Tropic.' "[43] What is relevant is that "the book must be accepted as a conscious effort to create a work of literary art."* The wording of the decision places a heavy stress upon an author's intention and strongly implies that a book is not to be declared obscene if its author is "attempting to be a literary artist." The court supports its conclusions concerning this "attempt" by reference to the assertion of "competent critics" that *Tropic of Cancer* has serious purpose and contains the author's attitudes about sex and culture. From this it would seem to follow that the conditions of redeeming social importance are met if it can be shown that an author intended to produce art and if literary critics will testify that he has expresed his opinions in his work. The Massachusetts court does not attempt to balance these redeeming qualities against the "gross offensiveness" of "almost all of 'Tropic.' "

In the *Jacobellis* case the work under consideration (the film *The Lovers*) did not receive the kind of critical support afforded *Tropic of Cancer*. The Supreme Court said: "The film was favor-

---

* The discussion that follows is not concerned with the validity of any of the judgments made about the novel. Its sole concern is with the legal criteria employed.

ably received in a number of national publications and disparaged in others, and was rated by at least two critics of national stature among the best films of the year in which it was produced."[44] As far as critical support is concerned, this, apparently, is enough.

The *Jacobellis* approach to obscenity cases is designed to foreclose, as much as words can foreclose, consideration of degrees of social and literary merit. And it is designed to prevent, as much as words can prevent, the weighing of the relative values of a work against the evils at which obscenity statutes are aimed.

These ends are achieved with some sacrifice of logic and clarity. The passage previously quoted from the *Jacobellis* decision (p. 70) begins with a reaffirmation of the *Roth* obscenity test. According to that test a work is legally obscene if its dominant theme appeals to the prurient interests of the average person. The Court then proceeds to assert that the work cannot be legally obscene if it contains *any* ideas or artistry. This reasoning appears to affirm —and then to deny—that the terms of the prurient interests test constitute the legal definition of obscenity. Logically, there would be three ways to avoid this ambiguity. The Court could have maintained that socially important works do not appeal to prurient interests. Of course, it could not say this and still maintain its minimal conception of social importance. The prurience test could have been revised to render it exclusive of materials containing any ideas or artistry. This is not done. Or, the Court could have said that the legally obscene is that material in which prurience outweighs social value. This solution is explicitly rejected. As a result, the *Roth* definition of obscenity is verbally reasserted—but in fact it is undermined or at least greatly diminished in significance. Indeed, the internal logic and the very meaning of the definition is now more than ever in doubt. What can it mean to consider the "appeal" of the "dominant theme" of a work if prurient appeal cannot be weighed against redeeming qualities? Surely any judgment on the *effects* of a work as a whole must involve some such weighing.

In *Jacobellis* v. *Ohio,* as in *Manual Enterprises* v. *Day,* the logic and clarity of the law is sacrificed in the interest of further restriction of obscenity regulation. It is difficult to see how anything other than the worst pornography can meet the three tests now arrayed against regulation. What kind of material other than hard-core pornography is prurient *and* patently offensive *and* utterly devoid of ideas or artistry?* If the Court has not avowed a hard-core pornography standard in the technical sense of that terminology, it appears to have achieved a similar result by other means.[45] And it has achieved this result by purporting to leave the concepts of *Roth* intact.

The legal situation is further confused by the manner in which the concepts now employed have achieved the status of constitutional law. They do not seem to represent the reasoning of any solid majority of the Court. The doctrine of patent offensiveness was announced by Justices Harlan and Stewart. Justice Brennan's concurring opinion, joined by the Chief Justice and Justice Douglas, makes no reference to "patent offensiveness" and rests upon very different grounds. In *Jacobellis* the Justice appears to have accepted the substance of the doctrine, though he does not refer to it by name. The *Jacobellis* decision was announced by two Justices. There are four concurring opinions (most of them embodying different approaches to the issues) † and two dissents.

The *Jacobellis* dissents, written by Chief Justice Warren and Justice Harlan, reflect considerable uneasiness with the trend of the decisions and the resultant posture of the law in this area. Both opinions indicate that the decisions have failed to provide lower courts and legislatures with the necessary guidance. Both Justices find it necessary to remark that there are public interests involved in the censorship of obscenity. The Chief Justice asserts that "we are called upon to reconcile the right of the Nation and of the States to maintain a decent society and, on the other hand, the right of individuals to express themselves freely in accordance with the guarantees of the First and Fourteenth Amendments."[46] Justice Harlan states the problem as one of "achieving a sensible accommodation between the public interest sought to be served by obscenity laws and protection of genuine rights of free expression."[47]

These Justices evidently do not think that recent judicial decisions have been providing for a "sensible accommodation." Chief

---

* One may wonder whether certain kinds of materials traditionally regarded as "hard-core" will meet these tests. See the discussion of the *Fanny Hill* case, *infra*, pp. 77–79.

† Justices Black and Douglas advocating the abandonment of censorship, Justice Stewart advocating a hard-core pornography test, Justice Goldberg emphasizing the character of the particular film in question, and Justice White concurring in the result without opinion.

Justice Warren would provide for it by allowing for the application of local community standards and by committing the enforcement of the *Roth* rule largely to state and lower federal courts. He would limit Supreme Court review of findings of obscenity to the question of whether such findings are supported by "sufficient evidence." Justice Harlan would continue to review the evidence in obscenity cases *de novo,* but he would differentiate between federal and state obscenity regulation, allowing to the latter a greater latitude than to the former. He would apply to federal regulation the *Roth* and *Manual Enterprises* tests, while holding the states to a less stringent test of "rationality."[48]

These suggestions are not without difficulties. The application of local community standards or a test of "rationality" could well result in the censorship of genuinely valuable materials. Justice Harlan's approach would in effect turn over the major censorship function to the states, by whom, perhaps, it cannot be adequately handled. It can be argued convincingly that the circulation of obscenity cannot be adequately controlled by states and localities.[49] Adoption of the Chief Justice's approach would amount to a decision *not* to face the central problem—the problem of "sensible accommodation" or "reconciliation" on a national level. Both of these proposed solutions are efforts to achieve by procedural readjustments that accommodation of public interests which ultimately can only be achieved by undertaking to determine what those interests are and by confronting the underlying issues. Chief Justice Warren and Justice Harlan have contributed to a series of decisions and judgments that are characterized by the avoidance of underlying issues and that lead to those confusions about which the Justices themselves complain.

The Supreme Court decisions in *Kingsley Pictures* through *Jacobellis* did not confront the problem of obscenity regulation under the First Amendment; they turned away from that problem. In case after case the Court declined to consider how the legitimate claims of free expression and the legitimate claims of public morality can be defined and harmonized. In case after case the Court proceeded as if its sole concern were to extend more and more protection to more and more categories of expression. The aims of obscenity censorship, as well as the social problems to which they may be addressed, were all but ignored in these decisions. In each decision the Justices concerned themselves with the terms and objects of a statute only to the end that its operation may be restricted. These one-sided judicial decisions were accompanied by a steady growth in the publication and circulation of increasingly salacious materials. Many new publications devoted to prurience appeared on the market, and many older publications became increasingly bold in their detailed presentations of lust, perversion, and violence.[50] The refusal to weigh these easily predictable consequences is the distinguishing feature of the cases considered above.

This libertarian one-sidedness represents a radical break with the liberalizing decisions of the past. A brief summary of the trend from *Kennerley* to *Jacobellis* should suffice to support this assertion. In *Kennerley,* Judge Learned Hand introduced the "present-day community conscience" standard in an effort to give social interests other than morality some weight in the legal scales. The judge wanted to protect society's interest in "truth and beauty."[51] The *Dennett* and *Ulysses* cases established standards protecting educational works and works of literary excellence, while permitting the law to reach "libidinous" materials. The *Levine* decision, aiming at a "passable compromise" between social interests in art and morality, established a balancing test: The salacious effect of a work is to be weighed against its aesthetic, or other, values. All of these decisions recognize a need to accommodate diverse public interests.[52] Their aim is to provide for the free expression of what is predominantly good and to permit the legal control of what is predominantly bad. The *Roth* case does not effect a sharp break with this tradition: some weighing and balancing of values is still indicated. *Roth* weighs the scale heavily in favor of free expression, however, and leaves unclarified the interests and purposes involved in obscenity regulation.

Out of the ambiguities of *Roth,* the *Manual Enterprises* and *Jacobellis* decisions have fashioned standards designed effectively to preclude any balancing of literary values against salaciousness and, hence, any weighing of the public interests involved on both sides of the obscenity issue. The smallest degree of artistic or intellectual content shall now prevail in the judicial scales over the greatest degree of vice. Can it reasonably be said that the effect of these provisions is to protect society's interest in "truth and beauty," in the expression of the human mind and imagination?

Whatever may be the interpretation of those who have framed these provisions, it is evident that their real effect is simply to protect expression as such.

Upon what rational grounds did the Court so subordinate the claims of public morality to the claims of free expression? It cannot be said that the claims of public morality have been examined and found to be groundless. The judicial decisions under consideration do not examine them. The Court has not adopted the view that obscenity has no harmful effects. It does not discuss the effects of obscenity. It does not undertake to show that prurient materials lacking in patent offensiveness are harmless. The possible effects of the materials involved in the *Kingsley Pictures, Manual Enterprises,* and *Jacobellis* cases are not considered in the majority opinions. These opinions do not contain any refutation of the contention that the circulation of obscenity constitutes a serious social problem. The rationale for obscenity regulation is nowhere examined and nowhere refuted.

Has the Court concluded that "censorship" is inherently so harmful and so dangerous that whatever the evils of obscenity, the evils of censorship are necessarily greater? If so, then this contention ought to be stated and supported. The written opinions suggest—without presenting any argument—that the values of art and culture are not safe unless the Manual Enterprises publications are also safe. But why is genuine art necessarily endangered by criteria which would permit the control of gross appeals to perverted sexuality? Have the Justices assumed that legislatures and courts are inherently unable to frame standards which would reach such material without reaching art?

Perhaps the values to which censorship is harmful are not those of art and culture, but those of free expression as such. Have the courts, then, concluded that freedom of speech and press must necessarily outweigh any public interests which may stand against it? It may be that freedom of speech is of far greater value to the community than any, or all, of its other ethical standards. It may be that society's interest in the written word—whether good or bad, true or false, beautiful or ugly—inevitably outweighs its interest in morality. Or, it may be that the moral norms from which censorship of obscenity proceeds are subjective, relative, and groundless and that therefore one is never justified in subordinating to them the values of free expression. These views, however, have never been asserted by a majority of the Justices. The Court does not avow them as the basis for its decisions.

Many of the attitudes sketched above are associated with the libertarian critique of censorship (and, therefore, with the judicial positions of Justices Douglas and Black). It follows from these attitudes that the regulation of obscenity should be greatly reduced and, if possible, abolished. In the cases we have considered the Court did not explicitly adopt the libertarian views, but it moved steadily toward the conclusions and policies which follow from them. The Court moved toward these conclusions and policies while continuing to affirm traditional principles and concepts (those of *Roth* and its liberal predecessors), while continuing to uphold the constitutionality of obscenity statutes, and while purporting to reassert the legitimacy of obscenity regulation. This duality is the root of the legal ambiguities and distortions noted in this chapter.

This duality is also the source of the difficulties inherent in subsequent decisions, particularly in the *Fanny Hill* case[53] and the *Ginzburg* case.[54] The former decision simply carries to its logical conclusion the doctrine enunciated in *Jacobellis* v. *Ohio*. In reversing the Massachusetts Supreme Judicial Court findings against the novel *Fanny Hill,* Justice Brennan said:

> The Supreme Judicial Court erred in holding that a book need not be "unqualifiedly worthless before it can be deemed obscene." A book cannot be proscribed unless it is found to be utterly without redeeming social value. This is so even though the book be found to possess the requisite prurient appeal and to be patently offensive. . . . Hence even on the view of the court below that *Memoirs* possessed only a modicum of social value, its judgment must be reversed.[55]

But the Massachusetts court did not find that the book possessed "a modicum of social value"; it found that the book possessed no redeeming social value whatever. The court listened to the testimony of literary critics concerning the literary value of the work, and it concludes that this testimony did not establish its social importance. This is what the Massachusetts Supreme Judicial Court said:

> We are mindful that there was expert testimony, much of which was strained, to the effect that *Memoirs* is a structural

novel with literary merit. . . . But the fact that the testimony may indicate this book has some minimal literary value does not mean that it is of any social importance. We do not interpret the "social importance" test as requiring that a book which appeals to prurient interests and is patently offensive must be unqualifiedly worthless before it can be deemed obscene.[56]

I offer, as the most plausible interpretation of the Massachusetts court's opinion, the following paraphrase: "We find that most of the experts' testimony concerning the literary merits of this book is far-fetched, representing perhaps a strained effort to ascribe merit to it. As judges, we are in no position to assert with certitude that these critics are simply wrong. But, even if the book can be said to possess such literary merits as they ascribe to it, these merits are very slight, and they do not establish the *social* value of the work. Such tenuous and minimal literary values as the book may be said to embody would not amount to *redeeming social* importance."

Justice Brennan's opinion constitutes a rejection of this last judicial effort to attach some meaning to the first two words in the expression "redeeming social importance." Since opposing factors may not be weighed, judges may not consider whether the values ascribed to a work are indeed "redemptive." And it would seem that they are also forbidden to consider whether the importance ascribed to a work is really "social" importance. Thus, it is asserted, in effect, that a book meets the "importance" test whenever literary men are willing to testify that it embodies qualities which are of interest to them.* Evidently such a work is to be protected, though its "dominant theme, taken as a whole" be both prurient and patently offensive. In this manner the Court goes to the verge of an explicit rejection of the *Roth* rule, while continuing to affirm that that rule governs obscenity cases.

In the *Fanny Hill* case the Court prevents Massachusetts from censoring a book which has been almost universally recognized and suppressed as pornography since its first publication 216 years

---

* For an extended survey and analysis of the testimony of literary critics in this case, see the dissenting opinion of Justice Clark. He concludes (as did the lower court) that this testimony has "no substance." He asserts: "It [the testimony] only indicates the lengths to which these experts go in their effort to give the book some semblance of value." 383 U.S. 413 (1966) at 450.

ago.* In *Ginzburg* v. *United States* the Court upholds the conviction of Ralph Ginzburg for circulating materials for which the judgment of obscenity is admittedly doubtful. Speaking for the majority, Justice Brennan said:

> In cases in which this Court has decided obscenity questions since *Roth,* it has regarded the materials as sufficient in themselves for the determination of the question. In the present case, however, the prosecution charged the offense in the context of the circumstances of production, sale and publicity, and assumed that, standing alone, the publications themselves might not be obscene. We agree that the question of obscenity may include consideration of the setting in which the publications were presented as an aid to determining the question of obscenity, and assume without deciding that the prosecution could not have succeeded otherwise. . . . We view the publications against a background of commercial exploitation of erotica solely for the sake of their prurient appeal.[57]

Thus the Court adds another standard to those previously established for the determination of obscenity cases—a standard which it designates by the term "pandering." Pandering is that kind of promotion and advertising of erotic literary materials which flagrantly exploits the sexually provocative or stimulating properties of such materials. It is publicity with "the leer of the sensualist," publicity designed to appeal to the salacious interests of potential customers. The *Ginzburg* decision did not hold that pandering is in itself an offense against the obscenity statute. Its explicit ruling is "that in close cases evidence of pandering may be probative with respect to the nature of the material in question." When material is highly erotic in character, but some doubt remains about the degree of its prurience, evidence that the purveyor has deliberately and heavily emphasized its prurient appeal may be decisive.

The *Ginzburg* ruling is not wholly without precedent. Prior to *Ginzburg* there were some federal court decisions, including *Grove Press* v. *Christenberry,* in which the circumstances of publication and promotion were considered relevant in some degree to the determination of obscenity.[58] But in the Supreme Court decisions since *Roth* there is nothing to suggest that pandering is a

* The "obscenity" of *Fanny Hill* is discussed in chapter 6.

major ingredient of the obscenity prohibited by the statute, and there is certainly nothing to suggest that pandering is a legal standard of importance equivalent to that of prurient interests and patent offensiveness. Before *Ginzburg* it was assumed that the decisive legal criteria are those concerning the nature of the literary materials in question. Judge Bryan, while taking into account the element of pandering, did not question this assumption. If the major precedents do not provide an adequate foundation for the new standard, neither does the language of the obscenity statute provide such foundation. The advertising provisions of that statute make it a crime to "give information" about where *obscenity* may be obtained.[59] But the Court appears to grant that Ginzburg's material, or most of it, is not in itself obscenity. How, then, does it become obscenity when associated with pandering, which is not in itself an offense against the statute?

I will not undertake an analysis of all the problems and implications of the *Ginzburg* decision; nor are we concerned here with all that can be said for and against its new standard. The questions requiring attention are these: (1) Why was this new and unexpected doctrine adopted at this time? and (2) To what extent, if any, does the *Ginzburg* decision reflect a retreat from or a modification of the Court's libertarian posture in this area?

As I have observed, in obscenity decisions since *Roth* the Court appeared to be drifting toward the extreme libertarian position without acknowledging that it was doing so (and, perhaps, without deliberate intention of doing so). While proclaiming its commitment to the concepts of *Roth,* the Court steadily undermined these concepts, rendering them increasingly ambiguous and unsuitable for the censorship of anything—except, perhaps, hardcore pornography. This tendency reached its culmination in the decision on *Fanny Hill,* rendered on the same day as *Ginzburg.* As a result, it would seem that the Court had nowhere to go except to a hard-core pornography standard or to a complete rejection of the *Roth* sanction for censorship. On the basis of this description of the legal situation, two interpretations of the *Ginzburg* decision are possible.

The *Ginzburg* decision may be read as an effort to avoid or postpone some of the logical consequences of previous decisions. It may represent an effort to find some way to avoid drawing the conclusions to which recent Court decisions point. The circumstances of the *Ginzburg* case would afford an opportunity to those who might wish to draw back from the brink of a hard-core pornography standard. In the promotion and circulation of his material Ginzburg did indeed conduct himself in a brazenly salacious manner.[60] He did indeed openly and blatantly flaunt his intention to violate community standards on sexual matters. In effect, he did proclaim the obscenity of his own material. Perhaps some of the Justices thought this an opportune moment to reaffirm the existence of public moral standards and thus to lend, by means of this reaffirmation, some support to what remains of *Roth*'s principles and purposes. The new standard proclaimed in the *Ginzburg* case may have been designed in part to prevent or postpone the complete collapse of these principles and purposes.

But the *Ginzburg* decision can also be read as an endeavor to disengage from the—now unworkable—prescriptions of *Roth*. It may represent an effort to move in a new direction—to turn away from censorship concerned with the obscenity of literary materials and to move toward "censorship" concerned primarily with the *conduct* of the purveyors. This course of action has been urged upon the Court in one form or another by a number of commentators in recent years.* It was advocated by Chief Justice Warren (a member of the *Ginzburg* majority) in his concurring opinion in

* See Paul and Schwartz, *Federal Censorship*. These authors argue that "obsceneness of itself should not mean illegality" (p. 212). They urge that the law should seek primarily to control conduct such as the "reckless commercial exploitation of obscenity" (p. 216). See also Louis B. Schwartz, "Morals Offenses and the Model Penal Code," *Columbia Law Review*, 63 (1963): 669. This article is cited by Justice Brennan in his *Ginsburg* opinion. Professor Schwartz suggests that efforts to control obscenity might reasonably be confined to "restraints on commercialization and restraints on *public* violation of standards that command virtually universal adherence" (p. 686, italics mine). As the concept of "variable obscenity," this approach was first systematically developed by Lockhart and McClure in 1960. They asserted that "material is to be judged by its appeal to and effect upon the audience to which the material is primarily directed. In this view material is never inherently obscene; instead, its obscenity varies with the circumstances of its dissemination. . . . Variable obscenity also makes it possible to reach, under obscenity statutes, the panderer who advertises and pushes non-pornographic material as if it were hard-core pornography, seeking out an audience of sexually immature. . . ." William B. Lockhart and Robert C. McClure, "Censorship of Obscenity: The Developing Constitutional Standards," *Minnesota Law Review* 45 (1960): 5, at 77.

Roth. The Chief Justice said: "It is not a book that is on trial; it is a person. The conduct of the defendant is the central issue, not the obscenity of a book or picture."[61]

The *Ginzburg* decision does not explicitly hold the defendant's conduct to be "the central issue," but it does pave the way for an increasing emphasis upon the behavior of the purveyor and a decreasing concern with the nature of his materials. This interpretation of *Ginzburg* finds some support in the text of the decision. Justice Brennan emphasizes the fact that a conviction for pandering "does not necessarily suppress the materials in question."[62] And, in explanation of what is wrong with pandering, he asserts that "such representation would tend to force public confrontation with the potentially offensive aspects of the work." If the Court wishes to adopt the policy proposed by the Chief Justice, it is now in a better position to argue that "forced public confrontation" is the primary evil involved in the circulation of obscenity. It is quite possible to envision the Court advancing from the *Ginzburg* doctrine to a position which would *require* evidence of pandering or some grossly offensive conduct to sustain a conviction for obscenity. Or, *Ginzburg* could lend itself to a doctrine which would require evidence of pandering in all cases except those involving the worst hard-core pornography.* Thus, working its way out of the difficulties fostered by its previous decisions, the Court may move still closer to the libertarian position and its central tenet that overt conduct is the only legitimate subject of legal control.†

The *Ginzburg* majority may have been searching for a way to avoid some of the more extreme implications of earlier decisions, and, as I think likely, some of its members may have intended to shift the emphasis in obscenity cases from the content of literary materials to the behavior of the defendant. At any rate, there is nothing in either of these interpretations of the decision, or in the language of the decision itself, to indicate a reversal of the libertarian trends in obscenity rulings or a determination to reassess the underlying premises which support this trend. *Ginzburg* does not extend the scope of obscenity regulation to include any ma-

---

* In *Mishkin v. New York,* 383 U.S. 502 (1966), decided on the same day as were the *Ginsburg* and *Fanny Hill* cases, the Court upheld a finding of obscenity under New York's "hard-core pornography" standard. Justice Brennan appears to have agreed with the New York courts that Mishkin's material was "hard-core."

† This libertarian doctrine is discussed in chapter 3.

terials previously held to be uncensorable. It is still the case that materials extremely prurient and offensive are provided with First Amendment protection. Literature more salacious than *Fanny Hill* and the Manual Enterprises publications may be freely and widely circulated as long as the purveyor does not conduct himself as did Ralph Ginzburg.

Some of the above-mentioned implications of the *Ginzburg* case become clearer when one considers the most recent rulings. In May 1967 in *Redrup* v. *New York* the Court handed down a brief *per curiam* opinion reversing judgments of obscenity in three cases. The *Redrup* opinion studiously avoids commitment to any particular definition of what is obscene material, but it does contain this significant statement:

> In none of these cases was there a claim that the statute in question reflected a specific and limited concern for juveniles. . . . In none was there any suggestion of an assault upon individual privacy by publication in a manner so obtrusive as to make it impossible for an unwilling individual to avoid exposure to it. . . . And in none was there evidence of the sort of "pandering" which the Court found significant in *Ginsburg v. United State.*[63]

Since *Ginzburg* and *Redrup* the Court has reversed convictions and findings of obscenity in a large number of cases, usually doing so without opinion or without much opinion. A marked exception to this trend concerns statutes carefully drawn to reflect "a specific and limited concern for juveniles."

In the recent case of *Ginsberg* v. *New York* the Court upheld a statute which prohibits the sale to persons under seventeen years of age of materials depicting "nudity," "sexual conduct," "sexual excitement," or "sado-masochistic abuse."* Speaking for the majority, Justice Brennan affirmed that the authority of the state over the conduct of children is broader than its authority over adults. The "girly" picture magazines at issue in this case would

---

* *Ginsberg* v. *New York,* 20 L. ed. 2d 195 (1968). The terms "nudity," "sexual conduct," "sexual excitement," and "sado-masochistic abuse" are defined in the statute with considerable precision. See Appendix to Justice Harlan's concurring opinion at pp. 207–08. On the same day as it decided the *Ginsberg* case, the Court struck down for unconstitutional vagueness a Dallas ordinance which allowed motion pictures to be classified as "not suitable for young persons" under sixteen years of age. *Interstate Circuit* v. *Dallas,* 20 L. ed. 225 (1968).

not be obscene for adults, and their sale to adults could not be prohibited.

The majority opinion contains two arguments in support of obscenity laws limited to the protection of children—one argument concerning the rights and claims of parents and the other concerning the special interest of the state in the welfare of the young. Says Justice Brennan:

> Constitutional interpretation has consistently recognized that parents' claims to authority in their own households to direct the rearing of their children is basic in the structure of our society. . . . The legislature could probably conclude that parents and others, teachers for example, who have this primary responsibility for children's well-being are entitled to the support of laws designed to aid discharge of that responsibility.[64]

Here it would seem that laws restricting children's access to "obscenity" are justified by reference to the parental role and rights in the education of children. This argument suggests that such laws are designed to protect a certain freedom—the freedom of parents and teachers to educate children as they see fit. The law protects this freedom by securing children from influences which are sharply contrary to parental views of what is good, and which would be very difficult for parents to control without aid from the larger community.

This argument surely makes some sense, but it is not enough—it cannot stand by itself. Ultra-libertarians or proponents of "the sexual revolution" would be quick to observe that laws such as this New York statute reflect a preference for some parents' views of what is good over other parents' views of what is good. If it can be said that the aim of such legislation is protection of parental freedom of choice in the rearing of children, it must also be said that the legislation is interested in the freedom of choice of those parents who hold the more traditional moral views about children's welfare. If parental rights and responsibilities are all that is involved, why should the claims of this group of parents receive the special solicitude of the law?

But Justice Brennan's opinion goes on to assert that "the state also has an independent interest in the well-being of its youth." The Justice is not able to find as a matter of established fact that obscenity is harmful to the young, but he concludes: "We do not demand of legislatures 'scientifically certain criteria of legislation.' ... We therefore cannot say that § 484-h [the New York statute] has no rational relation to the objective of safeguarding such minors from harm."[65]

This argument acknowledges a power of the state to see that children are "safeguarded from abuses,"[66] but it does not quite commit the Court to the view that obscenity is a source of abuses. With regard to the evil effects of salacious or sordid literature upon children, Justice Brennan appears unwilling to go much beyond the affirmation that the legislature's view of the matter is "not irrational."

At the time of this writing the Supreme Court has not yet finally committed itself to that course of action which *Ginzburg* v. *United States* and *Redrup* v. *New York* have opened up for it. The Court has not yet decided to confine the legal control of obscenity to the protection of children, the prevention of flagrant pandering, and, perhaps, restriction of unmitigated pornography. But one can well understand why Justices sorely beset with increasingly perplexing problems might find appealing that way of extricating themselves from "a constitutional disaster area."[67] In place of their present disagreements and confusions, the Justices might hope to build a stable majority around workable definitions of pandering, hard-core pornography, and the exploitation of youth's interest in sex. And it is probable that a majority of the public could be counted upon to support restrictions on these things. But this cannot be a solution to the problem of obscenity if it is arrived at without exploration of the basic issues.

Laws designed specifically to safeguard juveniles may be quite necessary and desirable. But it has not been established that the young are the only sufferers from obscenity or that their protection is the only public interest to which obscenity statutes are and should be addressed. Nor is it evident that laws confined to the protection of children could adequately protect them in the absence of any restrictions upon the adult world. For example, in a society permeated with obscenity—a society in which "anything goes" for adults—it would probably be fruitless to make laws limiting children's access to prurient writings and pictures. Finally, the argument which justifies such laws by reference to the rights of parents must eventually give way to a broader justification based on a view of what is good and bad for children. But this rationale is inadequately stated by the formulation that laws safeguarding children are valid because they are "not irrational." This formulation may suffice to save a statute for the time being, but the mind does not rest upon it with much confidence in its enduring capacity to justify.

With regard to the question of obscenity and adults, one should consider whether pandering and hard-core pornography are the only evils requiring legal restraints. One may ask why pandering should become a central consideration in the enforcement of obscenity laws, displacing the traditional concern with the character of the materials circulated. Such a change in censorship policy would follow from the assumption that the commercial exploitation of obscenity, or the obtrusive public display of things offensive to the majority, is the real evil. But this assumption should be carefully examined before it becomes the basis for legal standards.

Much can be said in favor of restraining those who would exploit prurient interests for profit—*if* there is something wrong with appealing to prurient interests. If there is no harm in the circulation and consumption of obscenity, it is not clear why it should be wrong for the purveyor of obscenity to make profit, as any businessman makes profit, by arousing a lively interest in his commodities. Much can be said in favor of laws against public lewdness which protect people from involuntary exposure to things which would shock or greatly offend them. But it has not yet been demonstrated that the primary reason for controlling obscenity is to safeguard non-consenting persons from offense to their sensibilities. Judges cannot reasonably assume, without argument, that obscenity is harmless to individuals and to society just because it is indulged in voluntarily and in private.

Likewise, it cannot simply be assumed that all forms of obscenity except hard-core pornography are harmless to the public interest when indulged in voluntarily and in private. What is called "hard-core" material is, perhaps, that form of obscenity which is most offensive to most people. But this is not a sufficient reason to suppose, prior to inquiry, that the circulation of hard-core pornography constitutes the whole problem or the major problem which obscenity poses for our society.

Legal standards aimed at the control of grossly offensive conduct or materials cannot function as a substitute for reasoning about the rationale for censorship. Legal rules are not self-sustaining; they require the support of adequate theory. The interpretation and application of a legal rule will be ambiguous if the reasons and arguments for it are confused or inadequate. Judge-made standards, such as those of "pandering" or "hard-core pornography," will be problematic to the extent that the rationale for the control of obscenity remains problematic.

The ambiguities and unresolved issues discussed in this chapter point to an urgent need for reflection upon the basic ingredients of the obscenity problem. It is appropriate to begin with a more careful examination of the libertarian ideas—those ideas which to a large extent underlie the recent tendencies of the Court and which continue to guide the reasoning of its members. Should the libertarian position become the acknowledged policy of the government, the law, and the country?

3

The First Amendment
and the Free Society:
Libertarian Views

The libertarian position consists, essentially, of two propositions: (1) that the censorship of obscenity contravenes the First Amendment and the principles which lie behind it, and (2) that obscenity is not harmful, or, at least, that the circulation of obscenity does not injure individuals or society to any significant degree. This chapter will be devoted primarily to examination of libertarian views of the First Amendment and the principles of a free society. The following chapter will be concerned with the effects of obscenity.

The views which are the subject of this chapter can be classified in two ways. One may distinguish between those arguments which rest or claim to rest primarily upon First Amendment considerations and those which rest largely upon considerations of political doctrine or philosophy. Among the former arguments one may differentiate between those which view the prohibitions of the First Amendment as in some sense absolute and those which view them as requiring the application of a more or less stringent "clear and present danger" test or a hard-core pornography test. This analysis will begin with the absolutist positions, and will move from constitutional considerations toward those of political philosophy.

In his dissent in the *Roth* case, Justice Douglas asserts that the First Amendment speaks "in terms absolute."[1] This view is elaborated by Justice Black in his concurring opinion in *Smith* v. *California:*

Certainly the First Amendment's language leaves no room for inference that abridgments of speech and press can be made just because they are slight. That Amendment provides, in simple words, that "Congress shall make no law abridging the freedom of speech, or of the press." I read "no law abridging" to mean "NO LAW ABRIDGING." The First Amendment, which is the supreme law of the land, has thus fixed its own value on freedom of speech and press by putting these freedoms wholly "beyond the reach of federal power to abridge." No other provision of the Constitution purports to dilute the scope of these unequivocal commands of the First Amendment. Consequently, I do not believe that any federal agencies, including Congress and this Court, have the authority to subordinate speech and press to what they think are "more important interests." The contrary notion is, in my judgment, Court-made, not Constitution-made.[2]

It should be added here that Justices Black and Douglas would have "these unequivocal commands" applied to the states on the same terms and with the same rigor as they would have them applied to the federal government. Justice Black has been foremost among those insisting that the Due Process Clause of the Fourteenth Amendment applies to the states the precise provisions of the Bill of Rights.[3]

Justice Black thus appears to argue that neither the federal government nor the states may restrict the right to speak or publish in any way or degree whatever. Further, he appears to regard his conclusions as arising necessarily from the clear and self-evident meaning of the constiutional text—from "simple words," and from principles that are "Constitution-made," not judge-made.

Now it is true that "no law" is absolute language—it admits of no exception—and that "no law abridging the freedom of speech, or of the press" is unequivocal. But the constitutional text does not define what constitutes an "abridgment," nor does it define the "freedom of speech and press" which it intends to protect. These are matters which require interpretation and about which men may, and do, differ. Justice Black has recently asserted that a state law the effect of which is to forbid a peaceful civil rights demonstration across the street from a courthouse does not abridge freedom of speech, and that picketing, "though it may be utilized to communicate ideas, is not speech."[4] It is, then, legitimate to ask whether obscenity is any part of that freedom of speech and press of which the First Amendment speaks and whether the removal of pornography from the mails abridges freedom of the press. For Justice Black, however, these questions are clearly answered in the affirmative by the unequivocal words of the First Amendment.

In 1960 Justice Black delivered a paper on the Bill of Rights in which he set forth his position at some length. He reiterated his oft-asserted convictions that "there *are* 'absolutes' in our Bill of Rights, and that they were put there on purpose by men who knew what words meant, and meant their prohibitions to be 'absolutes,' "[5] and that "the phrase 'Congress shall make no law' is composed of plain words easily understood."[6] In his discussion of other provisions of the Bill of Rights, however, Justice Black appears to grant that the words are not so "plain" and "easily understood" as to preclude judicial determination of their meaning and the possibility of divergent interpretations.

With regard to the Eighth Amendment Justice Black said:

> The Eighth Amendment forbids "excessive bail," "excessive fines" or the infliction of "cruel and unusual punishments." This is one of the less precise provisions. The Courts are required to determine the meaning of such general terms as "excessive" and "unusual." But surely that does not mean that admittedly "excessive bail," "excessive fines" or "cruel punishments" could be justified on the ground of competing public interest in carrying out some generally granted power like that given Congress to regulate commerce.[7]

Concerning the Fourth Amendment the Justice said:

> The use of the word "unreasonable" in this Amendment means of course that not *all* searches and seizures are prohibited. Only those which are *unreasonable* are unlawful. There may be a difference of opinion about whether a particular search or seizure is unreasonable and therefore forbidden by this Amendment. But if it is unreasonable it is absolutely prohibited.[8]

What, then, does Justice Black mean when he declares these provisions to be "absolute" and yet grants a necessary latitude for interpretation and difference of opinion? It would seem that his major purpose is to preclude the weighing and balancing of competing public interests where rights protected by the first eight amendments are concerned. These rights are "absolute" in the sense that they must take precedence over any considerations which may be thought to stand against them. The exercise of judicial judgment is confined to determining whether a certain punishment *is* "cruel and unusual" or whether a certain search and seizure *is* "unreasonable," that is, to determining whether the particular facts fall under the absolute principle or not. In the making of such judgments judges may have to determine the boundaries of a constitutional right, but they must not weigh the social values allegedly served by the act of government against the character of the particular rights claimed. Justice Black's absolutism can be read as an injunction to judges to engage in a certain kind of intellectual operation and avoid absolutely a certain other kind. They are to confine themselves to subsuming the facts involved in a particular act of government under the relevant constitutional standard or to relating the facts and the standard, and they are *not* to include as part of their determination a judgment concerning the values or ends which may be thought to justify the act of government.

But when he approaches the First Amendment, Justice Black does not appear to allow for even this degree of latitude for judgment. He does not seem to regard the terms of the First Amendment as problematic in the same way or to the same extent as are those of the Eighth and Fourth Amendments.[9] Now it may be that the terms "freedom of speech and press" and "abridging" are somewhat clearer and more precise than are the terms "unreasonable search and seizure" or "cruel and unusual punishment." But are they "plain words easily understood"? If so, they are not so easily applied. Is it self-evident that laws punishing the defamation of a race or class are abridgments of First Amendment rights?[10] Is it self-evident that the Manual Enterprises publications are part of that press the freedom of which the First Amendment seeks to secure? Perhaps Justice Black meant to say only that the words "Congress shall make no law" are plain and easily understood. If so, it is difficult to see how this would help us to know with certainty or with precision what is included within "freedom of speech and press."

Justice Black does not advocate an unlimited right to say anything, anywhere, in any manner. But his position does assert, at least, that the right to speak shall never turn upon a weighing of the values to be attained by restriction against the quality or content of the speech to be restricted. A regulation involving the restraint of expression shall not be justified because of its purpose or because of the character of the expression. It can be justified, if at all, only by a finding that the activity to be regulated does not fall within the category of "freedom of speech and press" or that the regulation is not in fact an "abridgment." But this presupposes that such findings can be reasonably made without any of the weighing and balancing which Justice Black forbids. In this regard the Justice's references to the Eighth and Fourth Amendments are instructive.

It would be universally agreed that the use of the rack and the screw would not be justified by evidence that such procedure would aid in the deterrence of crime. Crime and unusual punishments are forbidden. And the rack and the screw are recognized as being such punishments. But what is an "excessive fine"? Determination of this would turn upon examination of the specific facts. Some of these facts would concern the purpose of the fine, the social problem to which it may be addressed, and, perhaps, the persons upon whom the fine was imposed and why it was imposed on them. Likewise, inquiry concerning the "reasonableness" of a search and seizure cannot be isolated from a weighing of the public purpose to be served, on the one hand, and, on the other, the nature and value of that which was searched or seized in order to serve the public purpose. One would want to know what kind of crime or offense was involved, what peculiar problems there may be confronting the effort to detect and prevent such crimes, *and* the extent to which valuable privacy was involved. The systematic search of all automobiles in an area may become reasonable if the aim is to catch a dangerous criminal, and if the search is not conducted in flagrant violation of privacy. A forcible search of all homes and private papers in the area would, no doubt, be held unreasonable.

In both cases—that of the "excessive fine" and that of the "unreasonable search and seizure"—judges would be weighing and balancing; they would be considering the *degree* of officially imposed penalty, restraint, or search as against the end or conditions which may justify one of these actions. It is not necessarily the case that a slight search or seizure is condemned by the Fourth Amendment equally with a great one. For the degree of invasion of privacy is an important factor in the determination of how the terms of the amendment apply. It may well be found that, in certain circumstances, a "slight" invasion of privacy is not an invasion of that privacy which the Fourth Amendment protects by its term "unreasonable." Precisely the fact that a given invasion is "slight" might be the grounds for ruling it "reasonable."

These considerations do not become less compelling as one enters the area of First Amendment freedoms. The First Amendment forbids Congress to make any law "prohibiting the free exercise" of religion. Yet polygamy was made a crime even though it was a major tenet of a recognized religion. The outlawing of polygamy was upheld by reference to overriding public purpose—the preservation of the family structure upon which our society rests—and upon investigation of the character of polygamy.[11] Upon these and other grounds it was held that the prohibition of polygamy is not that "prohibition" which the First Amendment forbids.

If the consideration of diverse public interests and the weighing of degrees of restriction and of value are intrinsic ingredients of judgments determining the scope and application of other provisions of the Bill of Rights, why should it be otherwise with the terms "freedom of speech and press" or "abridging"? Justice Black has strong convictions about what is and what is not absolutely protected by these terms. But he cannot make good his contention that these convictions are dictated by the plain words of the First Amendment. If the peaceful picketing of an employer in a labor dispute is an exercise of First Amendment rights,* while peaceful picketing across the street from a court in a civil rights campaign is not, this must be because of considerations of "competing public interest"—and not because plain words so dictate.

It is not true, as Justice Black asserts, that "the area set off for individual freedom . . . was marked by boundaries precisely defined."[12] The words of the First Amendment do not define

---

* Justice Black joined the majority opinion in *Thornhill* v. *Alabama,* 310 U.S. 88 (1940), which held peaceful picketing in a labor dispute to be an act protected by the First Amendment. He dissented in *International Brotherhood of Teamsters* v. *Vogt,* 354 U.S. 284 (1957), a decision in which the court upheld an injunction against picketing.

their own boundaries. Men must determine their scope and application by the exercise of judgments of fact, of law, and of value. This is not to say that First Amendment rights, having been adjudged to be such, will then be balanced against competing considerations. Rather, it is to say that we cannot define these rights, we cannot determine what specific rights are granted by the general terms of the First Amendment, without engaging in the kinds of intellectual operations which Justice Black seeks to preclude. Judges will have to determine when a slight restraint upon speech constitutes an abridgment of the freedom of speech. This must involve judgments of value, as does any effort to define or apply terms which have ethical and political import. Such judgments may be more or less prominent, but they cannot be precluded. Thus the absolute language of the First Amendment does not of itself settle the problem of obscenity regulation.

But the views of Justice Black and Justice Douglas do not rest simply upon textual and semantic considerations. These Justices find in the First Amendment an underlying principle—a principle which distinguishes absolutely between speech and action. According to Justice Douglas, what the First Amendment dictates is that "government should be concerned with anti-social conduct, not with utterances."[13] "Utterances" shall be absolutely free; conduct alone is subject to government regulation. This, again, is not quite the same thing as an assertion that anyone may say anything, anywhere, in any manner. But it is at least an assertion that government may never concern itself directly with speech. Government may not outlaw a certain kind or form of expression, because it must never concern itself with the *content* of expression—with what is said or written. No form of expression shall be subject to regulation on the grounds of its intrinsic evil or its tendency to promote harmful consequences. Expression is subject to regulation only when it is so closely related to illegal action as to be inseparable from it. Since it cannot be demonstrated that obscenity is thus related to conduct, the First Amendment prohibits any effort to control it.

While Justices Black and Douglas' interpretation of the First Amendment claims ample support in the constitutional text, it also claims to be supported by the views and intentions of the men who gave us the First Amendment. Indeed, it is often asserted that the views of these Justices *are* the views of those founding fathers who were most closely associated with the First Amendment. In the literature and judicial decisions opposing the control of obscenity, quotations from James Madison and Thomas Jefferson are frequently advanced as conclusive evidence that the First Amendment was designed to be absolute and to legislate that sharp distinction between expression and conduct insisted upon by today's absolutists.[14] How are the doctrines of Madison and Jefferson related to those of Justices Black and Douglas and to the problem of obscenity control?

Madison's strongest and most explicit statements about the meaning of the First Amendment were made during the controversy over the Alien and Sedition Acts. In his *Report on the Virginia Resolution* of 1798, Madison said:

> Some degree of abuse is inseparable from the proper use of everything, and in no instance is this more true than in that of the press. It has accordingly been decided by the practice of the States, that it is better to leave a few of its noxious branches to their luxuriant growth than, by pruning them away, to injure the vigor of those yielding the proper fruits. And can the wisdom of this policy be doubted by any who reflect that to the press alone, checkered as it is with abuses, the world is indebted for all the triumphs which have been gained by reason and humanity over error and oppression; . . . the article of Amendment, instead of supposing in Congress a power that might be exercised over the press, provided its freedom was not abridged, was meant as a positive denial to Congress of any power whatever on the subject.
>
> . . . Is, then, the Federal Government, it will be asked, destitute of every authority for restraining the licentiousness of the press, and for shielding itself against the libellous attacks which may be made on those who administer it?
>
> The Constitution alone can answer this question. If no such power can be expressly delegated, and if it be not both necessary and proper to carry into execution an express power—above all, if it be expressly forbidden by a declaratory amendment to the Constitution—the answer must be that the Federal Government is destitute of all such authority.[15]

These views are, substantially, those expressed by Jefferson in his *Kentucky Resolutions* and in various writings. Although Jefferson did not speak of the scope of the First Amendment free press provisions in words quite as strong or as precise as these of Madison, it would be difficult to make a case for any significant difference between them on this subject.

The passage quoted denies, in terms unequivocal, that Congress has any power to control the press or any authority to restrain its "licentiousness." Madison's language strongly implies that the First Amendment does not permit a distinction between restraints which do and restraints which do not abridge the genuine freedom of the press—a distinction between liberty and license. In 1799 Madison explicitly rejected such a distinction.[16] It would appear that for Madison the "proper fruits" of an unrestrained press must necessarily outweigh the evils which result from its "noxious branches."

But this statement of Madison's views does not conclusively settle all relevant questions. The specific context in which Madison speaks is political. The restraints with which he is specifically concerned are restraints upon political criticism—the criticism of the government, of public officials, or of public agencies. The "licentiousness" to which he refers is primarily, if it is not entirely, the licentiousness of vituperative and defamatory political speech. What would Madison have thought of restraints having nothing to do with politics, upon forms of speech having nothing to do with government?

Madison's language is unequivocal—Congress may not exercise any power over the press. But this would answer our question unequivocally only if we could know with certainty what Madison means by "the press"—what classes of written or printed materials he means to designate by the term. Does "the press" mean only newspapers and journals, or does it mean anything produced by a printing press? A logical reading of this and other Madisonian texts would indicate that he is not speaking only of newspapers. It seems unlikely that Madison would think that it is to the newspaper that "the world is indebted for all the triumphs gained by reason and humanity over error and oppression." Madison appears to have a rather broad conception of that press whose products must be unrestrained. But we cannot know with certainty whether his conception would be so broad as to include all which today can be produced by the art of printing.

Madison and Jefferson would deny to the federal government any power to restrain the licentiousness of the press, but they would not deny that power to the states. In 1799 Madison said that "every libellous writing or expression can receive its punishment in the State Courts . . . whether it injured public officers or private citizens."[17] In his *Kentucky Resolutions* Jefferson asserted that the people of the states "retain to themselves the right of judging how far the licentiousness of speech and of the press may be abridged without lessening their useful freedom."[18] And in his famous letter to Abigail Adams, Jefferson wrote:

> Nor does the opinion of the unconstitutionality, and consequent nullity of that law [the Sedition Act], remove all restraint from the overwhelming torrent of slander which is confounding all vice and virtue, all truth and falsehood, in the United States. The power to do that is fully possessed by the several State Legislatures. . . . While we deny that Congress have a right to control the freedom of the press, we have ever asserted the right of the States and their exclusive right to do so.[19]

From these statements, and others from the same sources, it is evident that Madison's and Jefferson's opposition to the Sedition Act was not motivated solely by solicitude for freedom of speech and press. For Madison and Jefferson, the great evil of this act consisted in its infringement upon the inherent rights and powers of the states and in its tendency to promote a consolidated government. Their response to the Alien and Sedition Acts gave rise to their strongest statements about the scope of First Amendment rights. But in that response a concern for the prerogatives of the states blended with, if it did not take precedence over, a concern for free speech and press.

It is, then, of considerable significance that Madison and Jefferson held the capacity to impose some restraints upon speech and press to be among the inherent powers of the state governments and to belong to the reserved rights of the people of the states. Even though it be dangerous to endeavor to prune away the "noxious branches," Madison allows and Jefferson insists upon a power in the states to do so. They have not left us any comprehensive statement of the scope and limits of this power. It is clear that they would not look favorably upon frequent or severe state restraint of speech and press. But it is also clear that, in their view, the reserved rights of the states included at least the right to punish certain utterances of "seditious libel."[20]

It may be argued that these facts are not relevant to a discussion of the position taken today by Justices Black and Douglas, that these facts do not detract from the absolutism of the Madison-Jefferson view of the First Amendment, and that that amendment is now binding upon the states. That First Amendment which is binding on the states is, and ought to be, the real one— the one intended by the men who inspired and framed it. This argument, however, overlooks some important considerations. Even if it could be shown that the Madison-Jefferson conception of the First Amendment is absolute in the same sense and to the same extent as is the Black-Douglas conception of it, it was not Madison and Jefferson who made the First Amendment binding upon the states. Madison and Jefferson did not assert an unqualified immunity for all speech and press anywhere in the United States. They asserted, at most, such an immunity as against the federal government. Those seeking the abolition of all state laws controlling obscenity cannot claim to be resting simply on the doctrines of Madison and Jefferson.

But there is a further consideration bearing more significantly on the relation between the old and the new absolutists. Madison and Jefferson thought censorship extremely dangerous, but they did not deny that a power to restrain some forms of expression must reside somewhere in government. For Jefferson, "the confounding [of] all vice and virtue, all truth and falsehood" is an evil which can conceivably come within the cognizance of government. And a distinction between "free speech" and "licentious speech" is one which, on occasion, government may have to make. Jefferson would have these powers lodged in the states, which in his view constituted the primary governing agencies of the country —those closest to the people and primarily responsible for their welfare.

These conclusions, however, seem to be at variance with the spirit of Jeffersonian thought as it appears in so many of his more philosophic pronouncements. The following oft-quoted statements appear to establish that fundamental principle which Justices Black and Douglas find at the heart of the First Amendment. In his *Bill for Establishing Religious Freedom,* Jefferson said:

> To suffer the civil magistrate to intrude his powers into the field of opinion and to restrain the profession or propagation of principles, on the supposition of their ill-tendency, is a dangerous fallacy which at once destroys all religious liberty, . . . it is time

enough for the rightful purposes of civil government for its offices to interfere when principles break out into overt acts against peace and good order; and, finally, that truth is great and will prevail if left to herself, that she is the proper and sufficient antagonist to error, and has nothing to fear from the conflict, unless by human interposition disarmed of her natural weapons, free argument and debate[,] errors ceasing to be dangerous when it is permitted freely to contradict them.[21]

In 1814 Jefferson wrote in a letter:

> I am really mortified to be told that, in the United States of America, a fact like this [the sale of De Becourt's book *Sur La Création du Monde, un Système d'Organization Primitive*] can become the subject of inquiry, and of criminal inquiry too, as an offence against religion; that a question about the sale of a book can be brought before the civil magistrate. Is this, then, our freedom of religion? Are we to have a censor whose imprimatur shall say what books may be sold, and what we may buy? And who is thus to dogmatize religious opinions for our citizens? Whose foot is to be the measure to which ours are all to be stretched?[22]

In these statements Jefferson does not speak only of the federal government, he speaks of the "civil magistrate." It is government as such which is forbidden to intrude "into the field of opinion" or to determine what books may be sold. It is government as such which is confined to measures dealing with overt acts. These passages reflect that attitude toward the sufficiency of truth and the efficacy of reasoning which is usually associated with Jeffersonian philosophy. On the basis of these views could not "an overwhelming torrent of slander" be adequately met by "free argument and debate"? and could it legitimately be met in any other way?

It is significant that both of these Jeffersonian statements are made in a context of religious considerations. In the *Bill for Establishing Religious Freedom* he is specifically concerned with religious doctrinal controversy and with allegedly unorthodox opinions. In his letter of 1814, the book at issue is a philosophic or scientific treatise which is under official inquiry because of its alleged effects upon religious opinion. I do not intend to suggest that the meaning of Jefferson's words must be rigidly confined to their exact contexts. But one should not forget the subject about which Jefferson is speaking—as is often done in literature supporting the absolutist position by means of quotations from Jefferson. To do so is to run the risk of misunderstanding him and, perhaps, to expose him to charges of blatant self-contradiction. It is quite possible that in the mind of Jefferson the propagation of religious beliefs, or of philosophic ideas impinging upon religion, stands on a different moral and intellectual plane from that of "an overwhelming torrent of slander." For Jefferson, the sanctity of religious belief absolutely precludes the intrusion of the magistrate. Religious doctrines are not civil business. It is evident (in the letter of 1814) that what mortifies Jefferson is the possibility that citizens of the United States could be subjected to an official religious dogma whose imprimatur shall govern their religious opinions and determine what they can read.

But Jefferson does speak in the language of general principle. Do his principles establish the proposition of Justice Douglas that in all areas and in all respects "government should be concerned with anti-social conduct, not with utterances"?[23] And how much support do they provide for the corollary of this proposition— that obscene publications are beyond the reach of government?

It should be noted that the distinction which Jefferson makes is not quite the same as that which Justice Douglas makes. Jefferson differentiates between the propagation of opinion or principles and overt acts against public order. His subject is doctrines, principles, and beliefs, and his argument is that these are none of the magistrate's concern until such time as they result in breaches of the peace. Thus, Jefferson has not quite said that all "utterances" and "expressions" are outside the magistrate's sphere. This difference may be negligible in some contexts, but it is not negligible in the context of obscenity control. If Jefferson regards *all*, not just religious or philosophic, principles and opinions as beyond the scope of government, would he regard obscenity as embodying any principles and opinions? It would require some argument to show that materials now censored as obscenity involve the propagation of principles in the Jeffersonian sense of the term. Whenever Jefferson spoke of freedom of speech, press, and conscience he spoke in terms of truth and falsehood; that is, in terms of arguments addressed to the rational or spiritual faculties of man.[24] Would he think that suppression of obscene materials deprives citizens of any arguments or prevents the propagation of any opinions? We may speculate either that he would not think so, *or* that he would regard the censorship as more harmful than the obscenity. We cannot know the answer; we have no writings of Jefferson on the subject of salacious literature or, for that matter, on the subject of literature dealing with sex. This is another of those factors relevant to the intentions of the founders about which we cannot have certitude.

This discussion has been devoted to Madison and Jefferson because they are the founding fathers whose views are most often alleged to be identical with those of the present-day absolutists. But the views of Madison and Jefferson, whatever they may have been, cannot determine with finality what the First Amendment means or how it should be applied today. While Madison was the principle author of the First Amendment, and Jefferson one of its great sources of inspiration, there were many other founders involved in its passage, its ratification, and its interpretation. Though the ideas of Madison and Jefferson are entitled to great respect, the meaning of the First Amendment cannot depend on them alone. The attitudes of other important men, as well as those prevailing in the states which adopted the Amendment, are also factors which must enter into any judgment we can make of its original meaning.

There is strong evidence that most of these attitudes were not as libertarian as were those of Madison and Jefferson. In his recent study of the historical background of the First Amendment, Professor Leonard Levy concludes that, with the exception of Madison, the men who adopted the amendment did not even intend to abolish federal prosecution for seditious libel. He asserts of the framers that "few among them, if any at all, clearly understood what they meant by the free speech and press clause, and it is perhaps doubtful that those few agreed except in a generalized way and equally doubtful that they represented a consensus."[25]

Historians may or may not accept Levy's thesis. Some aspects of it may be overstated.* It is perhaps understandable that the framers would not, in the midst of crisis, address themselves with

---

* A portion of Levy's argument seems to rest on the premise that the true meaning of men's principles is to be understood by reference to the actions of those men, and he does not seem to take much account of the circumstances in which the actions were done. For instance, Levy notes that Congress and the states imposed considerable restraints upon loyalist expression and upon expression hostile to independence during the Revolution. He asserts that these actions constitute the "true meaning" of such libertarian declarations as that to the inhabitants of Quebec in 1774. Leonard Levy, *Legacy of Suppression* (Cambridge, Mass.: Harvard University Press, 1960), p. 188.

precision to the kinds of problems which most concern us today. And one need not conclude that, because the framers did not subscribe to our most libertarian doctrines, they therefore have left us a "legacy of suppression."

Levy's work reminds us, however, that we cannot rely on historical evidence—on evidence of the intentions of those who made the Constitution—in the way or to the extent that Justice Black would rely on it. The framers did not pronounce upon obscenity. But Justice Black and his supporters purport to find in the words of the Constitution, and in those of the men who made it, doctrines which dictate a precise solution to the problem. Words—past or present—will not do the work that Justice Black expects of them. The founding fathers did not address themselves to our problems; they could have no specific intentions about them. They could and did lay down "great outlines" and "important objects" which can guide present judgment but which cannot solve present problems.[26] There are many ways of forgetting "that it is a *constitution* we are expounding."

To take this position with regard to the intentions of the framers is not to deny the founding fathers any authority over us. One need not adopt judicial pragmatism. Nor is it desirable to avow, with Levy, that "the case for civil liberties need not be anchored in the past." It is too much to say that "no citizen, and certainly no jurist worthy of his position, would or should conclude his judgment on either a constitutional question or a matter of policy by an antiquarian examination of the original meaning of the freedom of speech-and-press clause."[27]

Of course, no one can "conclude" his judgment upon "antiquarian examination." But, as long as we have a Constitution to expound, such examination will be an important part of the judical process and of American political life. Antiquarian examination can teach us something. Madison and Jefferson were strongly opposed to political interference with the propagation of ideas, principles, or opinions.* To the extent that any censorship impinges upon such propagation, it is at least highly suspect. It must justify itself. Beyond this, problems are to be resolved by reference to precedent and consensus as these may be shaped by political doctrine and philosophy. Ultimately, there can be no

* It is unlikely that Professor Levy's libertarianism has escaped the influence of America's antiquarian concern with these men and their ideas.

position toward the obscenity problem which does not involve moral, political, social, and psychological premises.

There are two absolutist positions which rest, more or less openly, upon such premises. They are that of Morris Ernst and that of Alexander Meiklejohn. In his *Roth* brief, *amicus curiae*, Morris Ernst sets forth his views in their most systematic form.* He asserts that it is necessary to make a clear differentiation between three kinds of speech or three kinds of words: "seditious words," "merchandise words," and words concerned with "ideas." Seditious words are those which affect the preservation of governmental sovereignty. These may be restrained under a clear and present danger standard. "It would be absurd to plead that our Sovereign Rupublic is legislatively impotent to protect itself from attack." Merchandise words are concerned with commerce. They present no problem, since they "are merely the tools of things and *do not have as their sole or prime target the mere impact on the mind of man*" (italics mine). Words falling into the third area must be protected absolutely. "Here the First Amendment must be literally rendered, no abridgment is tolerable." What is the character of those words abridgment of which is intolerable? Says Ernst:

> This third sector is the sacred area of ideas for ideas' sake. This is the area of words which have as their real objective their ultimate resting place in the restless mind of man—that instrument made sacred in the constitutional terms by the First Amendment. . . . In this area we have not the Thing but the idea; not the package but the medium; not the paper, the ink, the binding, the film, but the thought. It is the thought, the idea—educational or entertaining—which, good or bad as judged by the whims of a passing generation, is the *res* of this area.

According to Ernst, this sacred area of ideas for their own sake includes materials characterized by obscenity, scandal, and sadism. They may not be subjected to any restraints whatever. Why not? Ernst makes no effort to state what are the ideas conveyed by obscenity, scandal, and sadism. He does not attempt to argue that expressions of this sort are written or spoken for the

---

* For the quotations which follow on pp. 103–4, see *Roth Briefs,* "Brief of Morris L. Ernst, *amicus curiae,*" at pp. 4–8.

purpose of conveying any thoughts. While Ernst appears to be at great pains to say what he means and does not mean by an "idea," the matter remains extremely obscure.[28]

Why is this third sector a "sacred area"? Ernst cannot easily answer that it is so because within this sector the mind of man is educated, developed, ennobled. He will not allow a distinction between education and entertainment—they both equally belong to the realm of ideas for ideas' sake. And judgments of the goodness or badness of an idea seem to be a matter for "the whims of a passing generation." Then is this area made sacred by the Constitution because within it there occur verbal events which have "an impact on the mind of man"? Are the prerequisites for the presence of an idea satisfied whenever some collection of words happen to influence the human mind, whether or not these words were intended to do so and no matter what the character of the influence? At any rate, this is the only definition of the term which would include all the forms of expression which Ernst insists are included within the absolutely protected realm.

Ernst's basic principle is "freedom for all that goes to the mind of man." While this could be a meaningful principle, it does not become one in the hands of Ernst. Upon examination, the realm of mind and of ideas turns out to be nothing more than what is left over when one has subtracted from the sum total of verbal expressions and impacts those having a seditious or commercial character. Within this residual realm all the distinctions which might make freedom meaningful are collapsed. In Ernst's formulations there is no room for differentiation between worthy and unworthy ideas, between materials which are designed to influence the mind and those which just happen to do so, between thinking and having one's thought affected, and even between that which is genuinely thought and that which is not, that which is genuinely mind and that which is not. Entertainment as such is not intended to influence thought, and it does not often influence thought. And if the pornography of sadism goes to the mind of man it does so by going first to passions and to primitive, unreflective symbolic processes. If Ernst's conception of "mind" has any definition, it seems to be this: the realm of mind includes everything except those activities which are concerned with external physical objects.

If this extremely vague and loose conception of "mind" be

conjoined with its corresponding vague and loose conception of "ideas," then the freedom which the First Amendment protects is the freedom to influence and be influenced in any manner by verbal expressions which are not seditious or commercial. The magistrate may control verbal expressions when they are concerned with commercial "things,"[29] but he must not control them when they appeal to sadistic impulses, because the latter expressions have an impact on that part of man's life which the Constitution has rendered sacred—that part which is not concerned with external physical objects. Freedom of speech and press deserve a better explanation than this.

Professor Alexander Meiklejohn adopts a very different line of argument. He is careful to make some of the distinctions the absence of which is so characteristic of Ernst's view. According to Meiklejohn, the Constitution differentiates sharply between two kinds of speech: that which is concerned with public interests, and that which is concerned with private interests. The First Amendment protects, and protects absolutely, all "public discussion,"[30] all speech about "public issues"[31] or about "the general welfare."[32] With regard to this kind of speech the language of the First Amendment is unqualified. "It admits of no exceptions. . . . That prohibition holds good in war as in peace, in danger as in security."[33] Speech directed toward our private interests and needs receives qualified protection from the Due Process Clause. Private speech may not be abridged without due process of law. Thus, libel and slander may be punished, but criticism of the government or the Constitution in wartime may not.

Meiklejohn's distinction is based upon his understanding of the meaning of self-government and America's commitment to it. American political society is based on our agreement that "We, the People" will govern ourselves. It follows from this that we cannot be denied access to any information or any points of view relevant to our self-governing powers and decisions. No public official can be in a position to dictate what viewpoints or arguments we shall hear, because we are the governors, and he governs only by our authority. Meiklejohn's model of democracy is that of the town meeting. In the town meeting the people will establish rules for orderly discussion. The rules will determine how, when, and where the people may be addressed. But there can be no control of what may be argued on any point before the house; no one may be denied a hearing because of his viewpoint. The people need to hear all relevant ideas. Says Meiklejohn:

> What is essential is not that everyone shall speak, but that everyone worth saying shall be said. . . . no suggestion of policy shall be denied a hearing because it is on one side of the issue rather than another. And this means that though citizens may, on other grounds, be barred from speaking, they may not be barred because their views are thought to be false or dangerous. . . . When men govern themselves, it is they—and no one else—who must pass judgment on unwisdom and unfairness and danger. And that means that unwise ideas must have a hearing as well as wise ones, unfair as well as fair, dangerous as well as safe, un-American a well as American. Just so far as, at any point, the citizens who are to decide an issue are denied an acquaintance with information or opinion or doubt or disbelief or criticism which is relevant to that issue, just so far the result must be ill-considered, ill-balanced planning for the general good. *It is that mutilation of the thinking process of the community against which the First Amendment to the Constitution is directed.* The principle of the freedom of speech springs from the necessities of the program of self-government. It is not a Law of Nature or of Reason in the abstract. It is a deduction from the basic American agreement that public issues shall be decided by universal suffrage [italics in original].[34]

Thus the First Amendment does not protect an individual's right to speak as much as it protects the citizen's right to hear. It protects the self-governing powers and functions of the people.

A number of questions may be raised about the premises of Meiklejohn's doctrine as well as about its applications. Why would it be illegitimate for the self-governing people to determine that they do not wish to hear a particular point of view? They may decide that they have heard enough, for instance, of communist doctrines and arguments, and they have made up their minds—they do not want to hear this anymore. They may decide that a certain idea is not worth hearing, and they do not wish to be bothered with it. Or, they may conclude, upon investigation and after discussion, that a certain kind of expression is unwise, harmful, and dangerous and ought to be severely restricted. Finally, they may wish to vote, with no investigation and discussion, to outlaw that expression simply because they do not like it.

In all these cases the people are "governing themselves." Meiklejohn would reply that they are not doing so wisely. How do they know that the viewpoints they reject without a hearing are not worth hearing and indeed are not precisely those which they ought to hear? And even if they have heard the communist doctrines many times before, how do they know that these doctrines are not applicable to the new problem which they face today, and how do they know that those wishing to expound these doctrines today do not have new insights? Finally, Meiklejohn *might* say, it is not reasonable to conclude once and for all, upon any investigation and discussion, that a certain class of expression is unwise, harmful, and dangerous.

But why are the sovereign people required to be reasonable? Meiklejohn says that we have made a fundamental agreement. But what agreement have we made—to govern ourselves, or to do so rationally? In Meiklejohn's theory these alternatives are not presented as alternatives; they are presented as being identical with each other or at least as being two aspects of the same thing. Logically, however, they are not necesarily two aspects of the same thing, and Meiklejohn does not demonstrate that they are.* As a result, Meiklejohn's theory actually contains two conceptions of self-government and two conceptions of the First Amendment which are never quite integrated in the theory. The First Amendment is designed to protect the prerequisites of popular sovereignty, *and* it is designed to protect the community's thinking process—to foster rationality. From the former concept it would surely follow that the government or its officials cannot, contrary to the wishes of the people, deny them access to any expression they may want to hear. But it would not follow that the people themselves may not, by means of government, deny themselves (or some of their members) access to expressions of which they disapprove.

Does democracy mean self-government, or intelligent self-government? If democracy means simply the former, then the people may censor with or without deliberation. But if democracy means the latter, does it necessarily follow that the people may not

---

* If it would be argued that self-government which is not intelligent will not survive, it may be answered that this proposition is not an absolute. The prophecy is most likely to be fulfilled in instances of *gross* unintelligence. At any rate, the sovereign people may prefer the present indulgence of their desires and aversions to the long-run survival of the Republic.

censor after deliberation? The intelligence of the people may lead them to decide that government should have some censorship powers and to vest these powers in government. The intelligence of the people may conceivably dictate that, under certain conditions, the values of self-government should be subordinated to other values; that *self*-government is not always the primary consideration. But for Meiklejohn self-government is always the primary consideration. He quotes the Preamble to the Constitution and follows with this statement:

> In those words it is agreed, and with every passing moment it is reagreed, that the people of the United States shall be self-governed. To that fundamental enactment all other provisions of the Constitution, all statutes, all administrative decrees, are subsidiary and dependent. All other purposes, whether individual or social, can find their legitimate scope and meaning only as they conform to the one basic purpose that the citizens of this nation shall make and obey their own laws, shall be at once their own subjects and their own masters.[35]

One may ask whether this is the understanding of the Constitution held by the authors of *The Federalist Papers*. It is highly questionable that Madison and Hamilton would have accorded this degree of priority to the first half of the dual concept "self-government." In *The Federalist* no. 37 Madison states the political problem as one of combining "in their due proportion" the requisites of "republican liberty" and the requisites of stable and energetic government.[36] It would seem that Meiklejohn reads the Preamble as if it said: "We, the People of the United States, in order to govern ourselves do ordain and establish the following means subordinate to this end."

The application of Meiklejohn's doctrine to the censorship of obscenity poses a special problem. Do obscene publications fall within the category of public speech or of private speech? Does literature treating of sex address itself to "public issues" in any significant sense? Do artistic forms of expression as such deal at all with those matters of the public interest about which the self-governing people is concerned?

These forms of expression do not appear to fall within Meiklejohn's definition of what constitutes absolutely protected speech. His doctrine of free speech is heavily weighted in the direction of political considerations. It is a political doctrine. *Free Speech*[37] and *Political Freedom,* the works in which his doctrine was originally set forth, employ political terms and examples almost exclusively. The author of these works speaks in terms of voting and of town-meeting discussions of community problems. He asserts that the First Amendment guarantee "is assured only to speech which bears, directly or indirectly, upon issues with which the voters have to deal."[38] It is difficult to see how literature dealing with sex would bear even indirectly upon such issues. Literature of this kind seldom addresses itself, even remotely, to political and public matters; rather, it is almost always concerned with the most private matters. It would seem, then, that it should receive only the qualified protection of the Due Process Clause.

In a more recent article, however, Meiklejohn asserts: "Literature and the arts must be protected by the First Amendment. They lead the way toward sensitive and informed appreciation and response to the values out of which the riches of the general welfare are created."[39]

Here it is Meiklejohn's argument that there are many forms of expression and communication which, though not concerned with public policy, provide an essential preparation for the proper performance of political functions. From these forms of expression the voter derives that intelligence and sensitivity to human values which are prerequisite for good political judgment. People do need literature and the arts "because they will be called upon to vote."[40] Upon this basis Meiklejohn condemns unequivocally the censorship of written and visual materials on grounds of obscenity.

In *Political Freedom* Meiklejohn thought it essential to render as sharp and clear as possible the distinction between that which is public and that which is private, between what belongs to the general welfare of the community and what belongs to the private welfare of individuals. Now it seems that, in the interest of free expression, he is willing to blur that distinction. The proper scope and the proper employment of his principles is now problematic. In his major works, Meiklejohn has interpreted his principle as requiring the denial of First Amendment protection to those forms of expression which are not "public" and which do not contribute to the development of self-governing citizens but rather inhibit their development. In 1948 Meiklejohn would have denied First Amendment protection to the radio. In *Free Speech* and again in *Political Freedom* Meiklejohn asserted of the radio:

It is not engaged in the task of enlarging and enriching human communication. It is engaged in making money. . . . The radio, as we now have it, is not cultivating those qualities of taste, of reasoned judgment, of integrity, of loyalty, of mutual understanding upon which the enterprise of self-government depends. On the contrary it is a mighty force for breaking them down. It corrupts both our morals and our intelligence. And that catastrophe is significant for our inquiry because it reveals how hollow may be the victories of freedom of speech when our acceptance of the principle is merely formalistic. Misguided by that formalism we Americans have given to the doctrine merely its negative meaning. We have used it for the protection of private, possessive interests with which it has no concern. It is misinterpretations such as this which, in our use of the radio, the moving picture, the newspaper and other forms of publication, are giving the name of "freedoms" to the most flagrant enslavements of our minds and wills.[41]

The author of these words was well aware that these media of communication and expression possessed potentials for public service. But he did not for that reason throw the mantle of absolute First Amendment protection over them. They were not in fact performing that public service. They were in fact serving private interests and inhibiting the growth of the virtues requisite for self-government.

How are Meiklejohn's later ideas related to these conclusions drawn by him as necessary inferences from his doctrine? The later Meiklejohn asserts that "the authority of citizens to decide what they shall . . . read and see . . . is 'reserved to the people,' each deciding for himself to whom he shall listen."[42] One cannot be certain that Meiklejohn would now extend the First Amendment's absolute protection to all those media of expression enumerated above, but his words point in that direction. Have these media changed their character—or has Meiklejohn changed his constitutional doctrine? Have these media moved from the service of private to the service of public interests and from the corruption of morals and intelligence to their promotion? Has Meiklejohn moved from a rigorous doctrine of public freedom for public ends toward a doctrine of the freedom of each individual to decide for himself? If the answer to these questions is no, then Meiklejohn's ideas require much clarification.

Justice Black, Morris Ernst, and Alexander Meiklejohn all

agree that the prohibitions of the First Amendment are absolute. But they are not in complete agreement on what the amendment prohibits and what it absolutely protects. Ernst would protect slanderous speech but not seditious speech. Meiklejohn would protect seditious speech but not slander. These differences in constitutional doctrine reflect important underlying differences. Likewise, there are differences, though perhaps lesser ones, among those who advocate some kind of "clear and present danger" or "hard-core pornography" test.

Judge Curtis Bok advances the most stringent test. He would hold written material legally obscene "only where there is a reasonable and demonstrable cause to believe that a crime or misdemeanor has been committed or is about to be committed as the perceptible result of the publication and distribution of the writing in question."[43] There must be a *demonstrable* causal connection between a particular writing and a particular criminal act. This rule would probably curtail the operation of obscenity statutes almost as effectively as would the absolutism of Justices Black and Douglas. Though Judge Frank substantially agrees with Judge Bok, he would substitute a somewhat less restrictive test. Under Judge Frank's test, a writing can be found legally obscene only if it falls into a class of materials which can be shown to have a "probability" of inducing either criminal behavior or "seriously anti-social conduct."[44]

In 1954 Lockhart and McClure offered a clear and present danger standard which also involves the consideration of effects upon conduct. But this test is more complicated. "One phase of the constitutional standard is 'clear' or 'probable' danger that the particular work under attack will lead to sex conduct deviating from the legal or otherwise currently established moral standards."[45] This "probable danger" would be balanced against other factors: the worth of the particular writing in question, the value of the class of literature to which it belongs, and the effect that banning the work may have on the freedom to write and read in this and related areas. Thus, if a thoroughly pornographic writing of no value is under consideration, a relatively slight "probability" of resultant antisocial conduct would be sufficient to justify suppression. But if the work has some value, a higher degree of "probability" would be required. If the work has considerable value, its suppression would be justified, if at all, only by a clear demonstration of a close causal connection between it and harmful conduct.

These judges and authors agree that censorship of obscenity is justified only where a causal nexus can be shown between written material and criminal or seriously harmful acts. The arguments upon which this view rests can be divided into two types: those concerned with the evils of censorship, and those concerned with the role of government in a free society.

The following are the "evils" of censorship most often cited in these arguments:

1. Censorship denies us access to the proper kind of information and insights concerning sexual life. It keeps us in ignorance and denies us the opportunity for responsible choice.

2. Censorship of obscenity has the character of "thought control."

3. It enervates the mind and spirit.

4. It is dangerously contagious. Once censorship gains a foothold in one area it inevitably spreads and grows.

Judge Bok asserts:

> I should prefer that my own three daughters meet the facts of life in my own library than behind a neighbor's barn, for I can face the adversary there directly. . . . Our daughters must live in the world and decide what sort of women they are to be, and we should be willing to prefer their deliberate and informed choice of decency rather than an innocence that continues to spring from ignorance. If that choice be made in the open sunlight it is more apt than when made in the shadow to fall on the side of honorable behavior.[46]

I do not wish to detract from the truths contained in Judge Bok's assertion. They are particularly compelling with regard to the books at issue in *Commonwealth* v. *Gordon*—among them, works of William Faulkner, James T. Farrell, and Erskine Caldwell. But there are qualifying truths. Not all obscene materials are safely confined in the libraries of men like Judge Bok. Many of these materials do indeed find their way "behind a neighbor's barn" and to the kinds of places indicated by this figure of speech. Judge Bok's daughters are, no doubt, quite safe. But not all children are the children of Judge Bok.

What leads us to think that those persons most likely to be reached by obscene materials are also likely to make "a deliberate and informed choice of decency"? Is even the average man naturally inclined to make it? It is undeniable that such a choice is preferable to ignorance and that ignorance is vulnerable to appeals "made in the shadow." But we are not confronted with only two alternatives: the unrestrained circulation of all written materials—including pornography—and ignorance. We can seek to make sure that the works of William Faulkner are available and pornography is not. And we have other ways of teaching and learning the facts of life.

Judge Bok's words reflect the Miltonian insight into the dignity of choice and the vacuity of a "cloistered virtue."[47] But Judge Bok does not take his stand simply on the dignity of choice. He does not say that chosen indecency and dishonor is better than innocent decency and honor. He expects the decision to be good. But he does not justify the expectation.

Judge Frank asserts:

> Any paternalistic guardianship by government of the thoughts of grown-up citizens enervates their spirit, keeps them immature, all too ready to adopt towards government the attitude that, in general, "papa knows best." If the government possesses the power to censor publications which arouse sexual thoughts, regardless of whether these thoughts tend probably to transform themselves into anti-social behavior, why may not the government censor political and religious publications regardless of any causal relation to any probable dangerous deeds?[48]

and:

> Governmental control of ideas or personal preferences is alien to a democracy. And the yearning to use governmental censorship of any kind is infectious. It may spread insidiously. Commencing with the suppression of books as obscene, it is not unlikely to develop into official lust for the power of thought-control in the areas of religion, politics and elsewhere.[49]

It is true that when government undertakes paternalistically to guard the thoughts of citizens, enervation may well result. This argument is suitably directed to those who would impose totalitarian ideologies upon a people by the devices of modern mass communication. But is it suitably directed to those who would control obscenity by the devices of the federal statute?

One cannot be certain whether Judge Frank thinks that the

censorship of obscenity *is* "thought-control"—or only that the terms upon which it is now conducted would justify "thought-control." At any rate, the first point to be made is an obvious one. Government does not here undertake to *impose* any thoughts on anyone. It seeks to prevent the dissemination of obscenity. A finding of obscenity will often turn on a finding that materials stimulate lustful thoughts or desires. The character of the "thoughts" with which government is concerned is indicated by the inevitable association of the term with terms like "lust" and "desires." Whatever may be the intellectual content of such thoughts, it is an intellectual content inseparable from certain passions. The statutes do not interdict concepts about sex or thoughts about sex as such.*

These considerations are relevant to a contention that the censorship of obscenity on grounds of the thoughts it promotes will justify the censorship of religious and political expression on the same grounds. A burden of proof is on Judge Frank to show that these thoughts are of the same kind or are so similar that reasonable men would have difficulty making the relevant distinctions. Reasonable men would take account of the character of the thoughts, the subject matter, and considerations of "redeeming value."[50]

If one takes the censorship of obscenity as it is, the argument about "enervation" is difficult to meet because it is hard to find evidence bearing upon it. It would probably be as difficult to prove this causal connection as that between obscenity and criminal conduct. From the 1870's to the 1930's, literature was under a censorship considerably more rigorous than that contemplated at the present. Were the American people enervated and rendered immature? Did they "adopt towards government officers the attitude that, in general, 'papa knows best' " any more than we do now? Perhaps it would be more defensible to say that some forms of censorship are enervating and that the circumstances and the ends in view are relevant to judgment on the matter.

But the viewpoint represented by Judge Frank regards censorship as such as containing an inherently imperialistic dynamism. It cannot be confined to worthless writings; it will spread and en-

---

* These observations are not intended to be my last word about the relation between censorship of obscenity and the opinions or thinking process of the community. They are, however, a sufficient answer to this aspect of Judge Frank's argument.

velop works of genius. It cannot be confined to literature; it will expand into politics and religion. Libertarians often appear to believe that once you begin to censor anything for any reason, there emerges an autonomous process of growth over which you can have little, if any, control.

This belief is supported in a number of ways. Impressive lists are presented showing how much of the world's valuable literature has at one time or another been subjected to censorship. Attention is directed to the personality and motivation of "the censor." It is often asserted that the censor is a person driven by irrational fears and wants which he projects upon the outside world. According to Judge Frank, the effort to control obscenity is inspired by those obsessed with "Victorian morality" and its attendant self-deceptions and corruptions. Lockhart and McClure observe that the censor is "often an emotionally disturbed person."[51] Justice Douglas, in terms less qualified than those of Judge Frank or Lockhart and McClure, simply assert that "censors are of course propelled by their own neuroses."[52] The dynamism of censorship is sometimes related to an inherent lust for power in government. Consequently, censorship cannot be confined by rational purpose because it is an inherently irrational process in which psychological complexes and desires for power combine under the guise of morality.

How much of this view can be accepted as valid? Such historical evidence as can be brought to bear on the matter often leads to mixed conclusions. Evidence concerning Victorian sex censorship in England may be taken as an example. This censorship was not confined to worthless obscenity—it reached into all areas of literary, poetic, and dramatic expression involving sex. But it did not "infect" the area of political and religious expression. As is well known, Victorian England was characterized by an ever widening toleration for criticism and unorthodoxy in matters of religion and politics. Censorship of expression in matters of sex did not spread and envelop this area.* And analysis even of the excesses of Victorian censorship and moralistic rigidity will reveal

* See Norman St. John-Stevas, *Obscenity and the Law,* p. 29. The author's analysis suggests an interesting connection between Victorian tolerance and Victorian intolerance. It suggests that some aspects of the sexual moralism of the age may have been a response to ceaseless change and increasing doubt in other areas of life. "Moral seriousness" provided "the stability of an age of doubt and revolution."

some motives and purposes which can hardly be condemned as simply irrational. That phenomenon was more complex than libertarian polemics would indicate.*

It cannot be denied that a very great number of important authors and works have historically been subjected to some kind of censorship. An impressive list of such authors and works can be compiled. But this evidence does not prove quite as much as it is thought to prove. It is not surprising that in the long history of Western civilization and others a large number of writings have come, in some way, to some extent, and for some length of time, under the eye of some censor. Of the writings on any particular libertarian list, a number of questions may be asked: What kind or degree of censorship was employed? By whom? For what audience? And for what length of time? It would be interesting to see a list of those same works, with the times and places wherein they have gone uncensored. Evidence bearing on these questions is seldom presented in any form which would render it susceptible to careful analysis and evaluation.[53] It is not suggested that such analysis and evaluation (if it could be made) would wholly nullify the libertarian contention about the nature of censorship. But neither is it self-evident that these contentions would be wholly supported.

There remains the libertarian postulate about the psychological dynamisms that drive "the censorious." This argument is, in my judgment, the least convincing, and the least worthy, of all those

---

* St. John-Stevas says: "There were reasonable grounds for the tenderness of the Victorian conscience on matters connected with sex. When the extent of Victorian pornography and prostitution is taken into account, it is possible to interpret the conventions about sex as a necessary means of self-defense, adopted to prevent subjugation by the underworld. Equally, 'respectability,' when considered against the actual background of social conditions, loses much of its stuffiness and hypocrisy, and can be reappraised as a valuable and even a moral social ideal. 'Respectability' not only protected middle-class standards, but enabled the skilled worker to rise above and keep himself distinct from the amorphous mass of the industrial proletariat" (ibid., pp. 39–40). Steven Marcus suggests that, while the Victorians paid a heavy price for their moralism, it did serve positive functions of a civilizing or humanizing sort in the lives of the lower classes. Says Marcus: "It is not usual nowadays to regard such values as chastity, propriety, modesty, even rigid prudery as positive moral values, but it is difficult to doubt that in the situation of the urban lower social classes they operated with positive force. The discipline and self-restraint which the exercise of such virtues required could not be but a giant step toward the humanization of a class of persons who had been traditionally regarded as almost of another species." Steven Marcus, *The Other Victorians,* p. 147.

on the libertarian side of the issue. While it can be shown that some or even many of those who have undertaken censorship have done so out of unworthy or unhealthy motives, it can hardly be shown that all have acted from such motives.[54] Least of all can it be demonstrated that wherever there is censorship, by whomever for whatever reason, there is mental illness or lust for domination. The "censor" is not a species the properties of which are to be found in all members. The control of written and verbal expression is undertaken by many different sorts of men, in many different circumstances, for many different reasons.

When placed in perspective the libertarian case against censorship retains some, but not all, of its force and its validity. The libertarian view of government and society must now be considered. A brief examination of Lockhart and McClure will lead us to the heart of that view.

Lockhart and McClure have had considerable influence on the course of judicial decisions, as well as on libertarian thought in this area.[55] Their most influential work is: "Literature, the Law of Obscenity, and the Constitution," written in 1954. In this work the authors set forth and criticize in systematic form what they regard as the four basic rationales for obscenity regulation. The following are the four "evils" which are often supposed to result from obscenity and at which regulation may conceivably aim. (1) The circulation of obscene literature may, in time, bring about a change in the moral standards of the community. (2) Persons will be shocked or offended by obscenity. (3) Obscenity stimulates lustful thought. (4) Obscenity promotes conduct contrary to the laws or moral standards of the community.[56] Lockhart and McClure proceed to analyze each rationale in terms of "clear and probable danger." They find that the first three "evils" cannot justify censorship under the Constitution and in a democracy. Either these are not really evils, or they do not pose such a clear and probable danger to substantial social interests as would justify restraint of expression. The danger that conduct contrary to law or accepted morality may be induced by obscenity would justify restraints, if that danger were sufficiently "clear" and "probable." The authors then propose their formulation of the clear and present danger test to be applied to materials challenged on these grounds.

In an article written in 1960 Lockhart and McClure reformulated this test, arriving at their concept of "variable obscenity."[57] They argue that, since there is no such thing as inherently obscene literature, materials must be judged by their appeal to and effect upon the audience to which they are directed. But it appears that the authors would confine this test to material which is, or is advertised as, hard-core pornography.[58]

In 1962 these authors wrote an article called "Why Obscene?" in which they seem to have completed their movement toward a hard-core pornography standard. Here they insist that, to meet the hard-core test, materials must be, not only highly erotic, but "grossly shocking" as well.[59] But Lockhart and McClure do not find it easy to justify censorship on this basis. They do not find sufficient evidence or information to support an acceptable rationale for the censorship of pornography. They conclude:

> Until that far off day when the social sciences have been able to furnish enough reliable knowledge to form a rational basis for obscenity censorship, perhaps the best we can do is to do what we might have to do anyway—to admit that in our way we are as bound by our culture as the members of primitive societies are in their way, that in our society there are outer limits of toleration for sexual expression. . . . This may come to no more than saying, as Zechariah Chaffee once noted, "We will permit what we will permit," which is going around in a circle, but for the time being it is the best we can do.[60]

This is to say that, until the social sciences can provide one, we will do without a reasonable test for censorship of obscenity and will rely instead upon feelings which we have because we cannot help having them. Gone is the clear and present danger standard with its heavy emphasis on a causal nexus between expression and harmful conduct. In its place is a standard which looks very much like that strongly rejected by Lockhart and McClure in their earlier work. They will now allow the censorship of material because it is highly offensive and "grossly shocking." In their 1954 article they said that "mere offensiveness cannot constitutionally justify censorship."[61] Now they will accept such a rationale because society will insist upon some censorship, and because this standard will provide the broadest scope for free expression tolerable to society. While the various constitutional doctrines offered by Lockhart and McClure may be somewhat inconsistent, they all reflect and are bound together by an underlying theory of the First Amendment and the free society.

In "Literature, the Law of Obscenity, and the Constitution," Lockhart and McClure say: "Certainly it is entirely appropriate for the *church* to discourage reading that turns the mind from spiritual to carnal thoughts, but under our constitutional system the *government* can scarcely claim authority to impose controls on literature for the purpose of directing men's minds away from the physical interests of life toward more spiritual and worthy thoughts."[62] This is because "the state can properly be concerned with controlling action that harms society, but ordinarily it must stop short of what men think and believe."[63]

The authors do not quite say that the state has *no* interest in "what men think and believe." It is evident that every President, every Congress, and every Supreme Court Justice is interested in the thinking and beliefs of citizens, not only with a view to being guided by them, but also with a view to guiding, influencing, or educating them. The Constitution-makers explicitly provided for this function when they designed our institutions.[64] And public education still seeks to promote certain common values and identifications by means of ceremonies such as the salute to the flag and by teaching aimed at instilling respect for American principles and traditions.[65]

It is true that "the state" ordinarily stops short of imposing any sanctions on the expression of thoughts and beliefs. And the law rarely acts directly with a view to them.[66] Such acts of government are open to grave suspicion in our system. But obscenity regulation need not be understood as an effort by government to direct "men's minds away from the physical interests of life toward more spiritual or worthy thoughts." As I have indicated, in its censorship of obscenity, government does not act with a view to directing the thoughts that citizens are thinking. It does not aim directly at anyone's thoughts, and it does not seek to promote "spiritual" thoughts. But it can be understood as aiming at some of those forces in society which shape moral standards. Censorship of obscenity can be understood as aiming at the control of some of those influences in modern mass society which operate to degrade moral standards and, ultimately, to debase moral character. As such, the objective of government would not be to turn men's minds toward more worthy thoughts, but to inhibit influences which corrupt that moral character which is a precondition for the emergence of any worthy thoughts.

Lockhart and McClure do not consider the corruption of character one of those possible "evils" to which obscenity statutes might be addressed. If it be granted them that "the state" is not concerned with the thoughts of citizens, do they believe that it has any interest in the character of citizens and in the moral standards which influence character? Do they believe that civil society has an interest in the promotion of any particular type of human character or in the maintenance of any particular kind of ethical values? Lockhart and McClure assert:

> The view that literature may be proscribed because of the risk that it may influence a change in the accepted moral standards of the community flies squarely in the face of the very purpose for guaranteeing freedom of expression. Back of this fundamental freedom lies the basic conviction that our democratic society must be free to perfect its own standards of conduct and belief— political, economic, social, religious, moral—through the heat of unrepressed controversy and debate. The remedy against those who attack currently accepted standards is spirited and intelligent defense of those standards, not censorship. . . . Only through unlimited examination and re-examination, attack and defense, can come the ultimate perfection of these standards, and the understanding and grasp of the reasons that alone will ensure their preservation, if sound.[67]

The authors speak continuously of the possibility of "change" in "accepted" moral standards. Government must not act to prevent such change from occurring. But do they recognize a possibility that change may take the form of degradation—that important values may be lost? Do they recognize a possibility that there may be some accepted standards which ought to be accepted and the loss of which would constitute a serious social injury? In their view, overt acts in violation of accepted morality are a social evil serious enough to warrant restraint of speech clearly inducing such acts.[68] But government must not act to restrain a continuous stream of expression—written, spoken, and visual—which might well lead, in time, to mass violation and to the disintegration of that morality. The law may punish violations of the moral code but, where expression is concerned, it must not seek in advance to protect the moral code from corrosion and destruction.

Lockhart and McClure insist that the only proper remedy against attacks on moral standards is "intelligent defense"; it is "controversy and debate." They often write as if they believed the problem—to the extent that they believe there is a problem—to be one of meeting arguments "challenging or questioning" prevailing ethics.[69] As has been indicated several times in these pages, prurient motion pictures, pornographic paperbacks, and obscene magazines do not make arguments which are to be met by intelligent defense. While they attack moral values, they do not challenge or question them in any sense relevant to what Lockhart and McClure are advocating. To the extent that they have an effect, it is most likely an effect upon feeling, upon motivations—ultimately upon character and the basic attitudes which arise from character. The nonlegal remedy most appropriate to such effects is not debate, but moral training.

The authors' essentially rationalistic or intellectualistic approach to the problem is most evident in these passages. They speak of the circulation of obscenity in our society as if it constituted an "examination and re-examination" of beliefs and standards. There is, of course, a controversy and debate going on in our society. It is going on between those who do and those who do not think that obscenity should be censored. But the relation between a salacious film or novel and its consumer can hardly be characterized in this way. The processes by which such materials circulate and have whatever effects they have cannot reasonably be viewed as a free exchange of ideas.

The rationalism of Lockhart and McClure does not consist only in their tendency to characterize the present situation in intellectualistic terms. And their libertarianism does not stop with the assertion that the First Amendment protects the right to criticize moral standards. They go farther than this. They suggest that the moral standards and beliefs of the community *ought* to be subjected to "unlimited examination and re-examination, attack and defense." Only thus can they be perfected.

Whatever Lockhart and McClure may mean by the "perfecting" of moral standards, what leads them to conclude that the ceaseless questioning and debate of our beliefs is more likely to lead to their perfection than to their dissolution? The authors' premises seem to be as follows. The only moral beliefs worth holding are those which rest upon reason. When men understand the reasons for their moral standards, then these standards will be preserved. When, by reasoning, they discover a better morality, they will be prepared to discard the old and adhere to the new and improved beliefs.* Thus Lockhart and McClure's argument seems to presuppose, not only that men hold their moral convictions upon the basis of their reasoning, but also that each man is intellectually capable of understanding the rational grounds for his and the community's convictions, of defending them when they are wrongly attacked, of adopting and making proper use of valid criticism, and of changing belief whenever reason dictates change. If the sanctity of the family and the moral primacy of fidelity over promiscuity are worth preserving, the great majority of citizens ought to be able to demonstrate to themselves why this is so and to reject fallacious opinions and prurient appeals.

Whether or not Lockhart and McClure actually hold all these premises, these are the premises which would have to be valid if their standing invitation to ceaseless questioning and controversy about basic moral standards is to result in the perfection rather than the weakening or destruction of the community's values. Even if men and communities were psychologically capable of holding their opinions about sex as tentatively as one would hold a scientific hypothesis,[70] it seems unlikely that many of the opinions now held would long survive the adoption of such an attitude.

The central problem arising out of the views of Lockhart and McClure is one concerning the character and the significance of society's moral framework. Does society need a moral framework, a public morality? Is there a public interest in the maintenance of any particular moral order? It is possible to derive from the writings of Lockhart and McClure three alternative answers to these questions. (1) Society as such does not have an interest in the maintenance of any particular norms. Society's primary interest is in the freedom to change. (2) There may be a public interest in the preservation of certain norms, but these are adequately secured by unrepressed discussion and debate. The free communication of ideas must necessarily result in the preservation of what is good and the rejection of what is bad. (3) Whatever the social significance of moral standards, and whatever their fate, government is forbidden to protect them by the restraint of free expression.

It is very difficult to determine which, if any, of these propo-

* Jefferson did not adopt this rationalistic approach to morality. He thought morality largely a matter of feeling or sensibility and not "a matter of science." Thomas Jefferson, *Living Thoughts of Jefferson,* p. 94.

sitions Lockhart and McClure would be willing to avow unequivocally and which of them they would regard as primary. They do not quite say that society's moral standards are expendable or that freedom of expression is more important than any such standards, but they often imply these propositions.[71] They do not quite say that moral truth must inevitably prevail in any open contest, but they often imply this proposition. It is, therefore, impossible to determine just where the theoretical side of their case rests. The theoretical side of their case is characterized by ambiguity about the crucial question: What is the public interest in moral norms and moral character, and how is that interest best served? They never clearly ask this question and they never clearly address themselves to it.

The avoidance of this issue and the ambiguity attendant upon such avoidance are characteristic of the libertarian position as a whole. Libertarian doctrines, however, will differ in accordance with the emphasis given to one or another of the three propositions listed above. In one form or another, these three propositions pervade the libertarian writings and doctrines.

In his *Roth* dissent Justice Douglas said:

> I can understand (and at times sympathize with) programs of civic groups and church groups to protect and defend the existing moral standards of the community. I can understand the motives of the Anthony Comstocks who would impose Victorian standards on the community. When speech alone is involved, I do not think that government, consistently with the First Amendment, can become the sponsor of any of these movements. I do not think that government, consistently with the First Amendment, can throw its weight behind one school or another. Government should be concerned with anti-social conduct, not with utterances. Thus, if the First Amendment guarantee of freedom of speech and press is to mean anything in this field, it must allow protests even against the moral code that the standard of the day sets for the community. In other words, literature should not be censored merely because it offends the moral code of the censor.[72]

Thus, moral standards are the concern of "groups" in society. Government stands aloof as these groups seek to advance, to protect, or to protest various private moralities. Government and law are not intrinsically concerned with the outcome. As Justice

Douglas sees the matter, the intervention of government in the area of morality can only be understood as government sponsorship of one or another of these various private associations. At best, it would be an illegitimate effort to defend, by means of law, the moral "standard of the day." Justice Douglas does not quite say that all of the community's moral norms are mere ephemeral standards of the day, but he does nothing to counter this relativistic tendency and effect of his words.

Justice Douglas does not have to decide, however, whether there are any norms based on something more solid than the transient opinions of the moment and, if so, whether these might require any attention from government. He has "the same confidence in the ability of our people to reject noxious literature as [he has] in their capacity to sort out the true from the false in theology, economics, politics, or in any other field."[73] Here confidence in the people relieves him of the necessity of taking a clear position on the status of public morality and its relation to law.

The moral relativism which is implicit in Justice Douglas' *Roth* opinion becomes quite explicit in his *Ginzburg* dissent. Speaking of literature designed to appeal to "masochists," the Justice asserts:

> Masochism is a desire to be punished or subdued. . . . the desire may be expressed in the longing to be whipped and lashed, bound and gagged, and cruelly treated. Why is it unlawful to cater to the needs of this group? They are, to be sure, somewhat offbeat, nonconformist, and odd. But we are not in the realm of criminal conduct, only ideas and tastes. Some like Chopin, others like "rock and roll." Some are "normal," some are masochistic, some deviant in other respects. . . . When the Court today speaks of "social value," does it mean a "value" to the majority? Why is not a minority "value" cognizable? . . . if the communication is of value to the masochistic community or to others of the deviant community, how can it be said to be "utterly without any redeeming social importance"? "Redeeming" to whom? "Importance" to whom?[74]

Thus, judgments about the human worth of masochistic or normal sexual life are based upon nothing more than arbitrary *tastes*. Masochists (and presumably sadists as well) are simply "nonconformists" whose likes and dislikes deviate from those which happen to prevail among the dominant majority. The community has no rational grounds for preferring the interests and values of the latter to those of the former. Indeed, according to this view, there is no community. Society is made up of a variety of "communities"—the masochistic, the sadistic, the homosexual, the "normal" (a term which Justice Douglas seldom fails to place in quotation marks)—all of which are, evidently, entitled to equal social status and esteem. In this manner, concepts such as "social value" are utterly relativized, as are other notions of value or worth. The distinction between healthy and perverted human relations, between things conducive to and things destructive of human development, is reduced to a matter of subjective preference. It then becomes impossible to say that any particular way of life is better, more desirable, or more conducive to social purposes than any other. The passage cited above comes closer than any judicial statement I know of to an outright denial of the existence of any valid social and ethical norms.

In his *Roth* opinion Justice Douglas affirmed that the people can be counted upon to reject "noxious literature." It is the implication of his *Ginzburg* opinion that there is no such thing as noxious literature and no moral reason why any forms of literature should be rejected by anyone. If personal tastes and values are to be regarded as equal, then a particular form of literature cannot be judged undesirable as long as some people desire it or can be induced to desire it. Now the present majority does not happen to have a taste for sado-masochistic literature and sado-masochistic experiences. Presumably there is no reason why they should not be induced, by advertising or other means, to acquire these tastes. There can be no public interest in the matter one way or the other. It would appear that the only public interest and the only moral imperative which escapes this general leveling of values is the requirement that individuals be left alone to live as they please.

Justice Douglas' defense of free expression rests sometimes on a doctrine of moral relativism and sometimes on assumptions about the inherent virtues of The People. Morris Ernst's defense of free expression does not rely upon any confidence in the capacity of the people to separate the good from the bad. He seems to be as skeptical about the wisdom of the majority as he is about distinctions between good and bad. Ernst's various writings constantly emphasize the irrational sources and the arbitrary or merely relative character of the moral standards prevailing in society at any given time.[75] He strongly suggests that society's standards on sex and allied subjects are nothing more than a collection of fears and taboos and that the majority is all too susceptible to these fears and all too willing to acquiesce in the taboos. According to Ernst, judgments about obscenity and non-obscenity are wholly matters of taste, of "the whims of a passing generation." And it seems that he holds almost all, if not all, of man's moral and aesthetic principles to be likewise relative.

But there is one standard of value about which Ernst is not at all skeptical; this is the value of "change." In Ernst's writings, change—the erosion of old values and their replacement by new ones—is always presented, not only as inevitable, but as unquestionably desirable. He repeatedly criticizes those who are slow to discard old beliefs, and he praises those who are disposed to "adopt the new in art and morality" and "carry out society's new attitudes."[76] For Ernst "new" is synonymous with "good." This is the only ethic which Ernst can consistently bring to the problem of obscenity and to the definition of the First Amendment.

Ernst does not provide his readers with much argument in defense of these assumptions which form the basis of his approach to censorship. Therefore one may continue to wonder whether it is really true that the standards of our socity on sexual matters have no more basis in reason or utility than the taboos of primitive tribesmen. And one may continue to doubt that an ethic which values change as a good in itself can help us to distinguish between desirable and undesirable changes.

Alexander Meiklejohn does not rest his case upon moral skepticism or upon unqualified confidence in the people. He insists that certain virtues are essential for the performance of self-governing functions. He knows that these virtues can be corroded and lost. He knows that the media of mass communication can "corrupt our morals and our intelligence"[77] and that literature and the arts may operate "for the building up of a way of life which we treasure or for tearing it down."[78]

Meiklejohn denies that his position rests in any degree upon faith in the inevitable triumph of truth:

> I have never been able to share the Miltonian faith that, in a fair fight between truth and error, truth is sure to win. . . . In my view "the people need free speech" because they have decided, in adopting, maintaining and interpreting their Constitution,

to govern themselves. And in order to make that self-government a reality rather than an illusion, in order that it may become as wise and efficient as its responsibilities require, the people must be self-educated in the ways of freedom.[79]

Thus Meiklejohn does not purport to ground his position in either skepticism or optimism about morality and truth. We need absolutely unfettered freedom of speech because of our unqualified commitment to self-government. But why must the sovereign people be exclusively self-educated in the ways of freedom? Why may they not decide that they need also to seek education in these ways by means of law? The control of expression by law is dangerous to the ways of freedom, but the people might intelligently decide that, under certain conditions, it is wiser to accept this danger rather than that resulting from unfettered free expression. Why can they not intelligently conclude that a certain kind of free expression is inimical to the virtues upon which the public safety and order depend? It appears that Meiklejohn would have to answer these questions in a way that commits him to a very optimistic conception of truth as it functions in a free society.

Meiklejohn insists that it is never legitimate to conclude that our interest in free expression must be subordinated to some other public interest. Freedom of expression and the public safety are never opposing interests; they *cannot* conflict. He asserts that "the integrity of public discussion and the care for the public safety are identical" and, therefore, that "the destruction of freedom is always unwise, that freedom is always expedient."[80] Freedom is always expedient because public discussion is the only safe and rational way to care for the public safety. These are the only foundations upon which truth can arise. Says Meiklejohn: " 'We, the People,' as we plan for the general welfare do not choose to be 'protected' from the 'search for truth.' On the contrary, we have made it our 'way of life,' our method of doing the work of sovereignty for which, as citizens, we are responsible."[81]

Freedom of speech can never stand opposed to any legitimate public interest. This is so because freedom of speech in inextricably linked to the "integrity of public discussion" and the "search for truth."

If this argument is to stand, a number of propositions must be presupposed: that free men do not need to be governed by anything but "truth," that the free expression guaranteed by the First

Amendment tends naturally to become a search for truth, and that the various searchings for truth of various free men cannot possibly endanger the public safety or any other public interest.

But it is not unthinkable that men may need to be governed through moral training backed, in some way, by law. And it is not self-evident that the mere opportunity for unlimited discussion will guarantee that the men making use of it will concern themselves with truth or will do so in a way which recognizes important public needs. It is quite possible (as Meiklejohn recognizes elsewhere) that they will employ public freedom for private ends, that they will employ passion and not reason in the discussion of issues, or, simply, that their speech about public interests will be uninformed and hence destructive of those interests.

Meiklejohn does not deny these possibilities. But much of his doctrine presupposes that they cannot occur often where discussion is really *free*. Much of his doctrine is based on the sanguine assumption that men, given the opportunity for free discussion, will not misuse it; that they will spontaneously search for truth and that they will find truth. Consequently, Meiklejohn has much in common with other libertarian writers in this area. He shares with them the tendency to identify the public good with the freedom to discuss the public good, and the successful search for political knowledge with the freedom to search for political knowledge.

Contemporary libertarians claim to find important support in the ideas of their great predecessors—John Milton and John Stuart Mill. Some attention must now be given to the question of how Milton and Mill are related to the contemporary doctrines.

Milton's *Areopagitica* was explicitly directed against a licensing system, a system of prior restraint. But his critique of censorship has broader application than this. He taught that the endeavor to get rid of vice by the control of printing is both harmful and impracticable. It is harmful because evil cannot be abolished, and the knowledge of it is therefore essential to the development of virtue. "Since . . . the knowledge and survey of vice is in this world so necessary to the constituting of human virtue, how can we more safely and with less danger scout into the regions of sin and falsity than by reading all manner of tractates and hearing all manner of reason."[82] Censorship is impracticable because it is impossible to secure virtue from all evil influences by the regulation of printing. "If we think to regulate printing, thereby to rectify manners, we must regulate all recreation and pastimes."[83] It is impossible to control the development of character and to guarantee virtue by censorship.

Those, however, who do not distinguish between appeals to reason and appeals to passion, between arguments about doctrine and incitements of prurience, will find no support in Milton. He argued against the constraint of learning and the fruits of learning. He taught that men should hear "all manner of reason." And those who are unconcerned or ambiguous about the need for a moral framework will find no support in Milton. He was neither unconcerned nor ambiguous about this. "That also which is impious or evil absolutely, either against faith or manners, no law can possibly permit, that tends not to unlaw itself."[84] Milton was not an "absolutist" about freedom of speech and press. It is almost inconceivable that Milton would have thought the censorship of obscenity a violation of his principles.

We do not know what John Stuart Mill would have thought of the legal control of salacious publications under contemporary conditions. He did not pronounce upon the censorship of obscenity. But any careful examination of his principles would lead to the conclusion that they condemn it. In *On Liberty* Mill said:

> The only purpose for which power can be rightly exercised over any member of a civilized community, against his will, is to prevent harm to others. His own good, either physical or moral, is not a sufficient warrant. He cannot rightfully be compelled to do or forbear because it will be better for him to do so, because it will make him happier, because, in the opinion of others, to do so would be wise, or even right. . . . Over himself, over his own mind and body, the individual is sovereign.[85]

Society may not coerce or restrain a man for his own good. It can only do so to prevent harm to others. What Mill meant by "harm" is some definite identifiable injury: either a physical injury, an injury to legal rights, or an injury to interests which, by common consent of society, are regarded as *rights*. Other conduct must be free from the restraints of law and the coercions of public opinion.

In this manner Mill endeavors to draw a line between the authority of society and the liberty of the individual, between what belongs to the public interest of the community and what belongs to the private life of the individual. All that is private which does not injuriously affect other persons or which does not so affect them without their consent. Within this sphere of liberty is the freedom to express any opinions; to develop any tastes and interests; to live our lives in our own way. Mill's first principle is the absolute right of each individual to live as he pleases, up to the point where his conduct violates the explicit rights of nonconsenting persons.

Mill regards this absolute liberty as essential for two reasons. (1) It is the indispensable precondition for any meaningful pursuit of truth and for the growth of any meaningful knowledge, and (2) it is the indispensable precondition for the development of human character. Genuine knowledge arises out of the conflict of opinions, and no one can be absolutely certain that the opinion he would suppress is not true or that the values he would condemn are not valid.[86] And it is only in choosing for ourselves how we will live that we achieve *individuality* of character, which is a major ingredient of human excellence and human well being. Hence, men must be allowed to choose. Mill writes: "As . . . there should be different opinions, so it is that there should be different experiments of living; that free scope should be given to varieties of character short of injury to others; and that the worth of different modes of life should be proved practically, when anyone thinks fit to try them. It is desirable, in short, that in things which do not primarily concern others, individuality should assert itself."[87]

Mill would prevent the community from imposing a conventional morality which would foreclose the "different experiments of living." He would do so in the name of those excellences of character which he called "individuality."

But it can be argued that, in the long pursuit of truth, we must surely have acquired some knowledge about what does and what does not conduce to the development of character. Surely we know that some "experiments" are worthless or harmful. If we do not know even this, then what is the value of the pursuit of truth? Are we to be always pursuing moral and political truth and never acquiring any? Mill would answer that we can never have such certainty of what is right as would justify the suppression of individuality. And it is never safe to invite men to impose their opinions on others, for the arrogance of dogmatism is great, and individuality is both precious and fragile.

But Mill himself is not without a conception of what does and does not constitute moral virtue. He is not asserting that just any kind of life is satisfactory as long as one likes it. What he envisioned is a society composed of persons vigorously and earnestly seeking values best suited to them and, in the process, developing those qualities of mind and personality which enhance human worth.[88] He envisoned men who might abandon a passive conformity in an active search for something better. He would not think highly of those who would deviate from social norms in order to live lives of passive indulgence in sensuality. He conceived of men breaking away from prevailing morality in order to develop and prove their own, possibly better, moral values. He would not consider it the proper fruit of his principles if people would abandon a prevailing ethic in order to have no ethic at all. Mill's individual is a person possessing active virtues: he searches; he experiments; he has, or seeks, a moral purpose; he is concerned about the good of others. This is the individuality which is supposed to be promoted by Mill's principles of free society.

But why is the removal of restraints more likely to promote this kind of individual than the kind of individual who lives for selfish momentary pleasures and rejects all moral purpose? Can it be said that the majority of those who evade the dictates of prevailing morality do so for the purposes and on the terms prescribed by Mill? Do most men who violate the norms of our society do so in order to experiment with a better way of life? Lord Devlin observes that Mill "did not really grapple with the fact that along the paths that depart from traditional morals, pimps leading the weak astray far outnumber spiritual explorers at the head of the strong."[89] Why did Mill fail to grapple with this fact?

Mill teaches that government and law must not be employed to impose or to maintain a common moral framework. And in *On Liberty* he often speaks as if such a framework were neither necessary nor desirable. But Mill presupposed a moral foundation—an ethical context—for all that occurs in society. This moral order need not be established by any deliberate acts. It is established by the inevitable movements of modern civilization. In *On Liberty* Mill presupposes a state of civilization in which "mankind have attained the capacity of being guided to their improvement by conviction or persuasion."[90] In *Utilitarianism* he describes the operation of the civilizing process. It operates constantly and progressively to bind men together and to expand the moral horizons of the individual.

> Not only does all strengthening of social ties, and all healthy growth of society give to each individual a stronger personal interest in practically consulting the welfare of others; it also leads him to identify his *feelings* more and more with their good. . . . This mode of conceiving ourselves and human life, as civilization goes on, is felt to be more and more natural. . . . In an improving state of the human mind, the influences are constantly on the increase which tend to generate in each individual a feeling of unity with all the rest.[91]

Thus, men are increasingly socialized by a movement which needs little attention from government. This process provides the ethical context within which we may be safely left to choose our own values, purposes, and pursuits. Men shaped by an ever improving civilization may be entrusted to conduct their moral experiments, to live as they please, with a minimum of external guidance. Civilization ensures that they will "please" to live civilized lives.

This assumption of an autonomous civilizing or socializing process lies at the base of much libertarian thinking on subjects such as that of obscenity. It provides a foundation for the pervasive confidence that freedom of expression cannot or will not have undesirable consequences.

The libertarian arguments on the subject of obscenity are many and various. To the extent that one can identify, amid this diversity, one homogeneous position, what can be said about it is that it is a complex combination of truths, partial truths, fallacies, and unexamined assumptions.

Libertarians rightly emphasize our constitutional and historical commitment to freedom of speech and press. Those Americans who have been most concerned with the First Amendment have always condemned unequivocally such censorship as would fall upon the pursuit of learning, the expression of ideas, or the expounding of doctrines. And it will always require intelligent effort to prevent censorship from invading these areas. Further, censorship is not our normal way of governing. Whatever its ends or subject matter, it must justify itself.

But the libertarians have not established that all censorship, whatever its ends or subject matter, is unequivocally evil. They have not established that freedom of expression, no matter what the character of the expression, must always be preferred to any ends which censorship may have in view. Nor have they established that freedom of expression is, in all situations and circumstances, identical with every aspect of the public interest. After the best of their arguments have been made and examined, there remains the possibility that some forms of speech and press may conflict with a legitimate public interest in morality.

On its theoretical side, the libertarian position is characterized by a considerable ambiguity concerning the nature of moral norms and their role in civil society. In libertarian writing, skepticism about moral standards is often combined with an almost unlimited confidence in "discussion" and "debate" about moral standards. And skepticism about ethical and political truth is often conjoined with an almost boundless faith in the search for such truth. Finally, fervent commitment to the free communication of ideas is accompanied by indiscriminate and imprecise use of the term "idea" and by vague or all-inclusive conceptions of what constitutes the communication of ideas.

These ambiguities can have consequences extending beyond the confines of the particular problem of obscenity regulation. The doctrines and conceptions with which they are associated are widely held, and they are influential. If our people should take seriously the discussion and debate of social problems, it is dangerous to teach them doctrines which exaggerate and at the same time undermine the role of discussion and debate. Further, a community which devotes itself to the communication of ideas ought not to become vague and confused about what it is devoting itself to. And it should not lose the capacity to distinguish a genuine search for truth about sexual morality from a morally indifferent sensuality.

There are several reasons why libertarian thinking may contribute to public confusion about these vital matters. With some exceptions, today's libertarian tends to be an ethical relativist with an absolute commitment to individual liberty. He tends to regard moral values as matters of subjective opinion or as temporary products of changing historical circumstances. But he is not at all skeptical about the moral claims of individual freedom. He does not regard these claims as a mere matter of opinion or a mere reflection of our particular and parochial culture. His relativism renders him highly dubious of any ethical standards which might serve to identify and define responsible public discussion and to differentiate a serious search for truth and an appeal to sensuality. And his absolute concern with "freedom" renders him unwilling to make these distinctions and delimitations. His purpose is best served by vague and all-embracing notions of free expression and communication of ideas.*

The relativistic tendency in contemporary libertarian thinking is frequently obscured by a somewhat contradictory tendency—an implicit, if unacknowledged, faith in the progress of civilization. Libertarian thinking often presupposes that the growth and spread of knowledge in society inevitably and progressively civilizes the members of society. This assumption permits the libertarian to believe that, whatever the moral interests of the community may be, these are spontaneously and adequately cared for by the ordinary processes of society. These interests do not require explicit attention or public policy addressed to their protection.

Thus, the libertarian's commitment to freedom, his relativism, and his faith in the development or results of civilization combine to foster an exclusive preoccupation with the values of personal freedom. A climate of opinion is created in which the concern for individual liberties supplants or assimilates all other moral concerns of the community. In such a climate, demands for freedom steadily escalate as minds lose the capacity and inclination to weigh competing considerations.

But the Idea of Progress is highly questionable in theory and in modern experience. If civilization does not inevitably perform the moral tasks which John Stuart Mill expected of it, then doctrines which assume that it does so will distort our analysis and interpretations of social problems.

And freedom itself may be endangered. Liberty itself may become meaningless when there are no ethical principles by which it can be interpreted and defined. Our freedom could come to

* Meiklejohn's earlier writing on freedom of speech is a notable and illuminating exception to these observations.

mean nothing more than the maximum opportunity for each individual to gratify whatever desires he may happen to have—no matter what they are or from what source they are derived. This would amount to the liberty of some persons to inflame or manipulate the passions of others and the liberty of these others to satisfy such artificial passions, limited only by the most minimal requirements of physical security and public order. It may be at least questioned whether this is our traditional American idea of a good society or a free society.

4

Effects of Obscenity:
The Arguments and the Evidence

The libertarian effort to define once and for all the limits of legal restraint upon free expression poses problems and raises questions which are unresolved in the libertarian doctrines. Yet, if the term "free society" is to have any meaning, there must be such limits and there must be principles by reference to which these limits may be determined. Most citizens would agree upon at least one of these principles: in a free society legal restraints must be justified by a showing of harmful consequences flowing from the activity to be restrained. Freedom of expression may not be limited on the basis of a mere feeling that the expression is undesirable, offensive, or even dangerous. There must be, at least, arguments and evidence leading to a conclusion that a particular form of expression has harmful effects upon substantial interests of other persons or of the community.

Does the circulation of obscenity have any such effects? This question is the subject of as much sustained controversy as any question in the field of obscenity control.

Lockhart and McClure assert that "the whole structure of obscenity censorship hinges upon the unproved assumption that 'obscene' literature is a significant factor in causing sexual deviation from the community standard."[1] According to these authors, this assumption is not only unproved, it is extremely tenuous and doubtful. What, then, are the injuries caused by obscene litera-

This chapter was published, in slightly altered form, in *Midway,* vol. 8, no. 4 (Spring 1968) © 1968 by the University of Chicago. Reprinted with permission.

ture? Why should the mere stimulation of thoughts and feelings about sex be considered in itself an evil? The authors ask the rhetorical question, "What are the possible harms?"[2]

Author and scholar Father Terrence J. Murphy asserts: "Obscenity, by its exaggerated and morbid emphasis on sex, its disproportionate details, its unrealistic presentation of social conduct and attitudes, the prominence it gives to the abnormal and perverted, runs contrary to the principles of mental health. Continued exposure to it is bound to produce adverse results in terms of mental health and social conduct."[3]

According to the proponents of censorship some of the "adverse results" of obscenity are juvenile delinquency, sex crime or others, and perversion. Many police and other officials associated with the prevention of crime see a direct link between the increasing circulation of obscenity and the alarming increase in delinquency, crimes of violence, and sexual deviation in our society. Says J. Edgar Hoover: "We know that an overwhelmingly large number of sex crimes are associated with pornography. We know that sex criminals read it, are clearly influenced by it."[4]

Opponents of censorship insist that these conclusions have no basis in scientific research and scientific knowledge concerning the causes of antisocial behavior. In the literature of opposition to censorship one of the works most frequently cited is that of Sheldon and Eleanor Glueck, *Unraveling Juvenile Delinquency*.[5] These authors, noted authorities on the subject of delinquency, carefully examined some ninety factors and influences that might lead to or explain it. They gave no consideration to obscenity or to reading material per se. The fact that researchers such as the Gluecks did not consider this factor worth investigating is offered as grounds for serious doubt about its significance. With regard to the antisocial conduct of adults, Judge Frank observes:

> To date there exist, I think, no thoroughgoing studies by competent persons which justify the conclusion that normal adults' reading or seeing of the "obscene" probably induces anti-social conduct. Such competent studies as have been made do conclude that so complex and numerous are the causes of sexual vice that it is impossible to assert with any assurance that "obscenity" represents a ponderable causal factor in sexually deviant adult behavior. . . . What little competent research has been done points definitely in a direction precisely opposite to that assumption.[6]

This controversy poses a number of problems for one who would weigh the evidence. Those who see and those who do not see harm in the circulation of obscenity tend to argue in different terms, to rely upon different kinds of evidence, and to resort to different kinds of experts. They disagree, not only about the effects of obscenity, but also about what kind of data are or could be relevant to judgment about it. Judge Frank demands "competent research" by "competent persons." But what is "competent research" on the subject of obscenity, and who are the persons competent to speak with authority on it? Judge Frank would not seriously consider the evidence gathered by J. Edgar Hoover; he would rely upon the findings (or non-findings) of social scientists such as Sheldon and Eleanor Glueck. And he would not give much weight to statements based merely upon experience—he would insist upon social science research explicitly addressed to the problem and, preferably, conducted under experimental conditions.

There is little systematic research on the subject of the sort Judge Frank requires. But there are many who have pronounced upon it with some claim to expertise. Among them are police officials, judges of juvenile courts, court psychiatrists, psychoanalysts, psychiatrists, those concerned with the correction of juvenile delinquents, those concerned with the scientific study of juvenile delinquency, sociologists, anthropologists, and researchers involved in the study of sexual behavior and attitudes.

What weight should be given by the citizen, the legislator, and the judge to the opinions or findings of these various kinds of specialists? And it may be asked whether these are the only significant kinds of expertise. For instance, one may reasonably ask why D. H. Lawrence should not be considered an expert on the effects of literature dealing with sex.[7] Finally, one must consider what is the proper role of historic or common experience in the formation of judgments upon social problems such as that posed by obscenity.

The controversy over the effects of obscene literature raises profound questions about the nature of social inquiry or social knowledge and about the proper roles of theoretical and practical knowledge. This chapter can only touch upon these issues; it can comment upon but it cannot undertake a solution to the problem of appropriate knowledge. The effort is made to present a representative sample, not an exhaustive coverage, of diverse views from various disciplines, to weigh these views, and to arrive at such reasonable judgments as can be made within the confines of this chapter and its author's understanding.

In addition to the validity of evidence, another problem confronting the student concerns the questions and the distinctions with which the evidence is to be approached. If obscenity is said to have some harmful effects, what kind of effects does it have and upon whom? Distinctions can be made between effects upon conduct, effects upon emotions, effects upon attitudes or opinions, effects upon moral character. One can consider such effects upon children or adults, upon the normal or the abnormal. While most of the evidence and opinions in this area involve effects upon children, and there is little scientific material concerning adults, the effort is made in this study to present materials and elicit opinions about both. For the purposes of this chapter, the most important distinction to be made is that between effects upon conduct and effects upon mind and character. While this distinction cannot be made absolutely (the two subjects will necessarily overlap), it governs the organization and analysis of the material which follows. The first part of the discussion will be addressed primarily to the arguments and evidence for and against the proposition that obscene literature promotes antisocial behavior. The second part will be devoted primarily to the influence of obscenity upon mind and character.

As has been observed, much of the support for obscenity control derives from those who deal professionally, in one capacity or another, with juvenile or adult crime. In 1954 the National Council of Juvenile Court Judges adopted a resolution on obscenity including this assertion: "The character of juvenile delinquency has changed as a consequence of the stimulation of these publications, being no longer the thoughtless, mischievous actions of children, but is reflected in acts of violence, armed robbery, rape, torture and even homicide to which the vicious and vile publications conditioned the minds of our children."[8]

Police and juvenile correction officials repeatedly point to case after case in which offenders have been found in possesion of obscene materials. The following statements are typical examples of this kind of evidence.

Inspector Ray Blick of the Metropolitan Police Department, District of Columbia, testified before the House Committee on Post Office and Civil Service:

> *Mr. Johnson:* Inspector Blick . . . in your mind [is] there . . . a connection between this growth in pornography and obscenity . . . and the increase in sex crimes?
>
> *Mr. Blick:* That is a hard question to answer for a number of reasons. We do not know what is in the mind of the individual who buys this material, so the only way we could answer that would be that around 75% of the perverts, those that are taken into custody, where we are fortunate enough to get in their apartments, . . . in those cases it is nothing for us to seize from one to twenty books of pornographic material.[9]

Inspector Harry Fox, Commanding Officer of the Juvenile Aid Division of the Philadelphia Police Department, told the Granahan Committee:

> I believe reading the material is going to stimulate them [youngsters] for the various sex acts for which we apprehend them. When we apprehend juveniles we search them. I wish I could lay before you all the obscene pictures that have been ripped out of magazines and valued as cherished possessions by these boys.[10]

Inspector Fox cited a number of cases in which adults had used pornographic materials to entice juveniles into sex acts. He asserted: "My men and I have questioned hundreds of these adults and the juveniles involved, and we believe . . . that this material acts as an aphrodisiac resulting in rapes, seductions, sodomy, indecent assaults and indecent exposure."

Captain Edward Blake of the Narcotics and Vice Unit of the Boston Police Department told the committee that pornography is frequently linked to crime and vice of every sort. "It has been my experience that once we get involved in a case of pornography, whether on the juvenile or adult level, if we dig long enough and hard enough we will come up with the most sordid situation."[11] The captain reported incidents of rape, the perversion of children by adults, the murder or suicide of children, homosexuality, and wife-swapping—all committed by people found to possess or use pornography.

Though these police officials repeatedly find that both juvenile and adult offenders are possessors and habitual readers of pornography, their testimony does not often establish a clear causal connection between the pornography and the criminal acts. Occasionally they are able to show a rather direct connection, as in this testimony of Captain Blake: "One child was found crucified. At the foot of the cross was a mound of pornography."[12] It can be argued, however, that most of the evidence supplied by the police is based upon an assumption unfounded in any study or any knowledge of the actual effects of the pornography on those they apprehend. Further, the police witnesses seldom present statistics, and when they do their statistics are, like those of Inspector Blick above, rather difficult to interpret.

The Granahan Committee also heard the testimony of some who are in a better position to observe and study delinquent and criminal offenders. Dr. Preston Sharp was Executive Director of the Youth Study Center in Philadelphia. The Youth Study Center conducted extensive interviews with delinquent boys and made several surveys of their reading habits. Dr. Sharp asserted: "There is no question that pictures and stories emphasizing sex exert a strong influence on many adults and youth. The degree of negative impact depends on the type of background of the person."[13] He believes that this negative impact is a result of the "imaginary sex activities" stimulated by the literature which may precipitate criminal acts. In some types of persons, obscene literature will stimulate an indulgence in fantasy which can lead to overt acts.

Dr. Nicholas Frignito, Medical Director and Chief Neuropsychiatrist of the County Court of Philadelphia, also testified in this vein. According to Dr. Frignito, the County Court subjects all delinquent children who come to it to sociological, psychological, and psychiatric studies. He observed that Court studies show that approximately 50 percent of all youths apprehended have indulged in pornography. He found a direct connection between the pornography and the youths' offenses: "Some of these children did not trangress sexually until they read suggestive stories and viewed lewd pictures in these . . . magazines."[14] Dr. Frignito also found the increasing rate of sex offenses among young adults of high school and college education to be connected with pornography. He told the committee that "this group represents the most avid users (or victims) of pornography."[15]

Dr. Frignito believes, as does Dr. Sharp, that the harmful

effect of obscenity result from its stimulation of imagination and desire which eventually must find some outlet. He asserts:

> Anti-social, delinquent and criminal activity frequently results from stimulation by pornography. This abnormal sexual stimulation creates such a demand for expression that gratification by vicarious means follows. . . . Boys and young men who have difficulty controlling the undue sexual simulation become sexually aggressive and generally incorrigible.[16]

In 1955 Dr. George W. Henry, Professor of Clinical Psychology at the Cornell University College of Medicine, appeared before the Kefauver Committee. He examined a magazine devoted to sado-masochistic materials and was questioned thereon:

> *Mr. Gaughan:* Doctor, I ask you, could children be sexually perverted by looking at, by studying and by dwelling upon photos of this nature and the contents of this book?
>
> *Dr. Henry:* Yes.
>
> *Chairman Kefauver:* Doctor, is it a very unwholesome influence, this sort of thing?
>
> *Dr. Henry:* It is.
>
> *Chairman Kefauver:* In your opinion the increase in sex crimes, deviations that we are having—does that result in part at least from the reading and looking at magazines and pictures of this kind by children?
>
> *Dr. Henry:* I would think that was an important factor in the increase.[17]

Those who deny or seriously doubt the harmful effects of obscenity would not be convinced by the testimony of Drs. Sharp, Frignito, and Henry. They would point to the absence of scientifically supported evidence in any of this testimony. Dr. Frignito reports that he finds pornography in the possession of juvenile and adult offenders. But he does not indicate that he has made any real study of the actual effect of this pornography upon their conduct as distinguished from the effects of other factors. He does not *demonstrate* that exposure to the pornography was a significant cause of the conduct but simply states his opinion that this is so. We have, at most, a clinical or experiential judgment and, perhaps, one that is colored by the criminal setting in which Dr. Frignito works. And even if Drs. Frignito and Sharp do succeed in showing that obscene materials have had some effect upon the type of persons with whom they usually deal, they offer no evidence to support a conclusion that average or normal persons would be so affected. Finally, it is open to serious question whether the opinions of Dr. Frignito, Sharp, and Henry represent the consensus in their professions.

If the evidence presented by law enforcement personnel, court psychiatrists, and some clinical psychiatrists can be said to lack scientific status, there exists at least one methodical and long-term study of the effects of some obscene materials upon children —Dr. Fredric Wertham's *Seduction of the Innocent*.[18] Dr. Wertham was senior psychiatrist for the Department of Hospitals in New York City; he directed the mental hygiene clinic at Bellevue Hospital and Queens Hospital Center and was in charge of the Court of General Sessions Psychiatric Clinic. Prior to writing *Seduction of the Innocent* he systematically studied comic books and their effects for over ten years, employing such methods as the in-depth interview, continuous consultations lasting for months (in some cases for years), statistical studies, the Rorschach Test, the Thematic Apperception Test, play therapy and group therapy sessions.

Wertham devotes his attention to "crime-comics"—those which emphasize and exploit violence and sex. According to him, the distinguishing feature of this type of comic book is its pornographic interweaving of violence and sex, cruelty and sensuality. He concludes that these materials definitely can be and often are a significant contributing factor in the causation of sexual maladjustment, delinquency, and acts of violence on the part of children and adolescents. He offers numerous examples of specific acts which can be directly connected with comic-book materials.* Of the moral world of the comic book and its consequences, Wertham states:

> The world of the comic book is the world of the strong, the ruthless, the bluffers, the shrewd deceiver, the torturer, and the

---

* The following are two of these examples:

"Three boys, six to eight years old, took a boy of seven, hanged him nude from a tree, his hands tied behind him, then burned him with matches. Probation officers investigating found that they were re-enacting a comic book plot" (p. 150).

"Take the fourteen-year-old Chicago boy who strangled an eight-year-old girl. He left fifty comic books in the room with his dead victim. They depicted all kinds of ways of abusing girls and killing people, including strangling" (pp. 245–46).

thief. All the emphasis is on exploits where somebody takes advantage of somebody else, violently, sexually or threateningly. It is no more the world of braves and squaws, but of punks and molls. Force and violence in any conceivable form are romanticized. Constructive and creative forces in children are channelled by comic books into destructive avenues.[19]

This destructive channeling can occur via one of two psychological mechanisms: a mechanism of imitation, and a stimulation-frustration-release mechanism. Children naturally seek someone to emulate and follow; they seek models. Those under the influence of comic books will often consciously imitate the violent or exploitive acts of comic book figures. This is often accompanied by a deeper psychological identification—children will endeavor not only to act out the exploits of their heroes but to be like them in thought and feeling.

On the other hand, constant exposure to comic-book materials could promote a buildup of emotional tension which may or may not find release in action. The result may be psychological harm or harmful behavior. Says Wertham: "The scenes of sadism, sex and crime in comic books arouse the child's emotions, but leave him only a limited scope of release in action. These actions can only be masturbatory or delinquent."[20]

Wertham does not contend that comic books must inevitably have those effects on all children exposed to them; nor does he contend that comic books are the only cause of the delinquency of those influenced by them. He recognizes that the effects of exposure to them will be conditioned by the child's environment and psychological dispositions. But he does insist that comic books are an important and harmful influence on many children; that in a very large number of cases this influence operates to promote or reinforce predispositions to destructiveness and that in some cases it can be shown to be a major and independent factor precipitating violent or other delinquent acts. Wertham summarizes his conclusions in this manner:

1. The crime comic-book format is an invitation to illiteracy.
2. Crime comic books create an atmosphere of cruelty and deceit.
3. They create a readiness for temptation.
4. They stimulate unwholesome fantasies.
5. They suggest criminal or sexually abnormal ideas.

6. They furnish the rationalization for them, which may be ethically even more harmful than the impulse.

7. They suggest the forms a delinquent impulse may take and supply details of technique.

8. They may tip the scale toward the maladjustment or delinquency.[21]

Thus crime comics are the source of many harms: psychological, intellectual, and moral. In a given case these harms may well add up to delinquent conduct. But prior to this conduct, or even in the absence of it, there has been damage done to mind and character. It is with this damage that Wertham is primarily concerned. We will return to this consideration later in the chapter.

The significance of Wertham's study for the problem of obscenity control is difficult to assess. Wertham confined his research to the impact of a very special type of obscene material upon children. He did not purport to pronounce upon all forms of obscenity, and he did not explicitly address himself to possible impacts upon adults. Yet his work does have relevance to the larger issues. If one accepts Wertham's findings, then one has accepted at least the proposition, denied by many, that the reading of some kinds of literature can be an important and independent cause of injury to some minds and of injurious conduct on the part of some human beings. Wertham's findings, however, are not universally accepted by those who address themselves to the subject of children's literature and its influence.[22] And, with regard to the direct connection between crime comics and delinquent behavior, it is open to question whether or not Wertham has overstated his case.

Other social scientists who have studied the subject support the view that evil social consequences flow from obscene literature. Among them one may cite Harvard sociologist Pitirim Sorokin, anthropologist Margaret Mead, and Ernest van den Haag, a psychoanalyst and professor of social philosophy. Sorokin's study, *The American Sexual Revolution,* employs a method of cross-cultural analysis.[23] He claims that the incidence of immoral or antisocial behavior is demonstrably greater in cultures or societies where the erotic sub-arts flourish than in those where these forms are kept under strict control. And he claims to be able to show conclusively that when a society moves from restraint toward permissiveness in this area a steady increase in such conduct tends to follow.

Mead and van den Haag do not carry this argument as far as does Sorokin. They are content to suggest that exposure to obscene materials affects some minds in ways which will ultimately result in socially undesirable patterns of conduct.[24]

Sorokin's method as well as his findings are open to dispute. Many social scientists would regard his cross-cultural approach as suspect, and the layman may wonder whether it is capable of yielding the kind of sweeping conclusions which Sorokin seeks to draw from it. His evidence may point toward these conclusions, but one may seriously doubt that they have been proved. Sorokin, Mead, and van den Haag do not conduct thoroughgoing studies of the effects of obscenity upon individual behavior. The dominant theme of their writings, and the main burden of their arguments, concerns the long-range effects of obscenity upon mind and culture. Their views, like all of those cited above, are controversial.

The case against the view that obscenity is dangerous may be briefly summarized as follows.

1. There is not one conclusive study supporting the assumption that the reading of obscene materials induces harmful behavior. This assumption remains at best wholly conjectural.

2. Such detailed research as we have points to the opposite conclusion, indicating that: (*a*) delinquents read very little; (*b*) the many and various influences in society that stimulate sexual desire are so much more prominent and potent than reading that reading is unlikely to have a degree of impact upon conduct worthy of attention; (*c*) the causes of misconduct are deeply rooted in the social environment and in psychological maladjustments in relation to which reading is at most a superficial influence.

3. Exposure to obscene materials is not only relatively harmless, it may well have positive therapeutic value—facilitating a release of tensions which might otherwise explode in action.

4. There is no way to determine what will be the effect of a given piece of literature upon a particular person or upon the average man. Responses to literature are highly variable and subjective.

Lockhart and McClure write:

> Although the whole structure of obscenity censorship hinges
> upon the unproved assumption that "obscene" literature is a sig-
> nificant factor in causing sexual deviation from the community
> standard, no report can be found of a single effort at genuine
> research to test this assumption by singling out as a factor for
> study the effect of sex literature upon sex conduct. Surely, meth-
> ods of social investigation have now progressed to the point
> where this can and should be done.[25]

Social scientists who have undertaken comprehensive surveys
of the literature in this field tend to agree with the first part of
Lockhart and McClure's assertion—there is no evidence and no
genuine research of the sort they specify. Marie Jahoda concludes
that, with regard to the alleged connection between antisocial
conduct and reading about sex and brutality, "there exists no
research evidence either to prove or to disprove this assumption
definitively."[26] A committee of Brown University psychologists
(Nissim Levy, Lewis Lipsitt, and Judith Rosenblith) supports
Jahoda's conclusions and goes on to assert that the arguments and
evidence put forth in support of censorship are wholly spurious.[27]
According to these psychologists, the proponents of censorship
simply assume, without evidence, that an allegedly high correlation between sex crime and the reading of lewd materials amounts
to a causal connection.

In place of such assumption and conjecture, Lockhart and
McClure call for rigorous experimental studies of the effects of
sex literature upon sex conduct. How could these studies be conducted in such a way as to yield scientifically conclusive evidence?

A large group of persons might be systematically exposed to
obscenity over a long period of time, while a similarly large control group is systematically isolated from all forms of obscenity.
Their respective patterns of conduct would then be observed and
analyzed. Even if such experiments could be conducted in our
society, the methodological problems would seem to be insu-
perable. How could one account for and control the differential
effects of environment and personal experiences before and during the experiment? Under the most exact experimental conditions would one not still be confronted with the same difficulties
we now have in determining just what portion of conduct is to

be accounted for by what social, psychological, and intellectual influences? The problem might even be aggravated by the introduction of a new causal factor most difficult to take adequate account of—the influence of the experiment itself upon the responses of participants.

If this plan of research would be thought farfetched, what other kinds of scientific study would meet the exacting requirements which libertarians so often bring to this subject? In *The Freedom to Read,* McKeon, Merton, and Gellhorn suggest that considerable progress has been made in the development of research techniques applicable to testing the effects of reading. The studies they cite, however, are all concerned primarily, if not exclusively, with psychological effects (e.g., with emotional response, attitudes, perception). The authors grant "the practical difficulties of developing suitable methods for assessing the psychological effects of the typically prolonged and intermittent experience of reading a book."[28] Surely one of the most important of these practical difficulties would be that of distinguishing adequately between immediate or ephemeral and long-term or profound effects. It is highly questionable whether the interview (a method frequently used in the study of responses to the mass media) could be used successfully to make this distinction. Even if extensive interviews could be supplemented by psychological tests it seems that the problem remains unsolved. What tests could establish conclusively that a given emotional or intellectual effect is (1) profound, (2) permanent, or (3) attributable to a book (or books) and nothing else?

These difficulties must be magnified manyfold in any effort to establish by these methods the effects of literary materials upon *conduct.* As is frequently pointed out by those opposed to censorship, the influences upon conduct are many, various, and intricate. As they are interwoven throughout a life history, the picture becomes complex indeed. What Lockhart and McClure are asking is that one specific element, reading of sex literature, be carefully separated out of this complex mosaic and that its effects upon another specific element, sex behavior, be carefully measured. Perhaps Lockhart and McClure would be willing to settle for statistical analysis of the results of well-conducted interviews. This method must rely heavily on the opinions of respondents concerning the impact of literature upon them. When the weaknesses of this approach are pointed out, those requiring the use of scientific method in this area have a final answer. Say the authors of *The Freedom to Read:* "Although the results obtained through such interviews are not rigorous, they are considerably more definite and substantial than the conjectures concerning the effects of books which now serve in place of any systematic evidence."[29]

The point of view we are exploring does not rest its case upon the mere absence of evidence concerning the harmful effects of obscenity. It goes on to argue that reliable research undermines the assumptions upon which censorship rests.

The Glueck study concludes that juvenile delinquents engage very little in reading and other non-active entertainments. Other studies concerned with influences upon sexual life indicate that the influence of reading is negligible. Alpert points to the results of a questionnaire circulated among college women graduates by the New York City Bureau of Social Hygiene. Of 409 responses to a question inquiring what they found most sexually stimulating, 9 said "music," 18 said "pictures," 29 said "dancing," 40 said "drama," 95 said "books," and 218 said "Man."[30] Psychologists Eberhard and Phyllis Kronhausen have made a list (based on the Kinsey study, *Sexual Behavior in the Human Male*) of forty-four sources of erotic stimulation in pre-adolescent boys. Among them are sitting in class, taking a shower, punishment, seeing females, thinking about females, physical contact with females, females in moving pictures, love stories in books.[31] Only four of the forty-four sources of stimulation could be in any way related to sex literature. The Kinsey Report found that only a slight majority of the men and women sampled reported any "erotic responses" from exposure to literature of a "romantic" or "sexual" variety:

Reading Literary Materials

Erotic Response	By Females	By Males
Definite and/or frequent	16%	21%
Some response	44%	38%
Never	40%	41%
Number of cases	5,699	3,952[32]

Commenting upon this study, Lockhart and McClure point to the fact that only 16 percent of the females and 21 percent of the males report any significant degree of stimulation from literature of all sorts, romantic as well as obscene.[33]

The question arises, What is the relevance and the validity of these and similar studies which appear so frequently in the literature of opposition to censorship? Does this research prove as much as it is thought to prove? It is not irrelevant to these questions that the Bureau of Social Hygiene and Kinsey reports rely on the methods of questionnaire and interview. The findings derived from this approach, when it is employed in this area, must depend substantially upon what people are willing to say about the factors which influence them in private matters and, perhaps more significantly, upon their awareness of those factors. But, whatever the limitations of the method, it may be pointed out that in the Bureau of Social Hygiene questionnaire 153 out of 409 respondents *did* assert that literature of some kind—pictures, drama, books—was most stimulating to them sexually. It is not surprising that the majority found men more stimulating than books. And the Kinsey Report *does* find that more than half of its respondents report sexual stimulation from literature. I make these observations only in order to suggest that these findings are problematic and are open to more than one interpretation. Further, the relevance of these studies to the effects of obscenity upon conduct is at least as questionable as is the relevance of police testimony.*

* Perhaps the most thorough and systematic study of the research literature on this subject is that conducted by Cairns, Paul, and Wishner. See Robert B. Cairns, James C. N. Paul, and Julius Wishner, "Sex Censorship: The Assumptions of Anti-Obscenity Laws and the Empirical Evidence," *Minnesota Law Review* 46 (May, 1962): 1009–41. These authors (two professors of psychology and a professor of law) carefully examined a large variety of research and experimental studies related to the effects of psychosexual stimuli conveyed by literature, pictures, and films. With regard to the question of sexual stimulation or "arousal" by such means, they summarize their conclusions thus:

"Despite the inadequacies of some of the investigations, we believe the results are consistent enough to suggest the following—which are offered, not as empirical laws, but as propositions which, thus far, appear to emerge from the evidence:

"(1) A significant portion of our society is sexually aroused to some extent by some form of sex stimuli in pictures and probably in books.

"(2) Portrayals of female nudity and of sexual activity lead to sexual arousal in many males—adolescents as well as adults. These materials arouse females far less frequently.

"(3) Females, on the other hand, are more frequently sexually aroused by complex stimuli which portray 'romantic' or 'love' relationships and which constitute, in general, less direct sexual cues.

The fact that students of juvenile delinquency such as the Gluecks find that delinquents seldom read must be weighed against the fact that law enforcement officials and court psychiatrists so frequently find them in possession of pornography. The layman is hard put to make a final judgment about this, but he can observe that one does not have to be much of a reader to be addicted to crime comics or pornographic magazines which contain many pictures and little text. As for the multifarious sex stimuli reported by the Kronhausens, the layman is in a position to ask how this bears upon the problem. It is well known since (or even before) Freud that pre-adolescents are stimulated in many ways. The Kronhausens make no effort to assess the relative importance of the various stimuli, including the literary ones, in the lives of the children.

Nonetheless, even after the many limitations of this kind of evidence have been observed, there remains to be confronted the underlying argument which it is designed to illustrate. Among all the various sexual stimulations which a human being undergoes, what can be the relative weight of obscene literature as a factor affecting conduct? Particularly in our society, a steady stream of such influences impinges upon the individual from all quarters. It is argued that the impact of sex literature must be quite trivial compared to all these.

This leads us to the most important argument against the thesis that obscenity is a cause of antisocial conduct. The Kronhausens state: "The body of clinical and psychological experience to date strongly points to much deeper causative factors in violent crime than reading."[34] The Kronhausens list several "deeper causative

---

"(4) Males differ among each other in terms of preference for and response to various types of sex stimuli. . . .

"(5) The environmental circumstances under which the sex stimuli are viewed may influence the extent to which the viewers will show evidence of sexual arousal. . . .

"(6) Exposure to certain types of sex stimuli is, for some persons, both males and females, a distinctively aversive experience" (p. 1032).

With regard to the significance of these findings for the larger question with which the obscenity controversy is concerned, the authors had this to say: "Granting that many obscene materials do arouse under many circumstances, we need to know more. We need to know how long the conditions of arousal last and how this stimulation might affect overt behavior, attitudes governing behavior and mental health" (p. 1034).

factors" in the promotion of delinquency: personal tension, defective discipline, insecurity, lack of home guidance, and emotional instability. "One notes immediately that all of these factors refer to deep seated emotional problems and disturbances in interpersonal relations, in comparison to which the reading of comics or even 'hard-core obscenity' appears a rather trifling surface concern."[35]

The causes of personal maladjustment, delinquency, and sex crime are deeply rooted in social and psychological disorders. Most social scientists who concern themselves with juvenile delinquency and adult crime do not regard literature as a highly relevant factor. They are concerned with social and economic deprivations, with unwholesome family relations, and with the psychological maladjustments arising from these. Psychologists and psychiatrists who study the sexual offender do not treat addiction to pornography as a cause of his offenses. In his comprehensive study, *The Sexual Offender and His Offenses,* Dr. Benjamin Karpman says that addition to pornography "is symbolic of undeveloped sexuality. . . . Pornography is a symptom not a disease."[36] In their study of sexual deviations London and Caprio assert that "people who are morbidly interested in or collect pornographic art and literature have a libido that is fixated at the paraphiliac level (auto-eroticism)."[37] Thus, the most highly professional research into sex crime and sexual deviation seems to support Walter Gellhorn's contention that an interest in pornography is the reflection of a man's personality, not the molder of it.[38]

Writers on this subject often cite Marie Jahoda's study of the research literature in this area. This is a summary of her rather cautious conclusions: Experts agree that there is no single cause for juvenile delinquency. Most of them regard early childhood experiences and later personal relations as far more determinative than vicarious experiences such as those provided by reading. Where such primary experiences combine to predispose a child to delinquency, reading experience could possibly function in one of two ways: it could serve as a "trigger-function" releasing an antisocial act, or it could stimulate fantasies which provide a substitute outlet for aggressions. There is no empirical evidence pointing to a predominance of one kind of effect over the other. In children who are insecure or maladjusted, excessive exposure to literature such as comic books may intensify those unhealthy dispositions which drove them to this literature. But "it should be noted that insofar as causal sequence is implied, insecurity and maladjustment in a child must precede this exposure to the written word in order to lead to these potential effects. Unfortunately, perhaps, the reading of Shakespeare's tragedies or of Andersen's and Grimm's fairy tales might do much the same."[39]

This view probably represents majority opinion in the social sciences. But Fredric Wertham strongly rejects it. Wertham agrees that exposure to crime comics can "trigger" the delinquent acts of the already maladjusted, but he denies that only the already maladjusted are subject to the damaging effects of this literature. Harmful addiction to comic books "occurs in children in all walks of life who are in no way psychologically predisposed. Of course, in children in bad circumstances it is apt to occur more frequently."[40] Wertham found large numbers of delinquent or aggressive comic-book readers who, according to his psychological tests and inquiries, were basically normal children not suffering from any deep-rooted maladjustments. In fact, he holds that it is *not* the most deeply disturbed children who read comic books and come under the influence of them.

Wertham takes to task authors who tend to divide children into two rigid categories: those who are "healthy" (and hence totally immune to the effects of bad literature), and those who are emotionally disturbed or insecure (and hence already predisposed to the evils for which bad literature is blamed). He insists that children do not fit neatly into the categories of "healthy" and "disturbed," "secure" and "insecure." Rather, the emotional life of most children comprises a delicate balance of various impulses, tendencies, and attitudes which can be affected in one direction or another by a variety of different causes. Bad literature can be one of these causes.

There appears to be a certain amount of common sense on Wertham's side of the issue. If it be the case that emotionally strong children will not be affected by vicious literature, while the emotionally disturbed are already predisposed to maladjustment, is it not also the case that most children (perhaps most adults as well) fall somewhere between these extremes? Can it be shown that most children (or adults) are "healthy," "stable," "strong," and "secure" as these terms are usually used in discourse about this subject? And it is well known that, whatever their family environment, children are highly susceptible to the influence of their extra-family environment—particularly that constituted by the interests and activities of their peers and older children. Perhaps even a secure child from a secure family would be susceptible to the influence of a comic-book saturated child society outside the home.

With regard to the "deeper causative factors" argument, Wertham asserts:

> You cannot at the outset reject one factor simply because on the surface it seems trivial. Sometimes the causes are near at hand and are overlooked for just that reason. . . . What people really mean when they use the let's-not-blame-any-one-factor argument is that they do not like this particular factor. It is new to them and for years they have been overlooking it. . . . They do not object to specific factors if they are intrinsic and noncommital and can be dated far enough back in a child's life. . . . But science does not mean a closed system of respectable causes, it means a mind open to all potentialities.[41]

The viewpoint represented by Wertham must be weighed as well as that represented by McKeon, Merton, and Gellhorn in their assertion that "the problem of delinquency [should] be seen, not as resulting from the one factor upon which attention happens to center, but as deriving from a wider complex of formative experiences and relations, little influenced, if at all, by the reading of books."[42]

Those who are skeptical about the effects of obscenity are quite right in warning us against a simplistic "one-factor interpretation" of complex social problems. Such warnings are always appropriate, since public debate on social issues is often vitiated by this fallacy. But some of the arguments employed against censorship are inclined toward an opposite fallacy, which might be called the "no-factor interpretation" of social problems. It is asserted that, since the causes of delinquency or crime are many and complex, it is impossible to blame one particular factor—such as the prevalence of obscenity. But this proposition would apply to any specific variable which could be advanced as a contributing cause. If, literally, we cannot blame any specific factor for contributing to an evil, then we cannot blame any collection of them for causing the evil. The problem is not resolved by attributing antisocial conduct to such vague and general influences as "deep-rooted psychological tensions," "the disintegration of social relations," or "a wider complex of formative experiences." These formulations are not really explanations of a phenomenon, they are abstractions and generalities. To transform them into explanations one must investigate more specific considerations.

Sometimes it is even asserted that salacious books, magazines, and films cannot be a cause of delinquency or crime because these evils are "rooted in the total structure of our society." This is true, but it is not very illuminating. We would be even less wise than we are now if we could learn nothing about particular social evils without tracing them back through ever widening causal sequences to "the total structure of our society." Indeed, the basic character of a community is responsible for the problems of juvenile and adult misbehavior which arise within it, but it is evident that these things can be partially understood through analysis of contributing and proximate causes.

There remain to be considered two further arguments employed in the literature of opposition to censorship. It is often contended that indulgence in obscenity can have positive therapeutic value as a safety valve through which harmful tendencies may be harmlessly discharged. Dr. Karpman writes: "Contrary to popular misconception, people who read salacious literature are less likely to become sexual offenders than those who do not, for the reason that such reading often neutralizes what aberrant sexual interests they may have."[43] According to the Kronhausens, the experience of obscenity through literature operates as a safety valve because it allows for "expressing anti-social impulses (sexual or otherwise) through the operation of fantasy instead of by direct action."[44] Impulses which are denied outlet (because of repression, psychological or social) achieve satisfaction through imaginations and fantasies, facilitated by pornography, of perverted or destructive behavior. Overt satisfaction then becomes unnecessary.

The Kronhausens report two case histories of psychiatric patients who were thoroughgoing addicts of sadistic pornography of the most extreme sort. Neither of these patients ever committed an overt sadistic act. When one of them, in an effort to reform, destroyed his collection of pornography, he became "so restless and disturbed that the therapist really feared serious consequences." When, with the therapist's consent, he began a new collection, "immediately he became quieter and able to function more effectively."[45] The Kronhausens offer this as an example of the successful operation of the safety-valve mechanism. They associate this mechanism with the well-known Aristotelian concept of "catharsis."

The safety-valve theory seems quite contrary to the ordinary, man-in-the-street understanding of human motivation and conduct, according to which one does not weaken or gain control of harmful impulses by stimulating them. Bad dispositions are thought to be overcome by activity *contrary* to them. Neither can the theory advanced by the Kronhausens legitimately claim the support of Aristotle and the classic doctrine of catharsis. Aristotelian catharsis is a purging of pity and fear, not of perverted sexual desires.[46] And Aristotle advocated for this purpose attendance upon works of art carefully prepared by dramatists and poets—not indiscriminate exposure to pornography. For the prevention of antisocial conduct Aristotle advocated virtuous acts and moral discipline.

Both common sense and Aristotelian teaching have sometimes had to yield to scientific knowledge. But the safety-valve theory can scarcely claim to have achieved the status of scientific knowledge. It is advanced by some social scientists and psychiatrists and repudiated by others. Says Margaret Mead: "Pornography is a most doubtful safety-valve. In extreme cases it may feed the perverted imagination of the doomed man who starts by pulling a little girl's braid and ends by cutting off a little girl's head, as each increasing stimulus loses its effectiveness and must be replaced by a more extreme one."[47] Says Wertham: "The getting-rid-of-aggression-by-comic-books argument has no clinical basis. The children with the most aggressive or violent fantasies or behavior are usually the most habitual readers of violent comic books."[48]

This disagreement seems to be rooted in opposing views about the role of fantasy and its effects upon mind and conduct. Karpman and the Kronhausens hold that dwelling in imagination upon a mixture of sex and cruelty often dissipates impulses to violent acts. Mead and Wertham, as well as Frignito and Sharp,[49] insist that this kind of fantasy more often stimulates and feeds such impulses, leading eventually to a psychic demand for their release in action. It may well be that the safety-valve mechanism does work in a number of cases. Therapists have used it under controlled conditions, and many people experience its operation in their own lives. But common experience continues to suggest that more harm than good ordinarily results from systematic indulgences in vicious thoughts, imaginations, and desires. At any rate, public policy cannot be reasonably based upon a tenuous and disputed theory of the role of fantasy in mental life. Public policy is more reasonably based upon an assumption like this: "Children do not need just an outlet, anyway, what they need is guidance to understanding, substitution and sublimation."[50] Is this statement any less true of adults?

It is sometimes argued that fears about the effects of obscenity are groundless, since we cannot reasonably determine how people will be affected by one kind of book or another. Judge Curtis Bok asserts that we cannot say in advance what will be the effect of a book on the "average man." According to the judge:

> It is impossible to say just what his reactions to a book actually are. . . . If he reads an obscene book when his sensuality is low, he will yawn over it or find its suggestibility leads him off on quite different paths. If he reads the Mechanics Lien Act while his sensuality is high, things will stand between him and the page which have no business there. How can anyone say that he will infallibly be affected one way or another by one book or another?[51]

It is the gist of this argument that the effects of reading are determined by the personal and subjective dispositions of the reader. It is quite true that such factors are operative in any reading experience. It is therefore impossible to be absolutely certain that an average reader will "infallibly" respond one way or another. But obscenity statutes do not rest upon such an assumption of unfailing mechanical cause and effect. They assume that a book which is designed to produce a certain kind of effect will ordinarily produce that effect in the average reader, or the reader for whom it is intended, in average situations. If so, then reasonable men can judge what is the likely effect of a book—its "tendency." This is the assumption upon which authors, including Judge Bok, write and readers read. Judge Bok can reasonably assume that his words will stimulate thought about censorship more often than they will stimulate lust.

The conception of reading suggested by Judge Bok is sometimes set forth in the terms of a scientific or quasi-scientific theory. Says Walter Gellhorn: "Certain psychological experiments suggest that one who finds pornographic elements in allegedly obscene books is very likely to discover them also in apparently innocuous books, through a process of self-selection and emphasis that the reader himself brings to the words. The same process of self-selection—this tendency to read and see what accords with preexisting interests—probably controls the effects of reading as well as the determination of what will be read."[52]

It is difficult to determine just how far Gellhorn intends to carry this concept of self-selection. Does he mean to assert that all readers see just what they want to see in the books they read—or only those readers who find obscenity in obscene books? If the former, then the enterprise of reading and writing would appear to be rather fruitless. Perhaps the concept of self-selection is intended to apply only to obscenity—"obscenity is in the eye of the beholder" (though it is not simply so with beauty and wisdom).

It is not to be denied that many habitual readers of the obscene will search for obscenity and find it in all sorts of reading matter. But is this evidence tending to show that all literary experience of the obscene is nothing more than the projection of the reader's subjective wants and interests upon the text? Is it not the case that writers of pornography intend to produce a prurient effect and that readers in fact experience this effect? The common sense of reading and writing certainly argues that this is so. And the Kronhausens find it to be so. They assert: "It seems to us undeniable that the vast majority of 'obscene' books fulfill their first and primary function of stimulating most readers erotically"; and, "We feel that 'hard-core obscenity' does stimulate in the vast majority of people what the law calls 'lascivious thoughts' and 'lustful desires.' "[53]

The argument that obscenity is in the eye of the beholder cannot be easily detached from a larger subjectivist view of reading experience and experience as such. It is not easy to argue that when we find the obscene in literature we have put it there ourselves, but when we find the beautiful it is there independently of us. Of course, in any reading experience there must be an interaction between reader and text. And it is often most difficult to determine by objective standards just what is obscene and what is beautiful. But these facts should not lead to the sweeping subjectivist conclusion that reading matter can have no influence upon a reader which is not wholly a product of dispositions already present in that reader—a conclusion which undermines the meaning of all literary activity. Says Ernest van den Haag:

> Communications and representations can have effects, desired or undesired, desirable or undesirable. Thus, the view that to the pure everything is pure, that obscenity is always the projection of the viewer or reader is surely mistaken. Though perceived subjectively, it is a quality of the object that is perceived, just as, for that matter, aesthetic merit is. . . . Difficulties of demonstration must not be confused with non-objectivity—even though they be of great practical moment in reaching consensus.[54]

People act upon literature but literature acts upon people. Shakespeare and Grimm's fairy tales have, more often than not, the kinds of effects they are designed to have. And pornography and crime comics have, more often than not, the kinds of effects they are designed to have.

What, then, are the effects of obscenity upon conduct? To what conclusions, if any, do the arguments and the evidence point?

In the controversy over this issue both sides often employ arguments which are inadequate and even unworthy. Very often passions or preconceptions govern the organization and analysis of evidence. This is not surprising in a controversy which must be, at bottom, political.

Proponents of censorship frequently infer disastrous consequences from the offensiveness of literary materials, without much effort to show a connection between the materials and the consequences. They substitute revulsion for analysis. Others assume that police testimony conclusively proves the case against obscenity, though they (and the police) frequently fail to distinguish between pornography and serious literature. They do not see the control of obscenity as a problem, and they do not make important distinctions.

Opponents of censorship very often assume that the whole weight of reason, evidence, and informed opinion is on their side. They demand scientific rigor, while submitting in support of their case research which is problematic, unanalyzed, and inconclusive. They buttress this evidence with propositions, such as the "safety-valve" and "self-selection" theories, which they do not adequately define, explore, or support and the implications of which remain unexamined.

It is not the case that the whole weight of reason, evidence, and informed opinion is on one side or another of this issue. Each side can appeal to the views of psychiatrists, psychologists, social scientists, and those professionally concerned with one aspect or another of crime and delinquency. It is my impression (though I cannot demonstrate it) that most academic social scientists and psychologists who pronounce upon the matter are highly skeptical of the harmful effects of obscenity, while this is not true of those trained in the social or psychological sciences who are in the public service and who are in some way associated with the prevention of crime. Psychiatrists and psychoanalysts who contribute to the discussion of this issue would seem to be more evenly divided. Little is proved by this, except that there is opinion on both sides which can reasonably claim to be heard.

The evidence presented by law enforcement officials and those who deal with delinquency in a criminal setting should have some weight in the citizen's thinking about obscenity. It cannot be said that these officials have proved their case, but it is wrong to say that their case has been disproved. Large numbers of offenders (we do not know how many) are found to have indulged in obscenity. But many offenders do not read obscenity, and there are many readers of obscenity who are not offenders. Police and court officials who testify before congressional committees seldom present figures concerning the percentages of those falling into each category.

In a recent study of sexual offenders the Kinsey Institute concludes: "Summing up the evidence, it would appear that the possession of pornography does not differentiate sex offenders from non-sex offenders."[55] Members of the Institute for Sex Research conducted systematic interviews with sexual offenders of various kinds and correlated the results with a survey of other types of offenders and a survey of non-offenders. The researchers did not find a correlation between exposure to pornography and sex crimes which they would regard as statistically significant. But this does not conclusively settle all the questions. Some of the offenders interviewed did testify to considerable use of pornography and did state that they were sexually stimuated by it to a substantial degree. With regard to the effects of sado-masochistic literary materials, the report says: "While it is probable that in a few cases such stimuli triggered an offense, it seems reasonable to believe that they do not play an important role in the precipitation of sex offenses in general, and at most only a minor role in sex offenses involving violence."[56] Even if the interview method were methodologically flawless, it would be too much to say (as some are saying) that this study finally disproves the existence of any causal connection between obscenity and sexual misconduct.[57]

It is still quite possible that some offenders have been stimulated to become such by their indulgence in obscenity. We do not find that all, or most, poor people become criminals or that all criminals are poor people, yet poverty is regarded as a cause of crime. Poverty is regarded as a cause of crime, though the cause-and-effect relationship can be proved to be operative in only a small minority of cases. But poverty has long been recognized as a source of crime. Common experience and social science join in regarding poverty as a deeper causative factor. There is no such agreement about exposure to corrupt literature.

As might be expected, most of the evidence gathered by police or psychiatrists is related to the effects of obscenity upon children or upon adults who may be considered abnormal. It is the disturbed child, juvenile delinquent, and the sexual criminal who come most frequently under study. On the basis of the material presented in this chapter it is at least an allowable judgment that some of these are influenced in harmful directions by pornography. If the pornography serves only as a "trigger function," this alone is not without some significance.

But there is little research evidence and not much more systematic inquiry on the problem of effects upon ordinary or normal adults. Some of the difficulties which must be involved in the conduct of such research have been observed. Yet the influence of obscenity on the ordinary adult is a basic issue; obscenity statutes are frequently defined in terms of the "average man."

In the absence of research evidence one may have recourse to opinions, such as that offered in court by Delaware State Psychiatrist M. A. Tamourianz. When asked about the effects of obscene motion pictures he said: "I have found that such films are not only detrimental to the youth, but detrimental to any human being who has normal endowments and is not particularly psychopathically inclined. It creates various deviations of thinking and emotional instability in regard to sex problems."[58]

One's classification of detrimental effects sometimes resulting from obscenity need not be confined to criminal acts or to the most extreme forms of antisocial conduct. It is arguable that some persons are stimulated by pornography to indulge in deviant forms of sexuality, to engage in "wife-swapping," or to resort to prostitutes.

A member of the anti-censorship school might answer that normal adults are not going to be seriously affected and they are certainly not going to be moved to antisocial actions by any obscene literature or art. A member of the pro-censorship school might reply that the requisites of "normality" are not so well established in theory or so often met in ordinary life as is presupposed in his opponent's argument. His opponent could retort that, whatever the definition of "normality" and whatever the percentage of those conforming to it, people are not impelled to violent or indecent acts by the stimulation of books or the mass media. If a film becomes the occasion for an antisocial act, we can be certain that the act is rooted in psychological or social influences in the life of that person and that therefore the film cannot be held responsible for it.

We are confronted once again with the "deeper causative factors" problem—which is the underlying problem. Ordinary experience and some expert opinion indicates that people can be significantly influenced by what they read in books, magazines, and newspapers and by what they see on the screen or the stage —particularly if the exposure to these media be frequent. And if beneficial influences are possible, so are harmful ones. But ordinary experience and much expert opinion indicate that people are influenced much more by the conditions in which they live (their economic conditions, family relations, work, and play) than by any literary experiences. Of course, the argument for censorship cannot establish the primacy of reading over social conditions and personal relations as an influence upon individual conduct. Therefore, it cannot be argued (if it is ever seriously argued) that an increase in the circulation of obscenity is the sole cause of delinquent, perverse, or criminal conduct. The most that can be claimed is that it is a contributing cause of sufficient magnitude to warrant attention.

How would this "contributing cause" usually operate? It is not (and probably cannot be) demonstrated that exposure to obscenity frequently operates as a clear, direct, and immediate cause of misconduct in average adults. And it is unlikely that, in any large percentage of cases, the misconduct of average children can be traced directly to the effects of reading or other literary experiences. Students of social and psychological processes who write of the evil effects of obscenity (such as Mead, Sorokin, and van den Haag) are not really talking about causation of this sort. Their primary concern is with influences upon attitudes, feelings, and inclinations which ultimately shape conduct. They are concerned with those effects of obscenity upon mind and character which, by processes too subtle to be measured, can operate to debase conduct. Tamourianz speaks of "deviations of thinking and emotional instability." In his *Roth* opinion Justice Harlan speaks of "an eroding effect on moral standards."[59] What can be said for the view that obscenity has effects of this kind?

One school of thought on this issue is represented by the views of psychiatrist and professor of psychiatry, D. W. Abse.[60] He regards obscenity as essentially a symbolic representation of infantile sexual and sadistic desires. He holds that indulgence in obscenity can operate to interfere with normal psycho-sexual development and contribute to "fixation" or "regression." He condemns "the pornography that simply encourages people to luxuriate in morbid, regressive sexual-sadistic fantasy and cultivates this morbidity in them, tending to arrest their development."[61]

In the work of Wertham an emphasis upon psychological development is combined with an emphasis upon moral development. He asserts:

> The most subtle and pervading effect of crime comics on children can be summarized in a single phrase: moral disarmament. I have studied this in children who do not commit overt acts of delinquency, who do not show any of the more conspicuous symptoms of emotional disorder and who may not have difficulty in school. The more subtle this influence is the more detrimental it may be. It has an influence on character, on attitude, on the

higher functions of social responsibility, on super-ego formation, and on the intuitive feeling for right and wrong. To put it more concretely, it consists chiefly of a blunting of the finer feelings of conscience, of mercy, of feeling for other people's suffering and of respect for women as women and not merely as sex objects to be bandied around or as luxury prizes to be fought over. Crime comics are such highly flavored fare that they affect children's taste for the finer influences of education, for art, for literature and for the decent and constructive relations between human beings and especially between the sexes.[62]

Wertham does not regard these "more subtle" influences upon moral values as irrelevant to the legitimate concerns of psychiatry or to the psychological development of human beings. He regards the "ethical image" which every person, child or adult, has of himself and of reality as "a cornerstone of mental health." Corruption of this ethical image is a major factor contributing to the distortion of personality.

Can exposure to obscenity promote this kind of moral-psychological deformation of human personality? Are adults vulnerable to it? I have had frequent occasion to refer to the paucity of scientific research on the consequences of obscenity. It is perhaps unnecessary to point out that the precise question raised here is the least researched of any in this field. Practically all the studies we have address themselves to grosser considerations—to factors promoting violent or criminal behavior, or to effects upon some of the more obvious aspects of personality development. Inquiry has been directed to such considerations as the causes of sexual perversion or aggression, but not to causes of the deterioration of moral perception and humane sensitivity.

The opponents of censorship rely heavily upon such inquiry. Their most frequent reliance is upon evidence and arguments tending to show that exposure to obscenity does not directly promote the grosser forms of harm. Typical of this reliance is the following citation appearing in Morris Ernst's brief in the *Roth* case: "In twenty-five years of practice, which includes ten years majoring in juvenile and adult court work, I have never been able to pin down a definite major causal influence between crime, violence, etc. as depicted in movies, cartoons, books or T.V. and the offensive behavior encountered in delinquency" (Dr. George

M. Lott, University Psychiatrist, State College, Pa., June 1, 1955).[63]

The oft-cited studies of Jahoda, the Gluecks, and the Brown University psychologists, as well as the statements of Dr. Karpman and other students of sexual pathology, are all concerned with the more flagrant and evident kinds of evil. These are evils which fit most obviously within a "clear and present danger" framework. Libertarian scholars are inclined to devote their attention to effects which allegedly pose a "clear and present danger." Such material as they provide that is relevant to the more subtle dangers is usually insubstantial and inconclusive. Questionnaires asking women what they find most sexually stimulating, the Kinsey statistics about sexual stimulation from literature, the Kronhausens' list of sexually interesting phenomena bear lightly and inconclusively on this larger problem. The "safety-valve" and "self-selection" arguments would be relevant to it, but these are, in this author's judgment, among the weakest of the anti-censorship arguments.

Libertarian writers do not explore very deeply the possible long-range effects of obscenity upon mind and character. Their failure to do so is perhaps rooted in the conviction that legislation with a view to such effects is forbidden by the First Amendment.

There is a body of literature somewhat relevant to the problem we are now considering. Studies have been made of the effects of reading and of the mass media upon the emotions, attitudes, and opinions of ordinary adults or young adults.

Waples, Berelson, and Bradshaw report on a number of experimental studies designed to test the effects of reading upon attitudes. Subjects, usually college students, were given textual passages to read. They were given attitude tests before and after the reading. According to the authors, "the studies have repeatedly shown that reading can change attitudes. They have also shown that certain reader traits and certain content elements will modify the effect of reading."[64] But the authors point to various limitations inherent in this method of investigation. The effects measured were those of short passages upon college students after a single reading.

In 1949 Joseph T. Klapper published a report of his extensive analysis of the research literature dealing with the effects of the mass media.[65] He reports the findings of Blumer and Hauser that motion pictures exercise a deep "emotional possession" of children, and he cites numerous other studies reporting changes in opinion and motivation induced by the various media. Nevertheless, "studies indicating the persuasiveness of the mass media can be paralleled by studies citing instances of mass media's failure to persuade."[66] He concludes:

> In sum, then, the pertinent literature indicates that material presented over any medium may be persuasively effective, but on the other hand, that it may not be effective. It is generally agreed that attitude changes consist more often of modification than of conversion and that, although some of these modifications wane after propaganda exposure is terminated, they are to some degree highly persistent. One series of experiments indicates that some attitude changes become intensified during the weeks following exposure. Some experimenters find brief exposure exactly as effective as cumulative exposure, while others find cumulative exposure more effective.[67]

These studies can hardly be regarded as conclusive. They do indicate that literary or mass-media experiences do (sometimes) modify attitudes and that such modification can (sometimes) be lasting. But they do not indicate how long-lasting are these changes, and how profound they are—how they affect basic opinion, values, and dispositions. It seems highly unlikely that research of this sort can ever produce scientifically conclusive answers to the questions with which we are concerned here. Their most serious limitations (both intrinsic and in relation to the obscenity problem) are suggested in Klapper's warning that "the empirical evidence must not be assumed to be valid in situations dissimilar to those described in the specific experiment."[68] The difficulties implied in this proviso would probably be at least as great in any similar experiments constructed to test the psychological or moral effects of obscenity.

With regard to the influence of obscenity upon mind and character, the research literature is as inconclusive as are the libertarian arguments. There is no significant body of tested opinion against the view that this influence of obscenity is harmful. Some investigations and some informed opinion support this view. Thus there is every reason to accord considerable weight to what might be called "the common sense of the matter"—to experience informed by reflection.

For present purposes I regard material deserving to be called "obscene" as that which (1) predominantly appeals to lust; (2) graphically presents and interweaves violence and sensuality; (3) graphically presents human beings as, to use the terms of Wertham, "sex objects to be bandied around." We must consider the likely effect upon average children and adults of frequent exposure to such obscenity through various media, including books, magazines, newspapers, advertising, and motion pictures.*

Informed opinion from Plato to Wertham has held that children can be powerfully influenced emotionally and intellectually by the stories they read and hear. It has always been thought dangerous to put sordid or demoralizing stories into the minds of children.

What about most adults? Are they immune to the impact of materials which appeal to their sensuality while depreciating traditional moral values and humane sensibilities? The current circulation of obscenity among us would strongly suggest that many are not immune to the *appeal* of such materials. And it is difficult to argue that the mere legal fact of adulthood renders us unsusceptible to any influence or impact from them. Some writers on the subject often speak as if adulthood in our society, and its corresponding freedom to choose, automatically carries with it the moral, psychological, and intellectual requisites of good choice. But it is common experience that many of our adults do not choose wisely or act well (by conventional moral standards) in matters relating to sex. Indeed, in our contemporary society there appears to be considerable uncertainty or confusion about what constitutes "good choice" in these matters.

But, it is said, normal adults are not influenced by stories as are children. They distinguish between fantasy and reality, and they are surely strong enough to avoid any harmful impact from mere words and pictures. Those who say this seldom wish to say that literary expression is powerless to obtain any hold on the normal human mind. What they usually want to say is that litera-

* It is legitimate to speak of frequent exposure, since the exposure is already considerable, and the libertarians would remove present restraints upon publication.

ture can have beneficial effects but not harmful ones. Passions may be aroused to good ends but not bad ones, and the mind may be inspired with noble thoughts but not base ones.

Such a view is not tenable. As has been observed several times in this chapter, people of all sorts are influenced by literary experiences—by the impressions received from words and pictures. And, ordinarily, the impressions received will be in accord with what the literature is designed to convey to the average or to the appropriate reader. Ordinary people can be moved, for good or ill, by "mere words."

As for the distinction between fantasy and reality, this distinction is often difficult to make, and it cannot reasonably be assumed that a large majority of us are highly skilled in making it. There is a considerable body of evidence, both scientific and experiential, which contravenes such an assumption. Numerous publishing and journalistic enterprises are built upon the exploitation of the harsh truth that some adults prefer fantasy and many are content to have their fantasies disguised as "facts." These desires are accommodated in "exposé," "true confession," "detective," or "men's adventure" magazines; in sensationalist newspapers such as the *National Informer* and even publications of higher repute. Those magazines which specialize in revealing to their readers the "inside dope" about the private lives of movie stars or "the real truth, candidly presented" about wife-swapping are hardly appealing to a taste for realistic understanding of human affairs. And it cannot be said that all consumers of such publications are mentally ill.

There are, then, good reasons for thinking that ordinary adults are not totally immune to the appeals and influences of obscenity. I suggest two ways in which these influences may operate.

They may operate upon deep-rooted passions and inclinations and, by means of them, affect attitudes and character. Those who habitually indulge in lascivious, morbid, or sadistic literature are encouraged to find satisfaction in lascivious, morbid, or sadistic experiences. Evidently such readers bring to this literature the wants which it fulfills. This much of the self-selection theory is true. But the theory fails to take account of factors more important than this. Desires and inclinations may not only be satisfied, they may also be reinforced or inflamed—one can become habituated to seeking unworthy satisfactions. The attitudes which lead one to "select" obscene experiences can be strengthened by repeated indulgence in such experiences.* On the other hand, if the opportunities for their indulgence are reduced, the unhealthy dispositions are more easily subject to modification or sublimation. If obscenity is not readily available, there is some prospect for healthier attitudes to win out over those which select obscenity.† For it is simply not true that an interest in the prurient can be as well and as easily satisfied by the reading of Shakespeare as by the reading of pornography.

The kind of influence under consideration can be, but need not be, described in psychoanalytic terms. Obscenity has always held a strong attraction, a fascination, for large numbers of people. The fascination lies in its appeal to powerful instincts or impulses, some of which are rooted in the natural endowment of man and some of which derive from tensions arising in human society. A man need not be particularly abnormal to be moved by appeals to dispositions which we all share and which few have completely mastered. It may be, as is asserted by Abse and others, that the essence of pornography is its stimulation of repressed infantile, hence perverse, wishes. According to this view, such wishes will remain to some extent operative in most men. Most men are, then, susceptible to a preoccupation with them, if not a regression to them. It may be, as is asserted by Freud and others,

---

* With regard to a possible "compulsion" for obscenity arising from frequent exposure, Cairns, Paul, and Wishner have this to say: "It may be that the obscene material is simply used in place of other material to satisfy a desire for sexual stimulation—a desire which will be fulfilled in any event. . . . But the evidence hardly negates other possibilities as well—including the hypothesis that the obscene material is both an artifact and a causative influence creating, in some, a stronger desire to view more obscenity. If, in fact, the seeking for obscenity becomes a 'compulsive' activity to some, this behavior may affect the individual's personality or his values and his attitudes toward sexual conduct or his health, happiness or efficiency. As yet, we cannot evaluate these hypotheses adequately. The data we have merely suggest that this may be an important and researchable area of investigation." Cairns, Paul, and Wishner, "Assumptions and Empirical Evidence," pp. 1036–37. What is suggested in the first sentence of this statement is undoubtedly true in some cases. But would it not make some difference where —with what kinds of material—one undertakes to satisfy his desire for sexual stimulation? If one can become habituated or predisposed to seek erotic satisfaction from literature, is it a matter of indifference whether the literature is *Romeo and Juliet* or sado-masochistic pornography?

† It is not suggested that such attitudes could win out if the entire social environment is against them.

that the sexual-sadistic dispositions derive in part from natural instincts and in part from an inevitable conflict between natural instinct and civilized restraints. If so, then the ordinary person remains somewhat vulnerable. The higher forms of character development are never completely secure, and they can be weakened by external factors which arouse the lower. At any rate, most of us are not wholly unresponsive to appeals to the lower passions, nor is it only the mentally ill or the abnormal who are capable of developing unworthy attitudes and interests. An obscenity-saturated literary environment could function as one factor in the activation and reinforcement of unworthy traits of character.

The unrestricted circulation of obscene literary materials could also operate to break down moral standards by undermining the convictions and the sensitivities which support them. Constant exposure to literary and visual materials which overemphasize sensuality and brutality, reduce love to sex, and blatantly expose to public view intimacies which have been thought sacred or private must eventually result in an erosion of moral standards.

The government's *Roth* brief asserts that "the common circulation of such material could hardly help but induce many to believe that their moral code was out of date."[69] People are influenced by what they think others believe and particularly by what they think are the common standards of the community. There are few individuals among us whose basic beliefs are the result of their own reasoning and whose moral opinions do not require the support of some stable public opinion. The free circulation of obscenity can, in time, lead many to the conclusion that there is nothing wrong with the values implicit in it—since their open promulgation is tolerated by the public. They will come to the conclusion that public standards have changed—or that there are no public standards. Private standards are hard put to withstand the effects of such an opinion. This may be particularly true of those moral standards which are difficult to maintain because they involve the restraint of passions or the sacrifice of pleasures.

But the results of obscenity need not be achieved in precisely this manner. Ethical beliefs may be undermined more indirectly. The ethical convictions of social man do not rest simply upon his explicit opinions. They rest also upon a delicate network of moral and aesthetic feelings, sensibilities, tastes—what Wertham calls "the intuitive feeling for right and wrong . . . the finer feelings of conscience, of mercy, of sympathy."[70] Such emotions and moral sentiments are indispensable supports for the higher or more subtle ethical judgments; it is by virtue of them that we feel respect for what is honorable and disgust for what is indecent— aspiring toward the former and recoiling from the latter. When sentiments of this kind are not developed, morality tends to degenerate into a collection of abstract precepts or a calculus of self-interest.[71] These "finer feelings" could be blunted and eroded by a steady stream of impressions which assault them. Men whose sensibilities are frequently assaulted by prurient and lurid impressions may become desensitized. Perhaps it will be thought paradoxical that obscenity, which appeals to and arouses the senses, is here regarded as a "desensitizer." But obscenity promotes the grosser passions; its corroding effect is upon the higher or more refined feelings—those upon which ethical and aesthetic discrimination depend. Men who are long accustomed to the experiences of the obscene may simply not *feel* the same way about ethical matters. This is what is meant by "an erosion of the moral fabric."

The libertarian is highly skeptical of all this. He is inclined to dismiss it as mere speculation. He is inclined to answer the advocate of censorship with arguments such as this one from Macaulay: "We find it difficult to believe that in a world so full of temptation as this, any gentleman whose life would have been virtuous if he had not read Aristophanes and Juvenal will be made vicious by reading them."[72]

This is not a proposition addressed to the real considerations which underlie any legitimate censorship. Aristophanes and Juvenal are not at issue, nor is that "gentleman" who is already well on the way to virtue. The argument is concerned with the "average man" who is neither virtuous nor vicious, but is capable of being moved in one direction or the other by the moral environment in which he lives. It is not asserted that Aristophanes and Juvenal can make a good man vicious. It is asserted that the widespread circulation of obscenity, particularly when legally protected, can so affect the moral atmosphere of the average man that virtuous dispositions are inhibited and vicious ones encouraged.

The moral environment consists largely of opinions, values, and sentiments tending to promote actions in accord with them.

A bad moral environment will promote evil in the same manner as a good moral environment is generally thought to promote good. It is upon such an assumption of cause and effect that parents are advised to provide good literature in the home and communities are advised to provide good libraries, serious motion pictures, and an ethically responsible press. It is assumed that these influences are a significant part of the cultural environment of a country, having, over a period of time, cumulative effects upon the quality of the individual's life. It is assumed that, over a period of time, cumulative effects are also produced by bad libraries, films, and newspapers.

Such effects as these are, of course, most difficult to measure, and surely they cannot be predicted with scientific accuracy. It is with regard to this kind of cause-and-effect relationship that the limits of scientific and specialized expertise become most evident. It cannot be demonstrated by any experimentation exactly in what way or to what extent good and bad literature affect the moral and intellectual life of a community. When this kind of problem is reached, science tends to give way to social philosophy and to sober reflection upon common experience.

There is a social philosophy according to which considerations of morality and immorality are never really relevant to the understanding of social problems. Morality and immorality are understood to be effects—but never causes—of social ills. Say the authors of *The Freedom to Read:* "The pressures for censorship arise from the practical problems characteristic of periods of crisis and change; but the arguments for censorship normally turn, not on inquiry into those problems and into means of solving them, but on the interrelated dangers of immorality, treason, irreligion, and error."[73] According to the views of these authors, it would not be reasonable to address oneself to immorality as a cause of the real "practical problems," and to wrong opinions or values promoted by literature as a cause of immorality. The causes are presumably to be found elsewhere in the social conditions, institutions, and personal relations of men.

There is another social philosophy according to which morality and immorality can profoundly affect the social conditions, institutions, and personal relations of men. And morality and immorality can be significantly influenced by opinions, attitudes, values, and feelings which literature conveys. Says Ernest van den

172

Haag: "In more than one sense, literature reveals and even creates good and evil. . . . Thus they [the books] can be helpful or harmful to any existing pattern of social organization and control and to the culture of which it is a part."[74] In this way literature and the arts are understood as "deeper causative factors." This view comes to us with a heavy weight of common and historic opinion behind it. It can be consistently denied only by those who are willing to argue that our beliefs, ethics, and moral feelings are not significant factors in the shaping of our social organization and the way we live.

Thus we arrive at a basic philosophic issue in the debate over the effects of obscenity. This issue concerns the significance to be attributed to "good and evil"—to moral character and its attributes as a determining factor in social life. There are social theories which regard the character of men who live in a community as a decisive fact about that community. And there are social theories which regard character as a secondary factor—derivative from economic, technological, and other material causes. Those who tend to view society from the former perspective are in a position to take seriously the possible effects of vicious literature. Those who view society from the latter perspective are predisposed to dismiss this consideration as irrelevant nonsense.

The viewpoint which separates man's economic activities and social institutions from his moral character and values, regarding the latter as a mere reflection or "superstructure" of the former, is a latecomer in the history of political thought. Traditional philosophic schools, which have disagreed about many things, have agreed that the way men organize their economic and social life is profoundly and reciprocally related to their views about good and bad. And one need not subscribe to the proposition that "the poets are the unacknowledged legislators of mankind" to take seriously the influence which literature and the arts can have upon our perceptions of good and bad. This influence does not become any less significant in an age of mass communication and mass media.

This study of the effects of obscenity leads to two sets of conclusions. With regard to the direct effects of salacious literature upon conduct, informed opinion is divided and the evidence is problematic. The evidence does not preclude a reasoned judgment that obscenity is sometimes a factor in the promotion of antisocial behavior. But the social importance or magnitude of such direct effects as can be shown remains open to dispute. The most socially significant issues concern the more subtle and long-term influences of obscenity upon mind and character—its moral effects. Obscenity can contribute to the debasement of moral standards and ultimately of character.

The assertion of this truth does not, however, resolve all issues. If obscenity poses for society what is essentially a moral problem, it remains to be established that government and law can legitimately address themselves to this problem. To what extent, if any, is "the state" legitimately concerned with the moral life of citizens, and more specifically, with that area of moral life which is related to sex? The following chapter considers the proper relation between law and morality and the philosophic rationale for censorship.

5

Law, Virtue, and Sex:
The Rationale for Censorship

The teachings of John Stuart Mill culminate in one massive conclusion: the law may not be used to punish acts which threaten
society's moral values; government may not act by coercive means
to protect the moral order as such. Coercion may be used only
against acts which are directly injurious to identifiable persons or
to the public peace and security. Mill's intellectual descendants
apply his principles in various ways and with varying degrees of
rigor. Judge Bok says: "The criminal law is not, in my opinion,
the 'custos morum' of the King's subjects, as *Regina* v. *Hicklin*
states: it is only the custodian of the peace and good order that
free men and women need for shaping their common destiny";[1]
and "censorship should be the proper activity of the community
rather than of the law."[2] In England the committee well known
as the Wolfenden Committee has asserted that "there must remain a realm of private morality and immorality which is, in brief
and crude terms, not the law's business."[3] Professor Louis Henkin
of Columbia University holds that the "sole or chief purpose" of
obscenity laws is "the preservation of a quasi-religious morality."
He asks: "Can government, which may not establish religion, or
interfere with the free exercise of religion and non-religion, enforce a morality rooted in religion?"[4]

Thus, it is frequently asserted that the function of law is to
provide for peace and security, while the moral interests of man
are exclusively in the care of agencies of society other than government. Public opinion will enforce its standards of decency
without the aid of law. Moral values and training must be, and

can most adequately be, provided by social institutions such as the family and the church. In addition, it is often suggested that sex and associated subjects belong largely, if not wholly, to the private side of life. This view sometimes takes the form of an assertion that sexual activity performed in private between consenting adults can be no concern of the organized public. It sometimes takes the form of a broader claim to the effect that sexual morality is a wholly private matter. Finally, it is contended that most of the laws purporting to deal with such matters can have no legitimate *secular* purpose and that the moral considerations from which censorship of obscenity proceeds are rooted, ultimately, in nothing more than religious beliefs and feelings. Since the state cannot coercively impose religious beliefs upon its citizens, it cannot impose ethical values which are based on religious beliefs.

The statute books of most nations contain many laws which constitute, or can be understood as constituting, attempts to enforce compliance with moral norms. These include laws against prostitution, brothel keeping, pimping, sodomy, bestiality, incest, homosexuality, adultery, fornication, bigamy, polygamy, abortion, suicide, euthanasia, cruelty to animals, dueling, gambling, narcotics, public indecency, and obscene publications.

Some of these prohibitions can be explained and defended in terms other than those of morality as such. It can be argued that when the law prohibits public indecency it is not concerned with the immorality of such acts, but with their offensiveness to others. The law seeks to prevent acts which will grievously offend nonconsenting persons and perhaps lead to breaches of the peace. Laws against bigamy may be represented primarily as efforts to prevent desertion or nonsupport of children or as efforts to protect religious sensibilities from outrage by a public act which desecrates the marriage ceremony. Laws against euthanasia, suicide, and abortion are sometimes placed in the same category as those which regulate drugs and narcotics—"paternalistic legislation" protecting people from physical destruction to which they may be led by ignorance or psychological weaknesses.[5]

But it cannot be denied that moral considerations have played and continue to play an important role in all the legislation enumerated above. It is generally understood that, whatever other purposes such laws may have, they are also designed to implement community ethical standards. Mill's principles would seem to require that this great mass of legislation be abolished—or at least radically reformed so that it no longer involves any legal enforcement of morality.

The Wolfenden Report on Homosexual Offenses and Prostitution argues for such reform in relation to the subjects with which it deals. The major conclusion of the *Report* is that "homosexual behavior between consenting adults in private should no longer be a criminal offense."[6] The Wolfenden Committee was strongly influenced by a humanitarian concern for the suffering which results when legal penalties are attached to homosexual activity. And the committee found no reason to assume that homosexual acts performed in private are in any way harmful to society. But, for our purposes here, the most important aspects of the *Report* are its general principles, which reach far beyond the particular subject of homosexuality. These general principles pronounce upon the functions of the law and the distinction between public and private interests.

The *Report* states that "it is not the duty of the law to concern itself with immorality as such. . . . It should confine itself to those activities which offend against public order and decency or expose the ordinary citizen to what is offensive or injurious."[7]

Thus the law is inherently unconcerned with the morality or immorality of men's acts or with the ethical character of social life. The law exists to protect individuals from various forms of personal injury, ranging from violence to psychological shock or offense, and to provide such general security as will remove the danger of these personal injuries. On these principles the committee holds that there should be no legal penalties for acts of prostitution—for the prostitute or her customer. Legal penalties should attach, rather, to solicitation in the streets, where the passerby may become an unwilling witness of something which he regards as indecent.* The law cannot be legitimately interested in the *immorality* of prostitution; prostitution can be a concern of the law only when it becomes a "public nuisance."

In affirming that there are certain acts or relations which are "not the law's business," the *Wolfenden Report* frequently uses the terms "private morality" and "private immorality." The com-

---

* Prostitution is not illegal in England, but solicitation in the streets is a punishable offense.

mittee does not clearly define these terms, and for its purpose it does not need to do. But the language of the *Report* often leaves the impression that private behavior—what is done in private between consenting adults—belongs to the realm of "private morals." Though the authors probably did not explicitly intend this, their arguments strongly suggest that the ethical standards which govern private activities are matters of personal choice and not matters of public interest.

The principles of the *Wolfenden Report* have received philosophic support from Professor H. L. A. Hart.[8] Hart is willing to compromise with the doctrines of John Stuart Mill in two respects. He is willing to compromise with the principle that no man may be coerced for his own good. He would allow "paternalistic legislation," legislation which employs threats of punishment to protect the individual against physical harms to which the individual himself might voluntarily submit. And Hart will apparently go further than Mill would have gone in permitting the penal law to be used to protect people from enforced public confrontation with activities repugnant to their moral feelings. But he would emphatically draw the line at what he regards as the core of Mill's teaching—that the law may not be used to "enforce morality as such."[9] Hart insists upon a sharp distinction "between inducing persons through fear of punishment to abstain from actions which are harmful to others, and inducing them to abstain from actions which deviate from accepted morality but harm no one."[10]

Among impermissible laws designed to enforce morality "as such," Hart would evidently include, not only those against homosexual behavior, but also those against incest, bestiality, and keeping a house for prostitution.[11] He does not explain why these and similar activities may be said to "harm no one." At any rate, Hart's argument appears to rest upon an absolute distinction between activities which are really harmful (such as indulgence in dangerous narcotics) and activities which are *merely* violations of the community's morality. Since the latter are intrinsically harmless, no man may be compelled by law to abstain from them.

If the doctrines of Mill's descendants are to be adopted, then the legal systems of most civilized nations will have to undergo some radical alterations. It is true that the recommendations of the *Wolfenden Report* are not always consistent wtih the principles which are laid down as their foundation. The *Report* vigorously supports legal penalties for such activities as "keeping a brothel" and "living on the earnings of prostitution" without any proviso that, to be punishable, such activities must involve disorderly conduct or offensive public behavior. Here the committee seems to recognize that prostitution involves or generates moral evils which are somehow "the law's business." Further, the committee regards the law as quite properly concerned to prevent the "corruption" of children or adults who are "specially vulnerable."[12] Once again the committee attributes to the law at least some limited interest in morality and immorality. But the fact that the followers of Mill are not always consistent does not render their legal doctrines any less significant or influential. It is therefore important to take these doctrines seriously and to consider what a system of law rigorously and consistently organized in accordance with them would be like.

Carried out to their logical conclusion, these doctrines would require of the criminal law (and presumably any law which may result in officially imposed penalties) a strict moral neutrality. Moral standards or judgments could not be used as criteria for determining what should be prohibited or punished. No act could be prohibited because of its unethical or vicious character. The law would tend to become little more than a body of convenient utilitarian rules for the protection of life and property and the prevention of violence, physical or psychological. Such rules would not embody any moral imperatives (except, perhaps, such minimal imperatives as are associated with physical security) or any preference for virtue over vice.

In the past hundred years the criminal laws of Western nations have undergone considerable liberalization. But they have not been divested of all moral content; they continue to distinguish in various ways between virtue and vice. The scale of punishments for various offenses continues to correspond to judgments of what is morally blamable. Judges still take account of considerations of moral responsibility in the interpretation and enforcement of statutes. In its diverse regulation of business, contracts, and divorce the law still finds way to throw its weight behind what is ethical and to place disabilities upon the wrongdoer. And, as I have noted, there remains on the statute books a multitude of restrictions designed to enforce ethical norms and to discourage vice in sexual and other matters. While perhaps some of these restrictions should be relaxed, they do testify to a persistent interest of "the state" in the moral life of men.

A defense of this interest against the strictures of Mill's descendants must undertake to show that the moral objectives of the law rest ultimately upon something more than arbitrary opinions or merely religious beliefs. And it must undertake to show that these objectives do not constitute an unjustifiable invasion of the private side of life.

In 1727 the English Court of the King's Bench decided the case of *Rex* v. *Curl,* recognizing, for the first time, the common law offense of "obscene libel." Curl was accused of publishing and distributing *The Nun in Her Smock,* a book with "several lewd passages." His attorney argued that "however the defendant may be punishable for this in the Spiritual Court as an offense contra bonas mores, yet it can't be a libel for which he is punishable in Temporal Court."[13]

The Court held unanimously that this was a temporal offense. Justice Probyn "inclined this to be punishable at common law, as an offense against the peace, in tending to weaken the bonds of civil society, virtue and morality."[14] Justice Reynolds endeavored to distinguish between acts of immorality which are "of spiritual cognizance only" and those of "a general immoral tendency" (such as Curl's publication) which constitute civil wrongs.

Undoubtedly, the issues in *Rex* v. *Curl* had religious overtones. But the Justices' opinions reflect considerable effort to present "obscene libel" in secular or political terms and to distinguish between immorality which is an offense against religion and immorality which is an offense against the civil interests of the commonwealth.

In 1961 the House of Lords heard the case of *Shaw* v. *Director of Public Prosecution.*[15] Shaw was indicted for composing and distributing *The Ladies Directory,* a magazine providing the names and addresses of prostitutes, nude photographs of them, and descriptions of their practices. He was charged with three offenses: (1) conspiring to corrupt public morals; (2) living on the earnings of prostitution; and (3) publishing an obscene article. The basic issues and major arguments of the case centered upon the question whether or not "conspiring to corrupt public morals" is an offense still known to the common law. Of the Lords who heard the case, all but one held in the affirmative. Viscount Simonds said: "In the sphere of criminal law, I entertain no doubt that there remains in the courts of law a residual power to enforce the supreme and fundamental purpose of the law to conserve not only the safety and order but also the moral welfare of the state, and that it is their duty to guard it against attacks which may be the more insidious because they are novel and unprepared for."[16]

Viscount Simonds' choice of language is significant. He holds not only that it is "a fundamental purpose of the law" to preserve the "moral welfare of the state," but also that this is an end distinguishable from the preservation of "safety and order." The moral well-being of the community is, equally with its peace and security, an object of the law's solicitude. It is suggested that the law is concerned with the former for its own sake and not simply as a precondition of the latter. It is also significant that, in the eyes of these judges, this basic consideration is not rendered obsolete by the advent of secularization and democracy. Viscount Simonds' opinion recognizes that Christianity no longer has the political status accorded it in earlier centuries. The moral function of the law is not based on specifically religious considerations, but on "fundamental assessments of human values and the purposes of society."[17]

American judges have expressed similar ideas in different language. In *Davis* v. *Beason* the Supreme Court upheld laws against the teaching of polygamy as "legislation for the punishment of acts inimical to the peace, good order and morals of society."[18] Laws which condemn the practice of polygamy on moral grounds continue to be upheld in American courts. An earlier case, *Trist* v. *Child,* contains a classic statement of the proposition that the republican state is particularly interested in the moral condition of citizens: "The foundation of a republic is the virtue of its citizens. They are at once sovereigns and subjects. As the foundation is undermined the structure is weakened. When it is destroyed the fabric must fall. Such is the voice of universal history."[19]

In *People* v. *Seltzer* Judge Robert Wagner expressed these views in what are perhaps more modern terms. He placed obscenity statutes in the category of health and welfare legislation, such as that prohibiting child labor, limiting the hours of employment, or providing for sanitary conditions in factories. He said:

> Just as it is of national concern and interest to protect their health, it is equally important to protect our youth against the corruption of their morals, so that we may do everything within governmental power to afford them physical, mental and moral virility and not have their development arrested during the formative period. It is a national duty to prevent the moral or physical weakening of the family—"The Nursery of Mankind."[20]

The nation is as much concerned with the moral health of the individual and the family as it is with their physical well-being. The family is the moral "nursery of mankind," but, for the successful performance of its tasks, it needs the support of law.

Such judicial pronouncements as these do not, of course, establish the case for the moral role of government and law in a secular society. They do indicate that judges have often affirmed the existence of this function and that, in doing so, they have not found it necessary to resort to religious beliefs and values. But they do not, and cannot, systematically explain why government must have this function, to what ends it should be exercised and what are its limits. As an introduction to the discussion of these issues I propose to examine briefly three typical rationales—three views of law, society, and ethics on the basis of which moral censorship may be justified.

According to the oldest of these views, the primary function of law is moral education; the ethical development of citizens is an inherent and ultimate aim of all political society. Says Aristotle: "This truth is attested by the experience of states: lawgivers make the citizens good by training them in habits of right action—this is the aim of all legislation, and if it fails to do this it is a failure; this is what distinguishes a good form of constitution from a bad one."[21]

This concept of law and government derives from a political and ethical philosophy which is far too complex for adequate treatment here. I will only indicate two of its distinctive features—its view of the ends of human society and its doctrine of virtue.

According to Aristotle's teaching, men are not in civil society simply for the preservation of life, liberty, and security. Men come together in political communities for the satisfaction of the whole range of human needs—the material (or "lower") as well as the moral (or "higher") needs. More precisely, while society exists to preserve life, its highest end is a good life—the cultivation in men of those qualities and capacities which are distinctively human. For the satisfaction of his various needs and the cultivation of his human faculties man requires certain virtues, such as courage, temperance or self-control, and justice. The development of the virtues involves acquisition of those qualities of character by means of which a man is enabled to discipline his passions and direct them to ends dictated by his reason. These are the properties which distinguish human life from animal life. Thus understood, the virtues can be said to derive from the demands of human nature, since human nature requires them in order to function as it is designed to function. But for the development of virtue most men need the discipline of law. The control and proper direction of the passions is not accomplished without authoritative guidance and encouragement from the community.[22]

What this classical view emphasizes, to use the language of Walter Berns, is "the role of the law in the civilizing process."[23] The law does not perform this civilizing function simply by its prevention or punishment of crime. The negative or coercive role of law is, ultimately, subordinate to its positive or educative role. Legislation seeks not merely to prevent the worst evils, but also to promote such higher forms of conduct and character as will serve the higher purposes of the community. Says Berns: "Since the way of a community depends upon citizens of a certain character, it must be the business of the law to promote that character."[24] Thus, "the formation of character is the principal duty of government."[25]

From this view it would follow that moral censorship is a legitimate activity of government. It is one of the means, though it is not the most important means, by which government performs its "principal duty." The censorship of materials appealing to the lower appetites would be a part (but only a part) of the external guidance required for the promotion of good character.

The theory under consideration involves concepts of human nature, society, and ethics which are rejected in much of modern thought. Its concept of virtue rests upon a doctrine of universally valid ethical ends which are discoverable by human reasoning and experience. Its concept of the role of law presupposes that political society is formed "by nature" to serve these ethical ends. These doctrines are the subject of profound philosophical dispute. They are rejected by those who deny the existence of any binding moral norms derivable from universal human needs. And they are rejected by those who deny that there are any natural ends of human activity other than those dictated by considerations of self-preservation.

H. L. A. Hart suggests that the only solid foundation for ethics is "the tacit assumption that the proper end of human activity is survival" and that when we raise any "question concerning *how* men should live together, we must assume that their aim is, generally speaking, to live."[26] Thus Hart is willing to recognize as requirements of man's nature only such moral norms as are concerned with the survival or preservation of life. What, then, is the status of those norms which involve the enhancement of life or the promotion of a good life? It follows from Hart's view of human nature that the status of such norms is highly problematic and that the aims of organized society can be most adequately described as "life, liberty and property."

There is an alternative to the classical rationale for censorship, an alternative which does not find it necessary to confront these philosophic dilemmas. It is not committed to a doctrine of human virtue or a theory of the natural purpose of political society. According to this view, censorship arises from a need, inherent in any community, whatever its purpose, for cohesion or unity. The very term "community" presupposes common beliefs and values which bind its members together and promote common actions or allegiances. The preservation of its common values is of deep concern to organized society. When they are seriously threatened, it is the duty of government to protect them. Says Ernest van den Haag:

> A society functions only if its members share a common body of values, and back of it, a common ethos. This permits some divergencies but also requires the society, if it is to remain viable, to protect the essential shared values. If this proposition is correct, as I believe, then Jefferson's society—which protects coercively only freedom, allowing people to make any use of it they want (to pursue and cultivate any values) as long as it does not interfere with the freedom of others—is an ideal that cannot be practiced. . . . The ethos may permit liberties—but not to the extent of endangering it. Certainly the right of censorship is implied. Within limits, freedom may be part of the ethos. But the ethos must include values beyond the mere universal distribution of the ability to choose (freedom), and these must be protected.[27]

This rationale differs from the former in its conception of what it is that censorship protects. According to it, censorship does not support virtue as such; it supports the "virtues" of a particular people—their most characteristic and most deeply cherished attitudes, convictions, values. These virtues may be good or bad in the light of some universal standard of human excellence. The attitudes embodied in a community's ethos may be more or less valid in the light of scientific or other truth. Says van den Haag: "In terms of social efficacy, it is not necessary at all that beliefs be true or demonstrably so. It is enough that they be held and that the holding of some such beliefs is needed for the moral solidarity of any society."[28] This rationale tends to abstract from considerations of the goodness or badness and the truth or falsity of the ethos from which censorship proceeds.

A similar view is reflected in some of the writings of the eminent British jurist Sir Patrick Devlin. Lord Devlin observes:

> I have said that a sense of right and wrong is necessary for the life of a community. It is not necessary that their appreciation of right and wrong, tested in the light of one set or another of those abstract propositions about which men forever dispute, should be correct. . . . What the lawmaker has to ascertain is not the true belief but the common belief.[29]

According to Lord Devlin, every community must rest upon moral agreement about such fundamental matters as monogamy or polygamy. In our society the lawmaker does not consider the intrinsic merits or defects of monogamy; he acts to preserve it as an institution essential to the structure of his society. When the lawmaker acts as a censor, his task is not the improvement but the preservation of "the essentials of his society."[30] This includes the protection of those aspects of its particular morality upon which there is fundamental consensus.

From the viewpoint represented by van den Haag and Devlin it can be concluded that government is profoundly interested in the morality of citizens. But government is indifferent to the intrinsic worth of the morality in which it is interested. The character of that morality is irrelevant to the ends for which censorship is used. Censorship may be properly employed in our society to restrict such forms of sensualism as are contrary to our deepest values—whatever they may be or from whatever source they may be derived. It may be properly employed in some other society to support or promote that very sensualism. And presumably, if the moral consensus changes from an endorsement of monogamy to an endorsement of polygamy, it becomes the task of censorship to safeguard the values associated with the latter.

There is a third rationale for the interest of government in morality. This doctrine would not regard it as a function of government to "make the citizens good" or simply to support such conceptions of goodness as they may happen to hold in common. According to it, there are certain minimal moral requisites for the proper performance of social and political duties. If these requisites are not met and the duties are improperly performed or not performed, then social life is debased and the form of government is endangered. Government may concern itself with morality, not in order to promote the virtuous character of individuals, but in order to prevent such a degree of vice as is incompatible with the health of society and the security of government. Paradoxically perhaps, Lord Devlin can also be cited as a proponent of this view. In his essay, "Mill on Liberty in Morals," he says:

> If apart from his assignable duties a man does not observe some standard of health and morality, society as a whole is impoverished, for such a man puts less than his share into the common well-being. The enforcement of an obligation of this sort can be distinguished from paternalism. The motive of paternalism is to do good to the individual: the motive of the other is to prevent the harm that would be done to society by the weakness or vice of too many of its members.[31]

It will be observed that this is not quite the same teaching as that embodied in the passages cited previously from Lord Devlin. The passage just quoted implies that there are certain human values or qualities of character which are generally advantageous and certain others which are always harmful to society, whatever may be the common beliefs prevailing in a particular society. If this is so, then the protection of a particular society's essential institutions may require something more (or something less) than the protection of whatever values a large majority of its members may happen to agree upon. Indeed, the latter will sometimes be incompatible with the former. The prevailing sense of right and wrong may be inadequate for the preservation of monogamy or some other "essentials of a society," or it may promote "vice" destructive of these essentials.

According to the argument now under consideration, the law is concerned with such morality as is a precondition for the willingness or capacity of men to contribute to the common tasks and interests of a community. The law is obliged to set such standards as will deter any large number of citizens from sinking below this level of morality. Devlin asserts:

> It is obvious that an individual may by unrestricted indulgence in vice so weaken himself that he ceases to be a useful member of society. It is obvious also that if a sufficient number of individuals so weaken themselves, society will thereby be weakened. . . . If the proportion grows sufficiently large, society will succumb either to its own disease or to external pressures. A nation of debauchees would not in 1940 have responded satisfactorily to Winston Churchill's call to blood and toil and sweat and tears.[32]

Those making this kind of argument seldom explain just what is meant by the "weakening" they speak of and how it is brought about. But their line of reasoning suggests two propositions. Excessive concern with the gratification of sensual desires, or extreme forms of such gratifications, weakens the higher faculties upon which self-control and social responsibility depend. And excessive preoccupation with sensual gratification results in the withdrawal of energies or interests from social concerns and their concentration upon selfish concerns. Thus a nation of thoroughgoing sensualists would not be able to respond to Churchill's call for sacrifice even if it wished to do so. The "citizens" would have lost the capacity to sacrifice immediate satisfaction to long-term ends. And they would be unwilling to do so. They would have lost the habit of taking an interest in the larger concerns of society. A nation can and must take measures to insure that its citizens will not sink to this subnormal and subpolitical level. In making its contribution to this end, the law would not take its bearings from the highest ethical norms, but from certain less rigorous standards of decency.

It would seem that this rationale harmonizes more easily with the principles and spirit of republican polity than do the first two rationales discussed above. Undoubted friends of liberal (though not libertarian) society have embraced it in one form or another.[33]

The argument that citizen responsibilities cannot be performed in the absence of certain virtues of self-discipline is most suitably addressed to polities in which the citizens participate in governing and in the making of public policy. A liberal government can be legitimately concerned with influences which undermine the moral requisites of its existence.

The point of view represented by Aristotle and by van den Haag appears to be less reconcilable with the liberal spirit. While the principles of the liberal polity need not be what libertarian writers say they are, it is a defining characteristic of such a polity that it seeks always to strike a balance in favor of liberty as against legal restraint. Laws passed with the avowed and explicit purpose of shaping character would not be well received by the liberal citizens. And laws passed for the sole purpose of preserving an existing ethos (whatever its contents) will be met by the criticism that the liberal mind is an open and not a closed mind.

It would appear that such censorship as is conducted in modern and liberal times cannot rely very heavily upon our first two rationales. Yet they cannot be reasonably ignored. For it can be argued that laws concerned with the prevention of widespread moral decay will not succeed in the absence of a more or less continuous concern with virtue. If citizens are taught that the promotion of good character is no function whatever of the political community, how are they likely to be affected by laws designed to prevent the grosser forms of moral debasement?

Further, the significance of common values—of a moral consensus—must be recognized even in a liberal society.[34] Communal life, at least decent communal life, requires mutual trust and respect. And it is a requisite for mutual trust and respect that certain fundamental attitudes and beliefs be held in common. No large body of men can be continuously bound together on the sole basis of the principle that values are a matter of personal choice. "The right to differ as to things that touch the heart of the existing order"[35] can be an important part of the public philosophy —but it cannot be the whole public philosophy or the first principle of it. This principle, if seriously adopted and acted upon as a first principle, could lead to such a diversification of choices and values as to render communal life extremely tenuous. Liberal societies do not, in fact, adopt "the right to differ" as the sole or most important item of their common faith. If decent social life requires that men believe something together, what they believe together must include a body of substantive values which are thought sufficiently important to warrant (at times) their imposition at the expense of dissent.*

The character of these values—what they are—is not, of course, irrelevant to the question of the legitimacy of their imposition. Van den Haag holds that the beliefs to which government lends its support need not be "true or demonstrably so." But if these beliefs are patently false (as are some doctrines of racism, for example) then an effort to support them by law can lead to the corruption of citizens—or to disrespect for law. If the morality to which the government lends its support is vicious, or irrational, or narrow and one-sided, similar results can be expected.

It is often the case, however, that salutary beliefs of great value to a community are not susceptible of proof. Many common

* There is a school of liberal thought which contends that common belief or moral consensus is neither necessary nor desirable in a free society. The arguments of this school are not convincing. Richard Wollheim says that in liberal doctrine "the identity, and the continuity, of a society resides not in the common possession of a single morality but in the mutual toleration of different moralities" ("Crime, Sin and Mr. Justice Devlin," p. 38). We may wonder what kind of mutual toleration would long sustain the "identity" of a society whose population is composed of dedicated Marxists, Fascists, and Constitutional-Democrats in equal proportions. Or, consider a society half of whose members believe in the sanctity of marriage and the sexual relation, while the other half are contemptuous of these values, believing instead in unlimited sensual gratification and in the desirability of public orgies. While such societies might survive in some sense, they could hardly be called communities. Groups of men deeply divided in their views of what is good will not trust or respect each other; their mutual suspicion or contempt will render sustained cooperation impossible. It is sometimes asserted that common belief on fundamental matters is unnecessary, because men in society are bound together, not by what they believe and value, but by their activities and institutions. For an example of this kind of argument, see Charles Frankel, *The Case for Modern Man* (New York: Harper & Brothers, 1955), chapter 5, "Liberal Society and Ultimate Values." Says Frankel: "The mutual understandings and common loyalties that sustain a social order emerge out of men's daily habits and routines, out of the concrete institutions that frame their lives," not out of common opinions and values (p. 84). Frankel does not undertake to explain how a people's social routines and institutions can be separated from and understood apart from its opinions and values. The various arguments denying the significance of moral consensus have one thing in common—their depreciation of the importance of what men think and believe.

opinions concerning the sanctity of sex, marriage, and the family, or concerning the dignity of human personality and the respect due it are not "demonstrably true." Perhaps it would be more accurate to say that decent convictions about these matters are often associated with and supported by numerous beliefs and attitudes which are questionable in the light of scientific or other knowledge. If government is to be allowed to lend its support to any community convictions, its support cannot be rigidly confined to those the validity of which can clearly be demonstrated.

Thus, there is a case to be made for legal protection of a community's particular virtues—if these have some reasonable connection with standards of good and bad which are more universally recognized. But for our times the most important argument to be made is that concerning the need for public standards designed to maintain the minimal moral requisites of decency, social responsibility, and citizenship.

It is often observed that standards of morality and immorality, obscenity and non-obscenity, differ widely from culture to culture. In some societies kissing in public is prohibited, while in others public acts of coitus are performed as religious ceremonies.[36] But, as anthropologist Margaret Mead observes, "every known human society exercises some explicit censorship over behavior relating to the human body, especially as that behavior involves or may involve sex."[37] There is no known society in which matters relating to sex and the human body are left wholly unregulated. And there is no known society in which the regulation of these things is left wholly to individuals or to spontaneous social activity.

The proper treatment of the physical or sensual side of life is a crucial and universal social problem. Says Mead: "Society has two problems—how to keep sex activity out of forbidden channels that will endanger the bodies and souls of others or the orderly co-operative processes of social life, *and* how to keep it flowing reliably in those channels where it is necessary if children are to be conceived and reared in homes where father and mother are tied together by the requisite amount of sexual interest"[38] (italics in original).

All human societies deal with these matters in essentially the same way: they establish public moral standards which are made binding on their members. These standards dictate what sexual acts may be performed and with whom; they establish the distinction between physical acts which may be done in public and those which may be done only in private; and they govern to some extent permissible verbal expression about such matters. My point here is twofold: (1) these standards have the character of *public* standards—they are imposed by society as such; and (2) these standards have the character of *moral* standards—violation of them is supposed to be attended by the appropriate feelings of guilt, shame, or disgust.

Why do we need to have public standards of decency? The issues which are the subject of such standards are highly perplexing and disturbing to the great majority of mankind. They concern the control and direction of powerful passions, the determination of the proper relation between the physical, social, and spiritual sides of life, and the moral judgments which are implicit in such terms as "higher" and "lower." No man (or very few) can resolve these problems alone, on the basis of his own private reasoning. Nor can he resolve them on the basis of a spontaneous "free exchange of ideas" with others. Therefore, we will always require some authoritative pronouncements on such subjects as: the proper character of the family, the nature of the marriage bond, the duties and rights of married persons, the human meaning of sex and its relation to love, and the extent to which the human body and its various functions should be revealed or concealed in public. In matters so problematic, men rely upon guidance from the community in which they live. They need public standards.

But why should public moral standards require the support of law? Why can we not rely for their promulgation and maintenance upon society or the community?

Whatever may be the case in primitive communities, in civilized communities "society" is not an autonomous, self-regulating entity. Society does not resolve its problems autonomously without authoritative direction. In civilized times it is the political community which most effectively represents the common ends and interests of society, and the political community characteristically acts by means of law. Indeed, in the absence of the political community and its laws, it would be most difficult to locate, amid the complex diversities which characterize modern life, anything deserving the name of "the society" or "the community."

Society as such cannot censor morals. Strictly speaking, society as such cannot make decisions and act purposively. Thus, when it is said that "censorship should be the proper activity of the community rather than the law,"[39] this can reasonably mean only that the contemporary public opinion should do it, the family should do it, or the church should do it. It is not to be denied that these can be influential agencies promoting moral restraint or ethical training. But are they alone capable of performing the community's civilizing and moralizing functions? And can they perform these functions without the support of law?

If public opinion is to be a moral influence, from whence is public opinion to receive its moral guidance? It is well known that on particular issues—the "issues of the day"—public opinion is often unstable, uncertain, and transitory. Ill-defined feelings and half-formed attitudes tend to become public opinion when positions are taken by influential persons—including statesmen, lawmakers, and judges. The formation of public opinion is profoundly influenced by action or positions taken in government and by laws —past, present, and prospective.

There is a more stable and more continuous "underlying" public opinion. Such opinion has more than one source, but surely one of its most important sources is to be found in tradition and customs which have been supported by (if not engendered by) the fundamental laws and principles of the country. Continuing public attitudes on many subjects (e.g., the rights of private property) may be traced in this manner to the Constitution and to the attitudes and decisions of such political men as Alexander Hamilton and John Marshall.

I dwell upon these commonplaces only in order to make the point that public opinion cannot be relied upon as if it were a self-dependent moral agent. The long-term or underlying public attitudes are what they are largely because of the context of social and political traditions in which they are formed. The public looks, in part, to the country's customs and laws for ethical and intellectual guidance. If there is now a body of public attitudes in support of moral decency, this must be, to a large extent, because there have been positions taken in the past in support of moral decency—positions resulting in or fostered by law. One may at least wonder what contemporary attitudes on moral matters would be if there had been no such decisions and no such laws.

Like the various public opinions, the family is but a part of civil society and is subject to the influences predominant therein. It would not be reasonable to expect "the home" to produce morally decent children if indecency prevailed in the society around it. The education promoted in the home could not withstand the influence of the surrounding moral environment, nor could the family as an institution avoid the effects of such an environment. For instance, the institution of monogamous marriage as we know it presupposes and requires some commitment to sexual fidelity. This is not to say that any lapse whatever from this commitment must be regarded as a "sin" which destroys a marriage. But, at least, there must be a belief in the obligation of faithfulness and efforts to live up to that obligation, if the family is to have the significance and perform the tasks which traditionally belong to it in our society. If, in the community at large, the commitment to fidelity as a norm were replaced by radical promiscuity, monogamy could not long retain its character. And the new institution, whatever moral training it might provide, could hardly continue to be a teacher of sexual fidelity. The family is not an autonomous social force capable of independently generating and sustaining values.

Traditionally, religious institutions have been such a source of values. For a number of reasons, they no longer have the political stature, the social influence, or the moral authority to perform for the community the civilizing functions which it requires.[40] The churches can teach morality, and they can lend their support to social movements concerned with morality, but they cannot be relied upon as a predominant influence upon character in modern society.

It is quite true that the social agencies under consideration are those most directly concerned with the promotion of virtue or decency. But inquiry shows that their success or failure is dependent upon factors or forces in society at large which they do not control.*

The community, then, cannot rely solely upon public opinion, the family, and the church to promulgate and maintain its public

---

* It is interesting to note that, while libertarian authors are insisting upon the exclusive moral role of family and church, increasing numbers of parents and churchmen are appealing to the law for support against obscenity. See chapter 1, *supra*. In general, see the Gathings, Kefauver, and Granahan Committee Reports.

morality. These agencies can shape the values which prevail in society, but, to a greater extent, they are shaped by these values.

Therefore, it must be a task of modern government and law to support and promote the public morality upon which a good social life depends. Censorship can serve this end in two ways: (1) by preventing or reducing some of the most corrupt influences and (2) by holding up an authoritative standard for the guidance of opinions and judgment.

Legitimate censorship is not designed to prevent the circulation of all literature which might have an immoral influence. It aims primarily at the most vicious materials. And it seeks, not directly to shape mind and character, but to contain some of those influences in modern society which shape mind and character in harmful ways. The effects of censorship upon these influences are not confined to the specific books or motion pictures which the censor condemns. Its more significant effects are those of deterrence. Publishers are deterred from publishing, and authors from writing, materials which cannot legally be circulated. Thus the results of legal censorship consist not in the confiscation of the relatively few obscene publications which the censor catches, but in the general reduction in the circulation of materials of that kind.

Laws against obscene publications may have a more subtle and, perhaps, more profound consequence. Such laws announce a moral decision of the community arrived at and issued through its official organs. They assert, in effect, that the organized community draws a line between the decent and the indecent, the permissible and the impermissible. Individuals may, of course, step over the line, but they are made aware that there is such a line. They are made aware that the community is committed to a distinction between what is right and what is not. In the long run this awareness must have an effect upon the moral attitudes and values of most people.

The coercive and preventing functions of censorship are thus supplemented by its hortatory and educative functions. Or perhaps it would be more correct to say that the latter are supplemented by the former. Libertarian authors are inclined to speak as if punishment were the heart of all legal censorship. They are inclined to refer to censorship exclusively as "the legal enforcement of morality." But there are some forms of censorship which do not involve criminal proceedings and need not involve any punishment at all. This is the case when the law employs purely administrative or civil proceedings for the condemnation or confiscation of obscene materials. Here the purveyor will receive no legal penalties unless he defies the orders of a court. And when the criminal law is used, punishment and the threat of punishment, while serving as a deterrent to specific acts against morality, are subordinate means to the larger educative ends. By its willingness to punish some violations of its morality, the community indicates that it is serious about that morality. Conceivably, a community could officially promulgate ethical standards without the slightest efforts to use coercion in support of them. It is all too likely that such standards would not be taken with sufficient seriousness by those most in need of guidance. Willingness to use coercion in their support is surely a prime indicator of the significance which society attaches to its various principles and purposes.[41] We do not know of any political community which has relied upon simple promulgation and exhortation for the implementation of its principles.

Laws against obscenity or other forms of vice serve to render community standards authoritative. They can also serve to clarify and define such standards. One need not presuppose that there would be no criteria of decency whatever in the absence of legislation. Individuals and groups do, obviously, have moral attitudes and values which they have not received from government. But attitudes and values which arise in "society" tend often to be vague, over-general, and contradictory. Individuals and social groups do not easily succeed in establishing the precise applications and limits of those general principles they hold in common. These principles, then, seldom constitute a clear and agreed-upon boundary line between decent and indecent activity. The law contributes to the drawing of boundary lines by its definition of such terms as "obscenity." The law thus helps to transform indistinct, indefinite, and personal moral feelings into public standards.

In the absence of public norms thus established, social attitudes (or public opinion) may remain ill-defined, inconclusive, and ineffectual. Or, they may vacillate between extremes of moral indifference and moralistic zealotry. As legal censorship is relaxed, the private standards of many citizens may also be relaxed. Other citizens may be aroused to replace legal censorship with a form of censorship considerably more repressive. Many authors have observed that as legal censorship is restricted the censorship activities of private groups tend often to increase.* And these groups can be far less discriminating in their moral and aesthetic judgments than is the law.

Communal standards, properly formulated, promulgated, and enforced will inhibit the emergence—and perhaps prevent the ascendancy—of immoderate or unreasonable private standards. A public moral philosophy, supported in part by law, can profoundly affect the dispositions and opinions by which social life is shaped. It can encourage civil or reasonable dispositions and opinions, and it can discourage those which are uncivil or unreasonable.

Can it be truly said that the organized community has no right to be thus concerned with the minds of citizens, with their "inner lives"? And can it be reasonably said that the operation of law must be strictly confined to overt antisocial conduct or to considerations of peace and security?

I have presented arguments showing that the political community cannot be indifferent to the moral values and the moral character of its members and why it cannot rely simply upon nonpolitical institutions to sustain values and character at a moral level consistent with its needs. Public standards are required, and private agencies cannot be confidently relied upon to provide them. In the absence of legal and political support, the capacity of such agencies to provide a communal morality would depend upon the many diverse influences—economic, social, psychological, and intellectual—which make them what they are. If civil society requires certain virtues in its members, it cannot afford to leave this to the determination of fortuitous circumstances and chance influences.

Of course, the law can punish indecent acts. This is the policy recommended to it by opponents of censorship—you may punish wrongful conduct, but you must never do anything involving the slightest degree of coercion to influence men's values or the char-

* Morris Ernst reports: "The great irony, however, is that while courts are restricting the powers of government in the field of so-called obscenity, the 'vigilantism' of private groups is on the increase. By 'vigilantism,' here, we are referring to all forms of essentially private pressure attempting to regulate what we read and see." *Censorship: The Search for the Obscene*, pp. 233–34. Ernst does not reflect very deeply upon this "irony."

acter of their private lives. But the threat of legal coercion will not sufficiently deter indecent acts when little attention has been given to the conditions which breed indecent men. If the law must restrain immoral conduct, then it cannot be indifferent to the influences which break down moral standards, weakening their hold upon conduct. If political society were to adopt a policy of legal coercion plus moral indifference, if it would seek by coercion to prevent immoral conduct while remaining neutral toward immoral character, two possible results are predictable. The penalties for bad conduct would have to be considerably increased; the coercive functions of the law would have to be made more effective. Or, the categories of punishable acts would have to be considerably reduced; society would have to lower its standards of conduct. If society is interested in the prevention of acts contrary to its moral standards, then it is neither reasonable nor safe to require it to wait until the acts have been done or are about to be done. A community with a large number of vicious citizens will have to control them by force—or the effort to control them will have to be abandoned.

Long before such a state of affairs is reached, the community is deeply interested in the morality of its citizens. Civilized social life requires not only that men observe certain decencies, but also that they believe in them. And political life requires not only that men perform certain duties, but also that they believe in them. The political education of every nation testifies to this communal interest in the minds, dispositions, and beliefs of its citizens.

These considerations are not less compelling when applied to the sensual or the sexual side of life. Every community must devote its attention to the discipline and direction of powerful natural impulses. Every social order must endeavor to give the sensual side of life its due while preventing undue or excessive preoccupation with it. The minds and energies of citizens must be available for the long-range pursuits and higher ends of the community. This requires socially imposed restraints upon the indulgence of the passions and, also, socially imposed standards and values concerning the indulgence of the passions.* Since the community cannot be indifferent to what its members do about

* For a statement of these propositions in psychoanalytic terms, see Freud, *Civilization and Its Discontents.*

the physical side of life, it cannot be wholly indifferent to what they feel and believe about it. Censorship of some kind or degree is implicit in these propositions.

There is a point of view on sex and society which is directly contrary to that expressed here and which is not without influence in our times. According to it, the public standards and socially imposed restraints of which this essay speaks are largely unnecessary. They can and ought to be reduced to bare minimum, if not abolished entirely. Such standards and restraints are held to be the causes of much of man's social and psychological ills. They place heavy restrictions upon the healthy satisfaction of natural desires; they promote guilt, fear, and repression, and they deny man that happiness which results from the spontaneous expression of his feelings and wants. Present-day morality should be replaced by an attitude toward sex which is highly tolerant and flexible, which de-emphasizes moral considerations, and which maximizes considerations of personal taste, personal choice, and personal satisfaction.[42]

Proponents of this view look forward to a "sexual revolution" which they see already in progress. They envision a "healthy," permissive society in which sexual relations are to be largely, or wholly, spontaneous and unregulated. They affirm as a first principle: "Man's right to use his body and his sexual organs in complete freedom as long as this occurs without violence, constraint or fraud against another person."[43]

While individuals may adopt this as a personal ethic, it is very doubtful that it could ever become, or long remain, the operating principle of a *civil society*. And even if it were possible for a society to adopt this as a governing principle, it is questionable that such a society could lay claim to the attributes of civilization. The healthy, permissive society may facilitate the spontaneous expression of desires and feelings, but would it promote the cultivation and education of its members?

Civilization has always been understood to involve the discipline and direction of natural or primary impulses. Civilization has always been understood to involve a moral and social organization of sexual life which does not rest simply upon considerations of personal enjoyment and personal self-expression. Says Margaret Mead: "It [the sexual problem] will never be solved, as some enthusiasts think, by spreading a 'sane, healthy attitude toward sex,' summed up in such home truths as 'Play, play with boys and girls all *together,* live in the sunshine.' " She continues: "Some patterning, some mystery is necessary. . . . Absence of pattern is unthinkable; without it human creatures, hardly to be called human beings, would vacillate between promiscuity and boredom, and society would be impossible to maintain."[44]

This is not to say that the socially imposed "patterns" should be harsh and repressive. It is neither necessary nor desirable that our communal standards embody the opinions of Victorians. But society must have some model of approved and nonapproved, esteemed and nonesteemed sexual behavior which reflects ends broader than those of individual satisfaction. In the absence of such values and distinctions, strongly affirmed and sometimes enforced by the community, it is difficult to see how social life could attain any coherence or how children could grow up without confusion and disorder in the soul. It is well known that children require for their personal development models of the honorable and the dishonorable, whatever some of our youth may say they need. As yet, there are few parents who are willing to provide their children with no guidance except the guidance—"choose for yourself." But in a society which affirms nothing except individual spontaneity, most parents would be unable to provide anything more.*

We know of no civil society which has yet established its fundamental law or ethical code upon the affirmation that any man may do just as he likes and live just as he pleases as long as he avoids "violence, constraint or fraud." This is hardly a mere accident of history, for the human community is always interested in something more than the prevention of violence, constraint, and fraud.

---

* This discussion of the "permissiveness and spontaneity" school of thought may call to mind the writings of Paul Goodman, who has been a strong critic of contemporary sexual ethics and an apparent advocate of the "sexual revolution." But it appears that what Goodman really advocates is "structured permissiveness" which he explains as follows: "permissiveness so that he [the child] can act without fear, shame and resentment, and learn by his mistakes; and a structure of firm parental morals and culture . . . with which he can identify when, in his anxiety and confusion, he needs security and guidance." Paul Goodman, *Utopian Essays and Practical Proposals,* p. 51. I submit that this serious thinker has not thought seriously enough about the indispensable prerequisites for the "structure" side of structured permissiveness.

Civil society cannot afford to be neutral toward the various forms and degrees of human sensuality which may emerge within it. It has a stake in the encouragement of some kinds of pleasures and desires and the discouragement of others. There can be, therefore, no absolute separation between the political and the sensual sides of life. Government cannot be wholly unconcerned with the sensual side of life.

It is often suggested that free society is exempt from these considerations and that the growth of political freedom necessarily involves increasing sexual liberty. The Kronhausens write: "Sexual freedom can be the privilege only of a free society. . . . The more actual democracy a society allows, the more sexual freedom is granted to its members."[45]

It is true that a free society seeks to confine the role of public authority and to provide broad scope for independent thought and action in such matters. But, though the role of public authority can be confined, it cannot be abolished; the latitude for freedom of thought and action can be broad, but it cannot be boundless. Free men still require external assistance in the control of their passions, and they still require public standards to guide them in the exercise of judgment on perplexing moral issues. Freedom itself may create problems which render such guidance all the more necessary.

Democracy cannot be characterized simply as the maximization of individual liberty in every area of life. And there are attributes and requisites of republican government which are not adequately expressed in the single word "freedom." The enterprise of self-government requires mutual respect and certain capacities for self-restraint, or, as these things used to be called, "civility." It depends upon a citizen body the members of which will devote their energies to long-range public interests and who can, when necessary, sacrifice personal comforts and personal satisfactions, perhaps personal happiness, for vital public interests. A people devoted exclusively to the satisfaction of sensual appetites is not, strictly speaking, a citizen body at all. It is a collection of private individuals, each concerned with his private gratifications.

Such individuals will not or cannot adequately fulfill their citizen responsibilities. Men who do not learn how to control their own appetites will not be able, or will not be willing, to control the government. And their relentless pursuit of self-centered gratifications produces interpersonal conflicts and social problems which provide a fertile field for the expansion of centralized government. The strivings and demands of undisciplined men create problems with which government must attempt to deal; problems which might not arise, or which would be soluble, among disciplined and public-spirited men. To the extent that individuals do not govern themselves, they must be governed by some external agency. Such men may be perfectly satisfied to let the government manage all public affairs, and many private affairs, as long as it provides them with opportunities for their personal pursuit of pleasures. This state of affairs would not be "actual democracy," though it might be "sexual freedom."

It is on the basis of considerations such as these that some political philosophers have emphasized the special connection between political freedom and moral virtue and have insisted that republican laws must address themselves to the maintenance of virtue.* A republic can and ought to concern itself with social influences which promote qualities of mind and character contrary to those necessary for its continued existence. It can take steps to provide that its citizens will not become a nation of sensualists. It need not sanction unlimited sexual freedom. It can make laws forbidding the circulation of the most corrupting kinds of salacious literature. And it can support, by means of law, those public standards of civility which are the foundation of good citizenship.

---

* Speaking of virtue in a republican state, Montesquieu says: "The love of our country is conducive to a purity of morals, and the latter is again conducive to the former. The less we are able to satisfy our private passions, the more we abandon ourselves to those of a general nature." *The Spirit of the Laws* (New York: Hafner, 1949), p. 40. Rousseau speaks frequently of "republican austerity." See his "Letter to d'Alembert"; see also his "Discourse on the Arts and Sciences" and "Discourse on Political Economy." Our own founding fathers were quite aware of this connection between moral character and republican freedom. Jefferson often spoke of "virtue" as an indispensable ingredient in the health of the republic. In a letter to Madison he affirmed that the will of the majority can be safely relied upon "as long as we remain virtuous." Thomas Jefferson, *The Living Thoughts of Thomas Jefferson,* ed. John Dewey, p. 56. In his Farewell Address, President Washington said: "Of all the dispositions and habits which lead to political prosperity, religion and morality are indispensable supports." Contemporary libertarian authors, while frequently appealing to the free-speech principles of the founders, consistently neglect this aspect of the founders' teachings and philosophy.

By the imposition of restraints such as these, republican government contributes to the cultivation of citizens who can wisely exercise freedom of choice in their private affairs and in their public affairs. Republican citizens are subjected to a mild form of moral discipline so that they will not have to be subjected to physical coercion. If this is a paradox, it is one which republicans can and ought to accept.

The foregoing arguments constitute, in this author's view, the essentials of the rationale for censorship. This statement of the rationale would not be complete, however, if it did not address itself more explicitly to one of the oldest and most persistent criticisms made against it.

In 1857, during the Parliamentary debate over Lord Campbell's Act, for the confiscation of obscene publications, a member of the House asserted that "a more preposterous bill had never been sent down from the House of Lords and that was saying a great deal. It was an attempt to make people virtuous by Act of Parliament."[46] Men cannot be made virtuous by law, or—to use the standard terminology—"You cannot legislate morality."

It is not always clear just what is intended to be conveyed by this proposition. There are three possibilities. You cannot legislate morality because: (1) If people want to do the immoral acts they will find a way to do them no matter what the law says. More precisely, laws against obscenity merely drive it "underground" where those who want it will find it. (2) Men do not become virtuous by compulsion. Genuine virtue must be the result of voluntary action. (3) The law cannot succeed in imposing a standard of morality higher than that which prevails in the community. Such morality as the law seeks to apply can be only that prevailing in the society of which the law is a part.

The first argument is highly speculative. It seems to presuppose that people will always find a way to do just exactly what they want to do and that the law is impotent to affect the desires that men have or to place impediments in the way of their satisfaction. I have suggested some of the ways in which obscenity laws can affect attitudes, and ultimately desires, and some of the ways in which they can obstruct the satisfaction of prurient interests. It is true that legislation cannot succeed in totally obliterating obscenity as long as people have a taste for it. A pornographic underworld will continue in business. But this argument is not as formidable as it is supposed to be. Effective laws will render obscenity much more difficult to obtain than it would otherwise be. The inveterate addict may manage to surmount the difficulties. The majority of those who are exposed to obscenity, or would be if there were no laws, are not, or are not yet, inveterate addicts.

But it is sometimes asserted that laws against obscenity only serve to arouse the desire for obscenity and stimulate efforts to obtain it. Official disapproval or restraint of prurience is held to be a primary cause of prurience. This is a variation of the "forbidden fruit" argument, which has some valid application to human affairs, as everyone knows. But to apply this as a sweeping generalization to all moral censorship and to regard it as the decisive factor outweighing all others, one would have to indulge oneself in some considerable assumptions about the way most people are constituted. It has not been demonstrated that most people are inveterate rebels against law and authority. And there are, after all, some evils in human affairs which are not the result of restraints imposed by law and authority.

It cannot be reasonably supposed that the average person will make every effort to acquire the "forbidden fruit," no matter how effectively or by what authority it is forbidden. The assumption that he will do so rests upon a view of human nature and motivation considerably more speculative than that upon which obscenity laws are based.

Maurice Girodias of the Olympia Press announces that "pornography is simply a consequence of censorship. Suppress censorship and pornography will disappear."[47] The observation is relevant that in recent decades the legal control of obscenity in the United States has been steadily relaxed, and the results are far from those that Girodias purports to expect.

The second argument—that compulsion cannot produce virtue —contains a truth which, however, has little relevance to any legitimate purposes of censorship. It is not to be denied that the highest or most genuine forms of virtue result from virtuous choices and voluntary self-discipline and not from fear of punishment. But the capacity for voluntary self-discipline and right choice does not arise by itself, independently of environment and training. Of those men who can choose the right without any external guidance, the vast majority have learned to do so through a long process of moral training and habituation. They have been exposed to a moral environment in which the good predominates over the bad, and they have at times been forced to refrain from undesirable acts. Such censorship as can lay claim to reasonableness does not purport to be a sufficient cause of virtue. It seeks only to affect the balance of good and evil in the moral environment by withdrawing some of the evil. To deter pornographers from interfering with this project, it threatens to punish them. The law does not coerce the pornographer in the hope of thereby making him good. It coerces him as a deterrent to pornographers and as a reaffirmation of its moral standard.

Law cannot force men to be good, but it can prevent some of the worst forms of evil, and it can point the way toward moral improvement by holding up a standard somewhat higher than that upon which many persons are acting. This moralizing role of law is exemplified in some recent American judicial history. The desegregation decisions of the United States Supreme Court[48] have had significant effects upon moral attitudes, values, and beliefs of many Americans. Of course, some have not been influenced by the decisions, and some have only reacted by intensifying racist attitudes. But as is indicated by the successful passage of civil rights legislation, a large number of Americans have been moved to regard this as a crucial moral issue. In this matter there are no grounds for asserting that the Court's decisions simply registered the strongly held convictions of the great majority. The decisions of the Court seem actually to have played a role in the formation and crystallization of ethical attitudes and moral feelings.

Finally, it is said that the morality on the basis of which the law acts can only be derived from the community in which it acts. Says Benjamin Cardozo: "Law accepts as the pattern of its justice the morality of the community whose conduct it assumes to regulate."[49] This proposition is, in part, an admonition to judges to refrain from imposing their own private moral values upon the public. It can also function as an admonition to lawmakers to refrain from attempting to impose on the community moral dictates which its members cannot possibly obey or which they are unlikely to obey. The law must not attempt to force upon the community ethical standards which are alien to it or which are too high to govern conduct in that community. In the performance of their ethical function judges and lawmakers must take account of contemporary community standards and contemporary social conditions. Failure to do so can result in widespread disobedience and disrespect for law, or it can result in human suffering.

It need not be presupposed, however, that the law must simply register or reflect the values actually prevailing in society and implicit in the conduct of its members. The law need not simply ratify the conduct of the majority; it can aim higher than that. Cardozo asserts:

> My own notion is that [the judge] would be under a duty to conform to the accepted standards of the community, the *mores* of the times. This does not mean, however, that a judge is power- less to raise the level of prevailing conduct. In one field or an- other of activity, practices in opposition to the sentiments and standards of the age may grow up and threaten to entrench them- selves if not dislodged. Despite their temporary hold, they do not stand comparison with accepted norms of morals. Indolence or passivity has tolerated what the considerate judgment of the com- munity condemns. In such cases, one of the highest functions of the judge is to establish the true relation between conduct and profession.[50]

The law may endeavor to raise the moral level of conduct which falls short of community standards even though the com- munity tolerates such conduct. If the legal definition of obscenity were to be determined on the basis of this principle, the judge would not have to exclude from the definition all forms of salacity which the community is willing to tolerate. He could hold up a higher moral standard based on an assessment of the real "senti- ments and standards of the age." But how does a judge determine what are the real sentiments and standards? And how is such a determination related to his ethical role? And in what way or to what extent is the moral function of the law confined to a ratifica- tion of the strongest or most genuine convictions of the age? Chap- ter 7 explores these questions in connection with the problem of contemporary community standards.

The idea that you cannot make people virtuous by an act of parliament is valid—if interpreted in a manner that renders it irrelevant to the rationale for censorship. It is not asserted that "parliament" can make men good by passing laws which com- mand them to become such. But the idea is usually employed to suggest that law can make no contribution to the virtue of men.

It implies that men are made good or bad by conditions in "society." For their moral improvement we must wait for "social progress" or for "changes in the minds and hearts of men." As far as the law is concerned, this view tends to see it as confronting men of two types: those who are already good and therefore will not be interested in obscenity, and those who are already predisposed to be interested in obscenity and cannot possibly be deflected from this interest. This simplistic view of human affairs is not a significant argument against the rationale for censorship.

The rationale for censorship conflicts sharply with the principles of John Stuart Mill and with the libertarian doctrines which are the offspring of these principles. But does it conflict sharply with the necessary and essential principles of liberal society and liberal government? It has been suggested here that the true definition of a liberal society need not be in every respect what libertarian authors say it is. I have argued that free society and republican government cannot wholly dispense with the function of censorship and with the purposes it serves. Finally, I have suggested that some doctrines and purposes of censorship can be more easily reconciled with liberalism than others.

Yet, even after these observations and qualifications have been made, there would still seem to be a considerable tension between the aims of censorship, as presented here, and liberalism, as it is usually understood. For, upon examination, it is evident that such censorship as can be rationally defended does not simply aim at the prevention of harmful conduct, or simply at the prevention of the grosser forms of social and psychological injury. Censorship performs some of its most important functions when it seeks to restrict influences which harmfully affect the wellsprings of conduct—the values and sensibilities, the mind and the character of men.

This harsh fact cannot be avoided by an assertion that: "To restrain the circulation of obscenity does not prevent any idea from being discussed and circulated. No book is obscene because of the ideas it contains, but rather from the way in which the matter is expressed."[51] It is true that the modern censorship of obscenity does not aim at "ideas" as such. Nor is it a kind of thought control, seeking to regulate the thoughts and feelings of citizens. These points are sufficient to meet and refute some of the less subtle and less discriminating of the libertarian criticisms of censorship. But, if the rationale presented here is valid, censorship does seek, ultimately, to have an effect upon attitudes, upon dispositions—emotional and intellectual—and even upon moral opinion. It does seek, at least, to control influences which have such effects. Thus, the rationale for censorship significantly involves government and law in the mental and moral life of man.

This essay does not undertake a comprehensive definition of "liberalism" or "liberal society." But it is evident that there is some tension between this involvement of government in the moral life and the liberal conception of what is public and what is private. The tension is not at great as libertarian writers allege, but it is there.

This fact is not a sufficient reason for the abandonment of all moral censorship. Our country is not only liberal—it is also democratic; it is also constitutional; it is also civilized. Our country is a liberal democracy, but it is also a civil society subject to the needs and purposes of civil life.

The foregoing interpretation of these needs and purposes leads to the conclusion that it is impossible to draw a firm and unchanging boundary line to separate what is public and what is private business and to define once and for all the limits of governmental activity. It is impossible to mark out in absolute terms and in detail certain moral enclaves into which the law is forever forbidden to enter regardless of the circumstances. For the moral character of society is a matter of vital public interest, and variable circumstances differentially affect that moral character.

But the values of privacy and freedom of the mind, so profoundly emphasized in the greatest liberal writings, must be respected and preserved. And there is good reason for careful attention to the operations and limits of an institution like censorship which is at variance with some of our most strongly held beliefs and with some of our most deeply engrained practices. I have, from time to time in these pages, suggested various criteria by which censorship in our society should be judged and delimited. Here these are assembled and, with some additions, offered as a body of general principles and guidelines.

A liberal society seeks to strike a balance in favor of free expression as against governmental restraint. Therefore, claims for the restraint of free expression must be subject to careful scrutiny.

They must be argued and justified. If the law seeks to influence opinion, this influence must be indirect. The government may not formulate an ideology and seek to impose it by law. When the law supports moral standards it must not endeavor to impose upon society standards alien to it or the standards of some particular group. Its legal standards should be flexible enough to take account of changes in social conditions and in community values.

Democratic principle requires that censorship operations and the criteria utilized in them should be open to public scrutiny. Democracy also requires that elected officials should from time to time look into the activities of censors and review the operations of the system.

The First Amendment requires that there shall be no censorship of genuine ideas about sex and related matters, or genuine argument concerning sexual morals—*or,* it requires a "clear and present danger" standard for the legal control of such ideas and argument. Further, it requires that the law take serious account of literary and other "redeeming social values." It is true that, where these principles are respected, the prevailing moral order is always in danger of peaceful overthrow or dissolution as a result of critical discussion and questioning. Public moral standards can be powerfully affected and eventually undermined by intellectual controversy over their fundamental premises. Thus, in the long run, the threat posed to the communal ethics by ideas and arguments contrary to it may be greater than the threat posed by obscenity and pornography. This risk is inherent in liberal democracy. Liberal democracy cannot undertake to deal with this kind of danger by means of censorship.

Due process of law requires that definitions of obscenity be arrived at (as much as possible) by rational processes and that definitions arrived at in lower courts be subject to review in federal courts and by the Supreme Court. Due process also requires that there be as much precision as is feasible in the definition of crimes associated with obscenity. Where the requisite precision cannot be obtained, civil proceedings against obscene publications are to be preferred to criminal proceedings.

A pluralist society endeavors to satisfy all the major social purposes and public interests of the community. Where these conflict, it seeks to weigh and balance diverse interests or values and to arrive at a reconciliation which does not wholly sacrifice any valid social aim. This is not to say that a pluralist society will accord equal respect to all values or ends with which any of its members may happen to be associated or that it will recognize as legitimate whatever is pursued as desirable by some sufficiently large "group." Some people value sado-masochistic experiences, and the Mafia or Syndicate is a large group. A viable pluralist society cannot be one in which all desires are equal and "anything goes." But genuine pluralism recognizes that the common good involves diverse goods, all of which are entitled to some accommodation.

There are public interests in morality and in freedom of expression, in the circulation of literature and in the preservation of certain community norms. To the greatest extent possible, obscenity should be defined and censorship conducted in such a way that real moral evils are attacked, genuine literature is protected, and community convictions are respected.

6

Definitions of Obscenity
and the Nature of the Obscene

Thus far I have been writing of "obscenity" without any systematic attention to the precise definition of the term or to the nature of the phenomena to which it refers. The concepts of obscenity relied upon in preceding chapters have been largely those appearing in ordinary discourse, public controversy, and legal decisions about the subject. While these may be adequate in the contexts in which they appear, they do not definitively answer the question: What is "obscene" and why?

Dictionary definitions of the term usually trace its etymology to the Latin *ob-caenum,* meaning "filth." Some commentators hold that the term originally designated that which is "off the scene"—not to be openly shown on the stage of life.[1] But what constitutes "filth"? And what things ought or ought not to be given public exhibition?

The fact that the answers to these questions are many and diverse has led some commentators to the conclusion that obscenity cannot be defined at all. Says Morris Ernst: "Many courts and commentators have attempted to define the concept; all have inevitably failed."[2] An Ohio state court has asserted:

> Obscenity is not a legal term. It cannot be defined so that it will mean the same to all people, all the time, everywhere. Obscenity is very much a figment of the imagination—an indefinable something in the minds of some and not in the minds of others, and it is not the same in the minds of the people of every clime and country, nor the same today that it was yesterday and will be tomorrow.[3]

There are others who flatly deny that obscenity is impossible or even difficult to define. They hold that everyone really knows what obscenity is. Pennsylvania Supreme Court Justice Michael Musmanno asks:

> What is indefinite about the word "obscene"? It is as indefinite as the word "cat." I doubt that there is a newspaper reader, radio listener or television watcher, no matter how meager his education or how much a stranger to books, who does not know the meaning of the word "obscene."[4]

It is a purpose of this chapter to show that obscenity is not impossible to define, though there are good reasons why its meaning can never be as obvious and as definite as that of the word "cat." To define something is to set forth its distinguishing or essential characteristics. The effort to do this for obscenity encounters two difficulties—one concerning precision or exactitude, and one concerning agreement or consensus. The latter difficulty is more formidable than the former.

Some scholars have succeeded in setting forth with a fair degree of precision what, in their view, is the essence of the obscene. But those who address themselves to the subject differ in their statements of what the essentials are. These differences arise, in part, from the fact that explicit concepts of obscenity are rooted in human experiences which are ultimately moral experiences. Moral values and moral perspectives are inevitably involved in the shaping of those human experiences out of which definitions of obscenity arise. Men do not succeed in defining their experiences of good and bad with scientific rigor, nor do they attain scientific certitude about their moral values. Therefore we continue to have different and divergent concepts of obscenity.

But these facts need not lead to the conclusion that nothing intelligible can be said about the subject and that any definition of obscenity is just as valid or invalid as any other. The term "obscenity" does refer to something that men experience. The various concepts of it do have something in common; they do have certain common attributes and elements which point, however indirectly, to an underlying human phenomenon. This discussion will begin with an explication of two such concepts which are systematically developed and applied to literature. Its ultimate objective is to present an interpretation of those factors and experiences which account for the endurance of the obscene in human life and to develop from these some criteria for the judgment of literature. Let us approach various definitions and conceptions of obscenity with two questions in view. (1) What do they contribute to our understanding of the nature of obscenity in literature and in life? and (2) To what extent can they be embodied in legal standards applicable to the problems and the needs of political society?

Some of the most systematic work in this area is that contributed by scholars in the Roman Catholic tradition. As Harold Gardiner, S.J., interprets that tradition, it requires that restrictions on liberty be "strictly" defined.[5] Therefore, he endeavors to present a precisely delimited concept of obscenity which would apply only to certain strictly defined sexual influences. He sets forth the essence of the Catholic definition in these terms: "It [obscenity] consists in the intrinsic tendency or bent of a work to arouse sexual passion, or, to put it more concretely, the motions of the genital apparatus which are preparatory to the complete act of sexual union."[6] Materials which do not tend to arouse *sexual* passions are not obscene, however objectionable they may be on other grounds.

But Gardiner's definition of obscenity is not confined to things which most palpably and intensely stimulate these "motions." Any deliberate arousal of the thoughts and feelings associated with them is also obscene—to the extent that the thoughts and feelings aroused are divorced from the sexual activity in marriage. In explanation of this proviso, Gardiner cites the views of another Catholic author:

> Pressing the button of a small electric switch can start the most powerful machinery. The least voluntary degree of sex activity is like a switch that brings into action beyond our power of control "primordial forces that move in the depths of our nature." If it is always gravely sinful to bring these forces into action, except in conformity to moral law (that is to say, in their proper activity in wedlock), it must be equally sinful to do what is to them the same as pressing the starting switch is to all the machinery connected with it. It does not matter whether this activity be physical or mental (bad thoughts), for both kinds have the same effect on the deeper forces connected with them, that is, of course, provided they are voluntary.[7]

Gardiner concludes: "This is called by the theologians 've-nereal pleasure,' and in summary we may say that if a work is to be called obscene it must, of its nature, be such as actually to arouse or calculated to arouse in the viewer or reader such ve-nereal pleasure. If the work is *not* of such a kind it may, indeed, be vulgar, disgusting, crude, unpleasant, what you will—but it will not be, in the strict sense which Canon Law obliges us to apply, obscene."[8]

Thus, all voluntary stimulations of "venereal pleasure" not re-lated to marital sex are obscene. The obscene in literature com-prises all works predominantly calculated to produce such pleasure.

This concept of obscenity illustrates that it is possible to an-alyze the subject with a certain degree of precision. But this definition is not as precise, nor are its terms as restricted, as its proponents suggest. It states only that *some* sexual activity (men-tal, emotional, or physical) must be stimulated. It does not under-take to establish criteria concerning the degree of sexual activity stimulated, the degree of venereal pleasure experienced, or the kind of venereal pleasure experienced. The theory does not facili-tate the making of such distinctions because, for it, these are not important considerations in the determination of what is obscene.

It is doubtful that this definition of obscenity could command the assent of any large percentage of Americans outside the Cath-olic faith. Do we ordinarily experience obscenity when confronted with an object the predominant tendency of which is to stimulate *some* sexual pleasure? Does the average man attribute obscenity to "the least voluntary degree of sexual activity" outside of mar-riage? This broad view of what constitutes obscenity rests heavily upon a doctrine of what constitutes sin which many do not hold.

Further, those who subscribe to this concept of obscenity often apply it to literature in conjunction with another and less strictly defined concept—that sin should never be made attractive. Gardiner has cited with approval the following statement by Gerald Kelly, S.J., setting forth standards for the judgment of literary works and theatrical productions:

> For such things to be obscene two elements are required: (a) their theme, or content, is of an impure or sexually exciting nature; and (b) their manner of presentation is such as to throw an attractive emphasis on that impure or sexually exciting ele-ment. For instance, adultery is a sin of impurity, so when a book

or play not only centers about adultery, but portrays it in an attractive manner, such a book or play is obscene.[9]

In the application of these criteria, everything would depend upon what is meant by an "attractive emphasis," and it is not clear that it means only "venereal pleasure." At any rate, it is evident that this view of obscenity is, like Gardiner's definition, closely tied to certain religious doctrines of sin. It does not rest primarily upon an analysis of what is by nature obscene. Rather, it tends to identify that which is obscene with that which is sexually immoral according to religious beliefs. It is not evident that an appealing presentation of adultery must always be obscene or would be experienced as such. Though adultery is immoral, it does not follow from this that it, or an incitement to it, is always obscene. And it does not follow that the sin involved in the voluntary arousal of sexual activity outside of marriage renders such activity obscene.

If the concept of obscenity under consideration is, in certain respects, too broad and inclusive, it may be, in other respects, too narrow and exclusive. It is concerned wholly with sexual impurity and sexual pleasure. It excludes from the definition of obscenity all experiences which are not predominantly sexual in character and all objects which do not promote sexual pleasure. It does not account for literary materials which stimulate disgust more than they stimulate pleasure or which appeal to an interest in things bestial or scatological. And it does not adequately account for what is sometimes referred to as "the obscenity of violence." A well-known Catholic thinker, John Courtney Murray, S.J., has evidenced considerable concern with the literary portrayal of violence. He writes:

> The image of the truly evil thing in the obscenities of our day is seen on the typical cover of the "tough" kind of pocket book—the semi-nude woman, with a smoking gun in her hand. The scene is one of impurity, but that is its lesser evil. The real evil is the violence in the impure scene. There is the perversion. If some restraint could be imposed upon this pornography of violence—so damning in its revelation of a vice in our culture—it would indeed be a moral achievement.[10]

Of course, the obscenity to which Murray refers does contain a sexual element. But, as he suggests, that is not its distinguishing attribute. Such material is not adequately identified by its sexual appeals. If it is in some sense obscene, this is not simply because it tends to arouse sexual passion and promote "venereal pleasure."

The Catholic definition of obscenity is, in some respects, quite close to that propounded in *Roth* v. *United States*. But the terms of the Catholic definition cannot be completely severed from their religious foundations. Its religious basis renders "venereal pleasure" a somewhat broader and more far-reaching concept than is the *Roth* concept of "lust." It seems highly unlikely that this definition of obscenity and the ethic upon which it is based can be made acceptable to a secular society and embodied in its law. A concept developed by canon lawyers and theologians with a view to Christian moral training can be useful for the guidance of private persons, but it cannot become a public standard for the United States in the twentieth century. Finally, while this definition might result in too much censorship, it might also result in the censorship of the wrong things. It may promote the censorship of some things that are not obscene, while leaving unrestrained other things which are obscene.

This is an alternative explanation of what obscenity is which tends to identify it with the pornographic. But those who take this approach provide a variety of definitions of pornography. According to one of these, the pornographic in human life consists in a preoccupation with infantile and, hence, perverted forms of sexuality. Thus, pornographic literature is characterized by its unrealistic emphasis upon the erogenic zones of the body which are predominant in early phases of psycho-sexual development; by its stimulation of auto-eroticism; and in general by its disassociation from reality.[11] According to D. H. Lawrence, "pornography is the attempt to insult sex, to do dirt on it," to degrade the sexual act and the human body.* Others regard pornography simply as that form of literature which is designed solely to function as an aphrodisiac.

The Kronhausens have systematically developed a definition of pornography which combines some, but not all, of the features mentioned above. Since the Kronhausens' approach is representa-

* Lawrence said: "Pornography is the attempt to insult sex, to do dirt on it. . . . The insult to the human body, the insult to a vital human relationship! Ugly and cheap they make the human nudity, ugly and degraded they make the sexual act, trivial and cheap and nasty." *Sex, Literature and Censorship,* p. 69.

tive of a widely held view of the subject, it will be considered in some detail. The main purpose of these authors is to establish a clear distinction between pornographic literature and "erotic realism." They assert:

> In pornography (hard-core obscenity) the main purpose is to *stimulate erotic response* in the reader. And that is all. In erotic realism, *truthful description* of the basic realities of life, as the individual experiences it, is of the essence, even if such portrayals (whether by reason of humor or revulsion, or any other cause) have a decidedly anti-erotic effect. But by the same token if, while writing realistically on the subject of sex, the author succeeds in moving his reader, this too is erotic realism, and it is axiomatic that the reader should respond erotically to such writing, just as the sensitive reader will respond by actually crying, to a sad scene, or by laughing when laughter is evoked.[12]

The Kronhausens proceed to establish this distinction by quot-ing from and analyzing a considerable number of works belonging to each of the two categories. As examples of materials falling into the first category they select ten books or booklets from the underworld of pornography. As examples of materials falling into the category of "erotic realism," they select such works as Mark Twain's "1601," Samuel Pepys' *Diary,* Poggio's *Facetiae,* Casanova's *Memoirs,* Frank Harris' *My Life and Loves,* Edmund Wilson's *Memoirs of Hecate County,* D. H. Lawrence's *Lady Chatterley's Lover,* and Henry Miller's *Tropic of Cancer.*

Since the pornographic works are designed to function as "psychological aphrodisiacs," they exhibit certain attributes which are the means to this end. This is a summary of some of the most prominent attributes of pornographic literature which the authors discuss:

1. Pornographic works build up erotic excitement by confronting the reader with a succession of increasingly stimulating scenes.

2. They heavily emphasize the physiological sex responses of the participants.

3. They heavily emphasize aberrant or forbidden forms of sexuality, including flagellation, incest, and homosexuality.

4. They contain defloration scenes with strong sadistic elements and to which the victims submit passively or with positive enjoyment. ("It is highly characteristic of these fantasies that, no

matter what the degree of agony inflicted, the girl invariably disclaims any concern over her pain.")[13]

5. They are utterly unrealistic in their presentation of the sexual activities, interests, and capacities of their characters. Women are portrayed as being constantly and insatiably concerned with sex. The sexual capacity of the male is grossly exaggerated. Parents condone and often participate in the sex activities of their children.

6. These features are all indicative of the "wish-fulfilling fantasy character" of pornographic literature.[14]

While pornographers are concerned with arousing and indulging the sexual fantasies of readers, authors of erotic realism are concerned with telling the truth as they understand it. Works of erotic realism are thus characterized by a "frankness and honesty" which does not distort but rather illuminates the sexual side of life.[15] Both forms of sex literature appeal to desires and impulses which have been repressed by a repressive society. But erotic realism can most effectively counteract the evils caused by repression. The Kronhausens assert:

> Erotic realism in literature constitutes an effective mental-health prophylactic against faulty attitudes surrounding sexuality. . . . erotic realism satisfies the natural and desirable interest in sex, without turning it into morbid channels, confusing and linking it with violence, or keeping it antiseptically detached from the physical sensations which should accompany it, and by connecting the sexual impulse with those love-feelings which are its highest perfection.[16]

While recognizing the usefulness of the distinction which the Kronhausens seek to make, and the criteria which they establish, one can ask whether this distinction is as broadly applicable as it purports to be. More precisely, one can question (1) whether all the qualities which the Kronhausens ascribe to pornography and erotic realism as such are really attributable to the literature they discuss, and (2) whether these two categories are an adequate basis for judgment about the various forms of literature which circulate in civil society.

While it may be the case that all of the erotic realists whom the Kronhausens discuss are attempting to portray life as it is, it does not follow from this generalization that they all provide a healthy prophylactic "against faulty attitudes surrounding sex" or that they are all engaged in connecting the sexual impulses "with those love feelings which are its highest perfection." While one can agree with the Kronhausens that Edmund Wilson deals with the details of sexual life "without ever degrading or embellishing them,"[17] it would not be universally agreed that the passages cited from Poggio, Casanova, and Frank Harris do not degrade or embellish them. It can reasonably be said that D. H. Lawrence is concerned with establishing the connection between sex and love, but this cannot reasonably be said of most of the other authors cited and the passages quoted by the Kronhausens.

The Kronhausens' fundamental distinction—that between realism and fantasy—is not as precise or as easy to apply as they suggest. It is not clear that the multifarious adventures of Casanova and Frank Harris present a realistic picture of sexual life, while pornography always distorts sexual life. The sadistic elements openly portrayed in some pornography are, as the Kronhausens observe, real and inherent elements of human life which are suppressed or disguised in other forms of literature. This pornography does not simply present wish-fulfilling fantasy; it also presents some aspects of reality.

Further, it may be doubted that "stimulation of erotic response" is an adequate or sufficiently comprehensive characterization of the aims and appeals of pornography. The Kronhausens observe the pervasive themes of brutality and bestiality in passages they cite, and in a great deal of literature of this type we can discern a more or less desperate and painful striving for total physical satisfaction. The Kronhausens do not sufficiently explore these themes, and their definition of the nature and objectives of pornography does not seem to take adequate account of such themes. It is not enough to say that this very important aspect of pornography is designed to stimulate sexual desires (even "infantile" sexual desires) and to function as an aphrodisiac. One wishes for a deeper investigation of this kind of appeal to sexual passions than the authors provide; one suspects that there is more to it than simply an endeavor to gratify erotic appetites.[18]

The Kronhausen argument leaves the impression that erotic realism and pornography are sharply defined and easily identifiable types of literature, with one set of qualities clearly ascribable to the one and another set clearly ascribable to the other. And it leaves the impression that there is one class of authors who are wholly concerned with catering to sex fantasies, while other authors who deal with sex are wholly concerned with speaking the truth about it. Finally, it leaves the impression that authors who have some desire to produce statements about reality necessarily succeed in producing realistic statements.*

What the Kronhausens say about erotic realism is largely true of D. H. Lawrence and Edmund Wilson. And what they say of pornography is largely true of—though it is not the last word about—the kind of pornography they examine. The Krohausens have succeeded in setting forth some useful criteria for judgment about a certain kind of obscenity and a certain kind of serious sex literature. But most of the literature encountered in our society falls somewhere between these extremes. We have works which combine, in varying degrees, reality and fantasy, prurience and intellectual sincerity. We have authors who intend to speak some truth and fail; we have authors with mixed motives; and we have authors who make a pretense of "frankness" and "honesty."

* In their second edition of this volume the authors have added a final chapter called "The Erotica of Tomorrow." Here they introduce a broad literary category which they call "quality erotica," a category within which they wish to include "erotic realism," "erotic autobiography," "erotic humor," "philosophic erotica," and "erotic surrealism" (p. 354). Presumably this category stands, over against "pornography," as excellent or worthy literature. Evidently, "erotic surrealism" does away with the distinction between realism and fantasy, since, "the erotic fantasies which it expresses are frequently indicative of the pathogenic effects of the traditional anti-sexualism in our culture against which this movement constitutes, among other things, a violent form of rebellion" (p. 356). As a prime example of this type of literature the authors point to the novel *The Story of O.* This is a story of a masochistically inclined young woman who is systematically brought into total bondage—first to her sadistic "lover" and then to an even more sadistic gentleman to whom her lover hands her over. Pauline Réage, *The Story of O,* trans. Sabine d'Estrée (Paris: Chez Jean-Jacques Pauvert, 1954). The Kronhausens do not explain why they regard this novel as an "outstanding" work (p. 362) or why it deserves to be called *quality* erotica. Nor do they undertake to explore the effects of their argument for "erotic surrealism" upon the rationale for their distinction between erotic realism and pornography. It will be remembered that they have praised erotic realism because its endeavors at truthful or realistic descriptions of sexual life constitute a healthy prophylactic against faulty attitudes concerning sexuality. And they have depreciated (or implied some depreciation of) pornography because of its indulgence in fantasy and because it directs our sexual interest into morbid channels, linking it with violence. Whether undermined or not, this distinction and argument is retained intact in the revised edition of *Pornography and the Law,* and, therefore, I treat it in this text as the primary argument of the book.

The criteria suggested by the Kronhausens would be of some value in some of these cases. All of that literature which is generally called pornography can be shown to embody one or more of the attributes which the Kronhausens ascribe to pornography. On the other hand, there is much material generally regarded as pornography in which many of these features are absent—in which, for instance, parents are not represented as condoning the vices of their children and women are not represented as enjoying or passively acquiescing in sadistic treatment. On the contrary, parents are sometimes represented as harshly repressive, and some pornography emphasizes the suffering and humiliation, rather than the enjoyment, of women subjected to sadistic treatment.

There are forms of literature widely distributed in our society to which the Kronhausen categories do not apply at all. How would they apply to the "men's adventure" magazines, the lurid tabloid, the sex (or "girly") magazines, the novels of Mickey Spillane, or motion pictures "realistically" presenting sex acts on the screen? I do not now suggest that all or any of these are clearly obscene; I only suggest that none of them is either "erotic realism" or "pornography."* And these categories could not be applied to them on the basis of judgments about the intentions (realistic or wish-fulfilling) of their authors.

The Kronhausen definition of obscenity actually does away with the concept of obscenity altogether. According to it, there is really no such thing as obscenity; there is only pornography. And the designation "pornography" is confined to materials which contain nothing but sexual episodes and which present these in the most gross and extreme forms, without any restraint whatever. The reader may wish to ask whether this is all there is to it; whether this is the only kind of material which can be legitimately called obscene and which can threaten the moral interests of society.

The concept of pornography under consideration can have only limited value for the purposes of the law and civil society. The Kronhausens do not undertake to establish that the various kinds of materials which are excluded from their definition of the term (and from that of erotic realism) are harmless to society. They

---

* Whether some of these would qualify as "erotic surrealism," I leave the reader to decide.

do not consider such materials, and they do not provide criteria by which they may be judged. The criteria which they do provide are not based primarily on a consideration of society's needs and problems. They are based primarily upon a psychologically oriented analysis of literary forms and literary purposes. This definition of pornography does not address itself to public problems but to the distinction between various forms of literary expression and the motives which underlie them. It is, essentially, a technical definition and, as such, is not sufficiently oriented toward public interest considerations to serve as a basis for public policy. Public policy cannot be determined on the basis of the information that the authors of one kind of literature are attempting to present life as it is, while authors of another kind are appealing to fantasy.

Public policy must be based largely upon assessments of social effects, social dangers, and social evils. There are good reasons for believing that that very special and narrow class of literature which the Kronhausens label "pornography" is not the kind of literature which is likely to do the greatest harm to society. There are good reasons for doubting that any very large percentage of Americans would be greatly interested in or much affected by this most extreme and crude form of pornography. It is a consequence of this technical definition of obscenity that attention is directed to the kind of literature which may be the most offensive—but probably is not the most dangerous—to the community.

There are two reasons why the problems confronting the law cannot be simply resolved by the adoption of a hard-core pornography standard for the legal definition of obscenity. The task of defining pornography is not free of difficulties or controversies. And the public interest to be served by the control of obscenity is not adequately served by the control of pornography alone.

There are several interpretations of what constitutes pornography. And these interpretations differ somewhat in the things they emphasize as its distinguishing features. The Kronhausen concept of it is not in complete harmony with that of D. H. Lawrence. According to the former view, pornography is that literature which is wholly designed to stimulate sexual excitement; according to the latter, it is that literature which is deliberately designed to debase sex. Some definitions of pornography tend to be broader and more inclusive than others. Consider these two ideas offered by Margaret Mead: "We may define pornography, cross-culturally, as words or acts or representations that are calculated to stimulate sex feelings independent of the presence of another loved and chosen human being"; *and* "The character of the daydream as distinct from reality is an essential element in pornography."[19] The latter proposition is in accord with the Kronhausens' emphasis on fantasy, but the former goes beyond this and covers more ground. It emphasizes the element of impersonal sex as the distinguishing characteristic of pornography.

In his very comprehensive study of Victorian pornography, Steven Marcus emphasizes "the sexuality of domination, . . . that conception of male sexuality in which the aggressive and sadistic components almost exclusively pervail." With regard to this view of sex, Marcus says: "It is also the form in which male sexuality is represented in the overwhelming majority of pornographic works written during the nineteenth and twentieth centuries."[20] Marcus' study suggests that one of the essential features of pornography is its association or identification of male sexuality with aggressive strivings for power and its consequent treatment of the female as a mere instrument for such strivings.

Of course, there is considerably less difference of opinion over the nature of pornography than there is over the nature of obscenity. The various definitions of pornography have a number of distinctive features in common. There is, if the expression be permissible, some hard core of agreement among students of the subject. But this does not mean that the courts can put an end to all the dilemmas and controversies in this area by defining obscenity as hard-core pornography. Men who agree upon some of the criteria we have been considering can still strongly disagree in their application of them to particular works. Sometimes it is a most difficult and controversial matter to decide whether or not a literary work is an aphrodisiac, a wish-fulfilling fantasy, or "dirt for dirt's sake."[21]

But I do not regard these problems of definition and identification as the primary reason for rejection of a hard-core pornography standard. These difficulties are not impossible to live with. The courts could minimize them somewhat by adopting one of the more rigorous or strict definitions of pornography, such as that advocated by the Kronhausens. And the judges could learn to put up with such ambiguities and differences of opinion as would remain under the strict definition.

Unfortunately, this solution would not be a solution to the problem of obscenity, properly understood. It does not adequately serve the ends for which the community seeks to control obscenity, whether these ends be understood in ordinary popular terms or in the terms of the rationale for censorship presented in the preceding chapter. The adoption of a rigorous pornography standard would amount to virtual abandonment of these ends and an official pronouncement that the community is willing to be subjected to a massive deluge of highly salacious books, magazines, newspapers, and films. The law's retreat to hard-core pornography would thus involve a substantial lowering of public standards. This depreciation of public standards, in addition to the increased circulation of obscenity, is likely to be at least as harmful to society as is hard-core pornography.*

Definitions of pornography, then, are not a substitute for inquiry into the nature of the obscene. And it would seem that moral

---

* It is worth noting that those who advocate a hard-core pornography standard seldom do so on the basis of a coherent rationale *for* the legal control of obscenity. What they want is a formula for reducing and confining censorship as much as is practicable. Professor C. Peter Magrath appears to be an exception to this assertion. See C. Peter Magrath, "The Obscenity Cases: Grapes of Roth," *1966 Supreme Court Review,* ed. Philip B. Kurland, pp. 7–77. Magrath seems to be urging the Court to adopt a hard-core pornography standard on the basis that there is a legitimate public interest to be served by control of obscenity. Magrath acknowledges that there are some grounds for believing that obscenity may be a contributing cause of antisocial conduct, and, further, he asserts that there are "justifications for obscenity laws that do not turn on the alleged impact of obscenity on behavior" (ibid., p. 55). But Magrath does not explain why a *hard-core pornography* standard is the appropriate legal response to these considerations. He does not undertake to show that it is hard-core pornography which is responsible for such antisocial conduct as may be said to flow from obscenity, and he does not undertake to demonstrate that those other "justifications" for obscenity laws to which he refers would be adequately served by laws restricted to hard-core pornography. Magrath may have succeeded in showing that, by adoption of the legal criterion he suggests, the Court can extricate itself from its "constitutional disaster area"; what he has not shown is that in doing so the Court will have significantly contributed to the solution of society's problem. I suggest that those who would try to make a sustained argument for a pornography standard on the basis of a public interest in moral values would find themselves logically compelled to go beyond a pornography standard.

perspectives and moral insights must enter into the analysis of both.

What, then, is obscenity? Gardiner and the Kronhausens agree in identifying it with some kind of sexual stimulation or sexual appeal. This is not wrong, but, as I have already suggested several times, it is not sufficient to account for all those phenomena in life and in literature in relation to which men experience and speak of "the obscene." For instance, it does not account for the experience of obscenity which underlies the following assertion by Richard Weaver:

> Picture magazines and tabloid newspapers place before the millions scenes and facts which violate every definition of humanity. How common is it today to see upon the front page of some organ destined for a hundred thousand homes the agonized face of a child run over in the street, the dying expression of a woman crushed by a subway train, tableaux of execution, scenes of intense private grief. These are the obscenities.[22]

What is (or may be) obscene about such scenes? They do not portray sex or appeal to an interest in sex. They are scenes of violence, agony, and death. But no one would say that violence, agony, and death are in themselves necessarily obscene. And Weaver would not complain about the portrayal of these phenomena in the fifth act of *Hamlet*. He does complain about a certain way of disclosing or looking at some of the most intimate private experiences of human beings. In the portrayals he condemns, the reader or viewer is invited to dwell upon the details—the physiological details—of human suffering and death. This invasion of aspects of life which are thought to be intensely private is not regarded by Weaver in terms of mere vulgarity or crudeness. He does not say that this is merely in "bad taste." He regards this as a violation of humanity and he places a moral judgment upon it.

Why should it be so regarded? The viewer of such scenes is a stranger to the persons who are undergoing the suffering and dying. He can have no personal interest in them. He is not invited by these portrayals to care about them as individuals. He is invited to dwell upon the physical aspects of their suffering and death. In these protrayals, not only are the most intimate aspects of human life revealed, but their human dimensions are reduced to their physical dimensions.

These reflections suggest two preliminary definiti
scenity: (1) obscenity consists in making public tha
private; it consists in an intrusion upon intimate physical
and acts or physical-emotional states; and (2) it consists i
radation of the human dimensions of life to a sub-human or
physical level. According to these definitions, obscenity is a certain
way of treating or viewing the physical aspects of human existence
and their relation to the rest of human existence. Thus, there can be
an obscene view of sex; there can also be obscene views of death,
of birth, of illness, and of acts such as that of eating or defecating. Obscenity makes a public exhibition of these phenomena and
does so in such a way that their larger human context is lost or
depreciated. Thus, there is a connection between our two preliminary definitions of obscenity: when the intimacies of life are
exposed to public view their human value may be depreciated,
or they may be exposed to public view in order to depreciate them
and to depreciate man.

These formulations are highly abstract and connotative. The
remainder of this chapter will be devoted to their explication,
clarification, and application.

The following observations of George Elliott strongly imply
that the essence of the obscene is its invasion of privacy.

> Psychologically, the trouble with pornography is that, in our
> culture at least, it offends the sense of separateness, of individ-
> uality, of privacy; it intrudes upon the rights of others. We have
> a certain sense of specialness about those voluntary bodily func-
> tions each must perform for himself—bathing, eating, defecat-
> ing, urinating, copulating. . . . Take eating, for example. There
> are few strong taboos around the act of eating, yet most people
> feel uneasy about being the only one at table who is, or who is
> not, eating, and there is an absolute difference between eating a
> rare steak washed down by plenty of red wine and watching a
> close-up movie of someone doing so. One wishes to draw back
> when one is actually or imaginatively too close to the mouth of
> a man enjoying his dinner; in exactly the same way one wishes
> to remove himself from the presence of a man and woman en-
> joying sexual intercourse.[23]

The element of obscenity here consists in one's being "too
close" to other persons performing intimate physical acts. But
why do we wish to avoid such closeness, or, more significantly, why

do we have such an aversion to being watched in the act of eating or of sexual intercourse? It is not an answer to this question to say that we are (puritanically) ashamed of eating and of sex. Nor is it a sufficient answer simply to say that in our culture these are private matters. Why do we insist upon making them private matters?

There are certain bodily acts which will tend to arouse disgust in an observer who is not involved in the act and is not, at the time, subject to its urgencies. What the observer sees is a human being governed by physiological urges and functions. Now, to the participants, the act of eating, or of sex, can have important personal and supra-biological meanings. But the outside observer cannot share the experience of these meanings; what he sees is simply the biological process. The personal values associated with such acts cannot survive such observation. The intrusion of a stranger or an outsider who neither knows nor cares about them tends to destroy them and reduce the act to its bare physiological properties. Thus, there are certain human experiences or values which can emerge and flourish only when the physical acts with which they are associated are sheltered from the gaze of nonparticipants. A man does not want outsiders looking at him while he is eating, because he does not want to be reduced in the eyes of others (and, hence, in his own eyes) to a collection of physical properties and reactions. The social proprieties which surround the act of eating serve as barriers against such reduction. The moral attitudes, aesthetic proprieties, and social forms which surround sexual life can serve a similar function.

Obscenity tears away these barriers, and what men experience when they are torn away can be appropriately termed obscene. From this line of argument it follows that obscenity is an aesthetic as well as a moral category. The revulsion (or enjoyment in revulsion) which often accompanies obscenity involves a combination of aesthetic and moral feelings. It also follows that there are degrees of obscenity. We do not feel as strongly about the public exposure of the private act of eating as we do about the public exposure of an act of sexual love or of a painful death. The grosser obscenities are those which invade the most important personal intimacies. It may be that the aesthetic ingredient in the obscene experience will be greatest where the minor intimacies are concerned, and the moral ingredient will be greatest where the major intimacies are concerned.

Obscenity is not merely an intrusion upon private things; it is an intrusion which degrades or dehumanizes those things and the persons involved with them. For the illustration of this thought it is useful to refer to literary examples. The three literary passages which follow are not presented as examples of obscene literature. It is not asserted that these passages (or the works from which they are taken) are themselves obscene. It is asserted that they illustrate the interpretation of obscenity set forth here.

In that portion of *Gulliver's Travels* called "A Voyage to Brobdingnag" there are passages highly illustrative of one facet of obscenity. Gulliver finds himself in a society composed of gigantic people who stand "as tall as an ordinary spire-steeple."[24] The average Brobdingnagian is about sixty feet tall. At one point Gulliver is compelled to watch a woman nursing a baby. He describes his reactions:

> I must confess no Object ever disgusted me so much as the Sight of her monstrous Breast, which I cannot tell what to compare with, so as to give the curious Reader an Idea of its Bulk, Shape and Color. It stood prominent six Foot, and could not be less than sixteen in circumference. The Nipple was about half the Bigness of my Head and the Hue both of that and the Dug so verified with Spots, Pimples and Freckles, that nothing could appear more nauseous: For I had a near Sight of her, She sitting down the more conveniently to give Suck, and I standing on the Table. This made me reflect upon the fair Skins of our *English* Ladies, who appear so beautiful to us, only because they are of our own Size and their Defects not to be seen but through a magnifying Glass, where we find by Experiment that the smoothest and whitest Skins look rough and coarse, and ill-colored.[25]

Gulliver is, evidently, "too close" to the physical intimacies described here. He sees too much in too great detail. The obscenity here consists in the fact that Gulliver is (and must be in his circumstances) so thoroughly absorbed in the physical details that he cannot see them in relation to their larger human context and meaning. He cannot see a woman nursing a baby, he can only see a monstrous breast and a huge nipple; he cannot long concentrate even upon a whole breast—so forcefully are the details thrust upon him. The human meaning of the event is broken down into its physical parts and these are further broken down into their parts. The "English Ladies" of Swift's day and the ladies of our own day cannot so easily be observed in this way. But an approximation to this can be achieved through the "magnifying glass" of obscenity. The endeavor to look at human beings in this way is obscene.

Gulliver's "disgust" is primarily aesthetic in character. Though moral considerations may be relevant, Swift does not stress them in his description of the event and his character's reaction to it. The ordinary reader would not experience a specifically moral revulsion.

In his short story "Erostratus," Jean-Paul Sartre presents a scene which must arouse both kinds of feelings. Erostratus engages a prostitute and takes her to a room. He does not remove his clothing. He requires her to remove her clothing and walk up and down the room while he gazes steadily at her. This follows:

> She let her underpants drop to her feet, then she picked them up and put them carefully on her dress together with her bra.
>
> "So you are a little vicious one, darling, a little lazy one?" she asked me. "You want your little woman to do all the work?"
>
> At the same time she stepped towards me and propping herself with her hands on the arms of my easy-chair she heavily tried to lower herself between my legs. But I pulled her up roughly.
>
> "None of that, none of that," I told her.
>
> She looked at me with surprise.
>
> "But what do you want me to do to you?"
>
> "Nothing. Walk, walk around, I do not want anything more."
>
> Awkwardly she started to walk up and down. Nothing bothers women more than walking around while they are naked. They are not used to putting down their heels on the floor. The whore curved her back and let her arms dangle. As far as I was concerned, I was in heaven. I was sitting in my arm-chair quietly and fully dressed, I had even kept my gloves on and this experienced woman had stripped herself on my command and was circling around me.
>
> She turned her head toward me and, in order to save appearances, she smiled at me coquettishly.
>
> "Do you think I am beautiful? Are you feasting your eyes?"
>
> "That's none of your business."
>
> "Tell me," she asked with sudden indignation, "Do you intend to make me walk around like this for a long time?"

"Sit down."

She sat down on the bed and we looked at each other silently. She had goose-pimples. You could hear the ticking of an alarm clock on the other side of the wall. All of a sudden I said to her:

"Spread your legs."

She hesitated for a quarter of a second, then she obeyed. I looked between her legs and sniffed. Then I started to laugh so loudly that tears came to my eyes. I told her simply:

"Do you realize?"

And I started to laugh again.

She looked at me with stupor, then she blushed violently and closed her legs.

"Son of a bitch," she said between her teeth.

However, I laughed even more and she jumped up and took her bra from the chair.

"Hey," I said to her, "we are not finished yet. I'll give you fifty francs in a minute, but I want something for my money."

Nervously she picked up her underpants.[26]

What Erostratus seeks to experience, what he wants to see, is precisely what I have called "the obscene." He does not want to see a woman; he wants to see a woman stripped of all human qualities and reduced to a "thing"—a sexual organ. He views this sexual organ in isolation, without any relation to its biological purposes or to the human life of which it is a part.[27] It is this stripping-down which accounts for the prostitute's moral outrage, and for the reader's experience of obscenity.

In his novel *Catch 22,* Joseph Heller presents a scene in which a young man is sliced by the propeller of an airplane:

Even people who were not there remembered vividly exactly what happened next. There was the briefest softest tsst! filtering audibly through the shattering, overwhelming howl of the plane's engines, and then there were just Kid Sampson's two pale skinny legs, still joined by strings somehow at the bloody truncated hips, standing stock-still on the raft for what seemed a full minute or two before they toppled over backward in the water finally with a faint, echoing splash and turned completely upside down so that only the grotesque toes and the plaster-white soles of Kid Sampson's feet remained in view.[28]

Later, the author observes, ironically, "now that bad weather had come, almost no one ever sneaked away alone any more to peek through the bushes like a pervert at the moldering stumps."[29]

These men were horror-struck at this event when it occurred. Why do they "sneak away alone" to see the remnants of its victim? Pervertedly, they seek to view, and to dwell upon, the severed and isolated parts of what was once a man. The obscene effect of this scene depends upon one's keeping in mind that these parts belonged just recently to a human being—Kid Sampson. The author achieves this effect by reminding the reader in various ways of this fact. What the reader apprehends with horror and what the author's characters ruminate upon with a mixture of horror, disgust, and enjoyment is the reduction of a man to an aggregate of disjointed and lifeless physical objects. This is the obscene way of looking at death.

Why do these men want to dwell upon death in this manner? Why does Erostratus want to experience obscenity? I do not undertake a thorough exploration of these matters here, except to suggest that the fascination with obscenity is not confined to the mentally ill, nor is it simply a manifestation of our culture alone. It is a pervasive phenomenon of human life. Obscenity is, at bottom, a certain view of, a certain posture toward, the basic conditions of human existence. It is always possible to take up this posture, it is always possible to take an obscene (as well as a nonobscene) view of sex, of death, of suffering, of the human body and its functions. The essence of the obscene view is its reductionistic isolation of these phenomena and its consequent depreciation of man.

In the broadest and most general terms, obscene literature is that literature which invites and stimulates the reader to adopt the obscene posture toward human existence—to engage in the reduction of man's values, functions, and ends to the animal or subhuman level. But this general definition of obscenity in literature requires considerable elaboration and qualification. A work cannot reasonably be regarded as obscene simply because it treats of things private and intimate. It is a major function of literature and the arts to treat of such matters. From an artistic point of view, there are no subjects per se which cannot become the subject matter of literature. And a work cannot be regarded as obscene simply because it adopts a "reductionistic" or materialist philosophy of life. For intelligent literary judgment in this area, everything depends upon the *way* in which these matters are treated and the *way* in which the mind of the reader or viewer is solicited.

In *Catch 22,* Heller presents a battle scene in which Yossarian, the book's hero, discovers that one of his comrades is mortally wounded:

> Yossarian ripped open the snaps of Snowden's flack suit and heard himself scream wildly as Snowden's insides slithered down to the floor in a soggy pile and just kept dripping out. A chunk of flack more than three inches big had shot into his other side just underneath the arm and blasted all the way through, drawing whole mottled quarts of Snowden along with it through the gigantic hole it made in his ribs as it blasted out. Yossarian screamed a second time and squeezed both hands over his eyes. His teeth were chattering in horror. He forced himself to look again. Here was God's plenty all right, he thought bitterly as he stared—liver, lungs, kidneys, ribs, stomach and bits of the stewed tomatoes Snowden had eaten that day for lunch. Yossarian . . . turned away dizzily and began to vomit, clutching his burning throat. . . .
>
> "I'm cold," Snowden whimpered. "I'm cold."
>
> "There, there," Yossarian mumbled mechanically in a voice too low to be heard. "There, there."
>
> Yossarian was cold too, and shivering uncontrollably. He felt goose pimples clacking all over him as he gazed down despondently at the grim secret Snowden had spilled all over the messy floor. It was easy to read the message in his entrails. Man was matter, that was Snowden's secret. Drop him out a window and he'll fall. Set fire to him and he'll burn. Bury him and he'll rot like other kinds of garbage. The spirit gone, man is garbage. That was Snowden's secret.[30]

"Man is garbage"—this is, in extreme form, the message conveyed by all obscene literature. In one way or another; in a greater or lesser degree, all obscene literature says this about man. But the passage just cited does not really convey this message, or, to the extent that it does so, it does not convey this message in an obscene manner. The reader is not stimulated or moved simply to believe and to feel that "man is garbage."

The difference between this passage and an obscene passage on the same subject lies in the emotional context in which this author presents the event and in the way he has his character respond. The event is presented in an emotional context which is largely one of compassion. The author does not depreciate the dying Snowden. He does not laugh at him or enjoy his suffering, and he does not invite the reader to do so. He does not present with a malicious leer the harsh and pitiful facts of life which Yossarian discovers.

It is true that Yossarian comes to a somewhat obscene conclusion about the nature of man. But he comes to it against his will. He hates this conclusion, and he recoils from the degrading factors that lead to it. The reader, identifying with Yossarian, is also likely to recoil. He is not invited by this passage to ruminate about the death of Snowden in the same manner as Heller's airmen ruminate about the decaying body of Kid Sampson or as Erostratus ruminates about his prostitute. The reader is not stimulated to give vent to morbid or bestial fantasies and feelings about death. He is stimulated to *think* about death in a human context.* While the reader is given an emotional experience of some of life's obscenities (and not simply an intellectual one), he is not encouraged to surrender to obscene desires and attitudes; he is encouraged to reflect upon the obscene side of life—as Yossarian does.

Here is, then, a fundamental distinction to be made between literature which treats of things private or of human debasement and literature which invades privacy and debases man. There is a distinction to be made between literature which deals with obscenity and literature which *is* obscene.

Genuine literature addresses the mind. It seeks to confront a reader or viewer with a problem; that is, it presents him with a picture of life which he must confront—intellectually as well as emotionally. That picture or representation, may be of things delicately private, but one is not thereby stimulated to revel in the invasion of private areas. That picture may be highly unflattering —or even degrading—to man, but one is not thereby invited to give vent to sordid thoughts and feelings of his own.

With regard to the distinction between art and pornography, James Joyce has written:

> The feelings excited by improper art are kinetic, desire or loathing. Desire urges us to possess, to go to something; loathing urges us to abandon, to go from something. The arts which excite them, pornographical or didactic, are therefore improper arts.

* In this discussion and in that which follows I refer to the "appropriate" reader, the one for whom the work is designed. By thinking in terms of such a reader we direct attention to the impact which a work is designed to have, and we abstract from considerations of its accidental impacts.

The aesthetic emotion is therefore static. The mind is arrested and raised above desire and loathing.*

When genuine literature treats of things intimately personal or of things ignoble, the feelings which it arouses are not the same as those which would be aroused by the direct experience of these things in ordinary life. They are, rather, "aesthetic" feelings—above ordinary desire and loathing. There are various artistic devices by which an author can contrive to promote an aesthetic experience of the objects he treats. The objects can be presented in such a way that the audience will contemplate them with a degree of detachment. Works can be designed so that the grosser physical aspects of the phenomena treated will be viewed from a certain distance. With regard to the aesthetic experience of art objects, Harold Gardiner observes that "the viewer of a still-life, let us say, of a table spread with succulent viands should not experience the reaction of having his mouth water."[31] Abraham Kaplan asserts:

> The aesthetic experience requires a kind of disinterest or detachment, a "psychic distance." . . . Only when we hold the work of art at arm's length is it artistic at all. The work *brings emotions to mind* or *presents them for contemplation.* . . . Sad music does not make us literally sad [italics mine].[32]

Thus, an artistic presentation of the sexual side of life is not designed to promote lust, and it does not tend to promote lust in those properly attuned to it. And a serious literary work treating of intimate physical facts does not make us literally disgusted. Rather, the feelings which such works arouse are aesthetic emotions—focused upon and governed by the particular plot and the particular characters presented. A sexual scene should not stimulate desire or loathing as such, it should stimulate an interest in the characters—in what they are doing and undergoing. More precisely, when such passions are aroused by good literature, they are subordinated to and determined by one's interest in the particular problems portrayed and in the human problems which these are

* James Joyce, *A Portrait of the Artist as a Young Man* (New York: Viking Press, 1916), p. 205. In this passage it is Joyce's character Stephen Dedalus who speaks. But Stephen's aesthetic views are, in part, those of Joyce himself.

designed to represent. Art is not primarily concerned with making us *want* something; it is primarily concerned with making us *see* something.

When a work tends to promote lust or disgust to a high degree, then it is not good art or it is not genuine art. Literary art teaches by promoting an experience of some aspect of life and presenting that experience for contemplation and interpretation. The predominance of lust or disgust is incompatible with that detachment which is a prerequisite for the interpretation of experience. Therefore good literature cannot literally invade man's private affairs and it does not promote an obscene experience of life.

Obscene literature may be defined as that literature which presents, graphically and in detail, a degrading picture of human life and invites the reader or viewer, not to contemplate that picture, but to wallow in it. Thus, while we can identify obscenity with a certain view of man, I would not identify it simply with an *idea* about man. Obscenity is a depreciating view of intimate or physical things which is accompanied by desire or loathing.

The writings of Freud about sado-masochism are not obscene, but an obscene novel could be written on the basis of them. The obscene novel would *portray* the physical phenomena of sado-masochism, and it would do so in vivid detail. It would not maintain aesthetic or intellectual distance between it readers and these details. Its readers would not be invited to reflect upon the nature of degrading human experiences, but, simply, to have such experiences. Its readers would not be stimulated to reflect upon an *idea* about the reduction of human things to physical things, they would be stimulated to indulge themselves in feelings and in fantasies which dwell upon this reduction. Literary materials are obscene to the extent that this is their dominant tendency.

It must be acknowledged that this definition of obscenity, and the distinctions embodied in it, is not wholly free of vagueness or ambiguity. It cannot serve by itself to distinguish, with absolute clarity and precision, between obscene literature and that art which deals with the obscene. The application of this definition to some forms of literature must be attended with considerable practical difficulties. But I submit that it does serve to identify the underlying elements of obscenity, and it can serve as a guide to moral and literary judgment.

The concepts presented here can help to explain what makes

the difference between an obscene and a non-obscene treatment of those aspects of life which are the subject matter of obscenity. The passage previously cited from *Gulliver's Travels* does not plunge the reader into imaginative preoccupation with the "disgusting" details which Gulliver perceives. Though the reader may well share some of Gulliver's responses, his attention is not fixated upon these things. His attention and interest is quickly diverted to Gulliver himself—to Gulliver's comments and insights and to his further adventures and prospects.

In some productions of the "underground theater" the audience is presented with close-up shots in which the camera focuses upon people eating, copulating, or defecating. There is no plot and no characterization of any meaningful sort; there are no persons in whose adventures, prospects, or insights the audience is interested. In the "exploitation film" (definitely "aboveground" and now making its way into some conventional theaters) a thin, scarcely developed story is the vehicle for action scenes involving almost complete nudity and graphic sex. Both types of film provide the audience, not with an aesthetic or contemplative experience, but with a direct experience of the obscene.

In Act V of *Hamlet*—in the well-known "graveyard scene"—Hamlet comments upon death and upon its inevitable reduction of the human spirit to such stuff as may provide food for worms or "stop a bunghole."[33] The act concludes with a scene of violence and carnage. This is not obscene.

In one edition of the *National Enquirer* the headline tells us that a man has killed his son and fed the corpse to pigs.[34] There is a photograph of the "the reconstructed head" of the boy. Inside, there is an article describing how "more than seventy of the slobbering animals hungrily devoured Alfio's severed arms, legs and torso." There is also a close-up photo of a man cut in half by a "man-eating tiger," and a photo of the blood-soaked body of a man murdered by his son. The story accompanying the latter informs the reader that "the shots blasted his father's head from different directions." In some writings of Mickey Spillane a naked woman will appear with a gun in her hand, ready to kill the man who has been her lover. The naked woman will be violently overpowered, beaten, shot to death, or burned alive. Sometimes a woman will meet violent death while in a passionate embrace. Such materials are obscene.

In Act V of *Hamlet* the audience is exposed to contemplations about the ultimate degradation of man to brute matter. The audience sees the details of this degradation through the eyes of Hamlet—a character in whose doings and sufferings it is deeply interested and whose reflections impart to these details, and to the carnage which follows, the dimensions of tragedy.

In the material cited from the *National Enquirer* such details are presented directly to the reader. They are not presented for contemplation; nor are they presented in relation to any persons in whom the reader can have a human interest. There is nothing which stands between the reader and the spectacle of human beings reduced to brute force and decaying matter. The reader does not reflect upon the human condition; he leers at scenes of dehumanization.

In the writings of Mickey Spillane physical details are not so blatantly presented. But a picture is often presented in which human eroticism is associated with, or identified with, brute violence, and the death of a human being is rendered as insignificant as the death of an animal. In many passages the reader is invited to ruminate upon this degradation of love and death while under the influence of physical and psychological desires which the scenes arouse. Violence is obscene when it is presented in such a way as to reduce persons to a brutish or animal-like condition and to invite the observer to enjoy the reduction.

We now turn to the consideration of specifically erotic literature. It follows from the concepts set forth in this chapter that the novel *Lady Chatterley's Lover* cannot reasonably be labeled obscene, while the novel *Fanny Hill* can reasonably be labeled obscene. In order to indicate how the criteria developed here can be applied to such works, one relatively long passage will be cited from each.

The following passage presents the first love scene between Constance Chatterley and her husband's gamekeeper, Mellors. In despair over the emptiness of her life, Constance Chatterley has wandered to the vicinity of Mellors' hut. While they converse, Mellors is apprehensive, as sympathy and desire rise up within him.

> He glanced apprehensively at her. Her face was averted, and she was crying blindly, in all the anguish of her generation's forlornness. His heart melted suddenly, like a drop of fire, and he put out his hand and laid his fingers on her knee.

"You shouldn't cry," he said softly.

But then she put her hands over her face and felt that really her heart was broken and nothing mattered any more.

He laid his hand on her shoulder, and softly, gently, it began to travel down the curve of her back, blindly, with a blind stroking motion, to the curve of her crouching loins. And there his hand softly, softly, stroked the curve of her flank, in the blind instinctive caress.

She had found her scrap of handkerchief and was blindly trying to dry her face.

"Shall you come to the hut?" he said, in a quiet, neutral voice.

And closing his hand softly on her upper arm, he drew her up and led her slowly to the hut, not letting go of her till she was inside. Then he cleared aside the chair and table, and took a brown soldier's blanket from the tool chest, spreading it slowly. She glanced at his face, as she stood motionless.

His face was pale and without expression, like that of a man submitting to fate.

"You lie there," he said softly, and he shut the door, so that it was dark, quite dark.

With a queer obedience, she lay down on the blanket. Then she felt the soft, groping, helplessly desirous hand touching her body, feeling for her face. The hand stroked her face softly, softly with infinite soothing and assurance, and at last there was the soft touch of a kiss on her cheek.

She lay quite still, in a sort of sleep, in a sort of dream. Then she quivered as she felt his hand groping softly, yet with queer thwarted clumsiness among her clothing. Yet the hand knew, too, how to unclothe her where it wanted. He drew down the thin silk sheath, slowly, carefully right down and over her feet. Then with a quiver of exquisite pleasure he touched the warm, soft body, and touched her navel for a moment in a kiss. And he had to come into her at once, to enter the peace on earth of her soft quiescent body. It was the moment of pure peace for him, the entry into the body of the woman.[35]

This passage describes an intimate physical act, and it does so in some detail. But, seen in the context of the whole work, it does not grossly invade the private side of life and it does not strip the private things of their human meaning and value. This is, evidently, a kind of love scene. While some of the physical aspects of love are presented, the emphasis here is upon the compassionate or affectional side. The physical details are presented in order to promote understanding of these particular persons on the one hand and, on the other, of the human meaning of sexual life. The sensual details are designed to help the reader explore the nature of Constance and Mellors' suffering and the nature of the "generation's forlornness." And they are designed to show that love is rooted ultimately in a mysterious physical compassion which can point toward "peace on earth" in spite of the generation's forlornness. There are eight such passages in the book, occupying at most, some 25 pages in a novel of 280 pages. It can hardly be said that their design and cumulative effect is such as to reduce love to sex and sex to its physiological dimensions. When physical acts are presented, they are always presented in their human context; their supra-biological meanings are never lost or depreciated.

Lawrence does not make a public display of the private side of sexuality. He does contrive to keep his readers at a certain distance from the physical intimacies he describes. He does this, in part, by presenting no more sensual detail than is necessary for the understanding of his characters and his teaching. Thus, the reader is not encouraged to wallow in these details for their own sake (though, of course, he may succeed in doing so); he is encouraged, rather, to relate them to the lives of Constance and Mellors. To the extent that erotic feelings are aroused, such feelings are necessary concomitants of insight into the actions and passions of such characters as these. No matter what the intensity of the sexual scenes presented, the reader is never encouraged to forget how they are related to the problems and aspirations of two human beings in a "forlorn" world. This does not stimulate depersonalized sexual desire. It does not present human beings as mere sexual objects. And it does not strip away human purposes and values in order to reveal mere animal functions.[36]

The following selection is taken from a passage (four pages long) describing an act of coitus between Fanny Hill and a young man whom she has persuaded to seduce her. This describes the conclusion of the act:

> As soon, then, as he had made a short pause, waking, as it were, out of the trance of pleasure, . . . he still kept his post, yet unsated with enjoyment, and solacing in these so new delights; 'til his stiffness, which had scarce perceptibly remitted, being thoroughly recovered to him, who had not once unsheath'd, he proceeded afresh to cleave and open to himself an entire entry into me, which was not a little made easy to him by the balsamic

injection with which he had just plentifully moisten'd the whole internals of the passage. Redoubling, then, the active energy of his thrusts, favoured by the fervid appetite of my motions, the soft oiled wards can no longer stand so effectual a picklock, but yield, and open him an entrance. And now, with conspiring nature, and my industry, strong to aid him, he pierces, penetrates, and at length, winning his way inch by inch, gets entirely in, and finally mighty thrust sheaths it up to the guard: on the information of which, from the close jointure of our bodies (insomuch that the hair on both sides perfectly interweav'd and incircl'd together), the eyes of the transported youth sparkl'd with more joyous fires, and all his looks and motions acknowledged excess of pleasure, which now I began to share, for I felt him in my very vitals! I was quite sick now with delight! stir'd beyond bearing with its furious agitations within me, and gorged and cramm'd, even to surfeit. Thus I lay gasping, panting under him, til his broken breathings, faltering accents, eyes twinkling with humid fires, lunges more furious, and an increased stiffness, gave me to hail the approaches of the second period: it came . . . and the sweet youth, overpower'd with the extasy, died away in my arms, melting in a flood that shot in genial warmth into the innermost recesses of my body; every conduit of which, dedicated to that pleasure, was on flow to mix with it. Thus we continued for some instants, lost, breathless, senseless of every thing, and in every part but those favourite ones of nature, in which all that we enjoyed of life and sensation was now totally concentre'd.[37]

The reader of this chapter is invited to compare closely this passage with that of D. H. Lawrence cited previously, and to compare them in the larger contexts of the two works. In this passage the physiological phenomena of sex are considerably more obtrusive than is the case in Lawrence's writing. The reader is much closer to the physical act of Fanny Hill and her partner than he is to that of Constance and Mellors.

Further, this act is not presented with a view to the exploration of character or the explication of a teaching. It can scarcely be said that the novel has any characters. The author has not done very much to develop the personality of the various figures who appear in the book, and the reader is not likely to have much interest in who they are and what happens to them. The action of the story is primarily a succession of such scenes as the above. Such non-erotic scenes as are presented are little more than preludes and stepping stones to the erotic ones. While one may become interested in some of the nonsexual actions or descriptions for their own sake, these are far from constituting a dominant theme, and they do not weigh very heavily against the overwhelmingly erotic impact of the total work. The book embodies no explicit teaching. Its non-explicit teaching is that to experience the maximum of physical sensation is the end of life. The reader does not confront this as a teaching; rather, he simply experiences the sensations. As a whole, the story is hardly more than a platform for the detailed presentation of various sexual encounters, ranging from ordinary coitus, to lesbianism, to flagellation, to intercourse publicly performed.[38]

It is not suggested that *Fanny Hill* is the worst kind of obscenity. The participants in its sexual episodes do observe certain delicacies, as does the author's commentary, and the book does not, on the whole, identify sex with brutality. But it is suggested that the book intrusively invades important personal intimacies and does so in such a way as to reduce their human to their physiological properties. Indeed, the physical side of sex is itself broken down into some of its most elemental motions and functions. Love becomes sex, and sex becomes an interaction of organs and parts of organs.

The reader is presented with a series of obtrusive sexual images which are so unrelated to any aesthetic end, so unrelated to plot and character, that they can only arouse depersonalized desire. The reader is not concerned with Fanny and her partners. In most of the scenes Fanny and her partners are simply sexual objects which stimulate in him the desire for sexual objects. This is the obscene way of presenting sex.

When such obscene portrayal of sex is carried very far one may be said to have arrived at pornography. Speaking of a nineteenth-century pornographic novel called *The Lustful Turk,* Steven Marcus says: "It concentrates upon this [male sexual] organ and what it can do: the organ becomes the person, and the woman ceases to be a woman and is transformed into an object, an object upon which the penis works its destructive yet delightful effects." Commenting upon this phenomenon, Marcus observes: "From organs and objects it is but one step to machines."[39] He cites this passage from *The Lustful Turk:*

> Stretched almost to suffocation on the rack of pleasure, its point stung her so much that, catching at length the rage from my furious driving, she went wholly out of her mind, her sense concentrating in the favorite part of her body, the whole of which was so luxuriously filled and employed. There alone she existed, all lost in those delicious transports, those ecstasies of the senses. . . . In short she was a machine (like any other piece of machinery) obeying the impulse of the key that so potently set her in motion, till the sense of pleasure foaming to a height drove the shower that was to allay this hurricane. She kept me faithful company, going off with the old symptoms. . . . And now in getting off her, she lay motionless, pleasure-filled—stretched and drenched—quite spent and gasping for breath, without any other sensations of life than in those exquisite vibrations that trembled yet on the strings of delight, which had been so ravishingly touched. . . .[40]

The reader will note how, from the beginning, he is invited to enjoy the ingredient of pain which is present in this woman's pleasure ("stretched almost to suffocation," "rack of pleasure," "its point stung her"). But the interweaving of pleasure and pain is not the heart of this passage's pornography; nor is it even the brutality of the passage that constitutes its essential pornographic appeal. The woman whose behavior is the subject of this passage was a proud English girl of good family;* now she is a machine— a mere instrument at the disposal of her master, or, at least, he has the power to turn her into such a machine at his will. She has been beaten and raped into the submission and passivity described above, and—most significant for the pornographer's intent— she has been forced to *desire* this submission and passivity. We are presented here with the spectacle of a human being who is, or is made to be, "wholly out of her mind." She has become nothing more than a body, but even this body has lost its autonomy—it has become a thing, or collection of things, completely controlled

---

* It seems essential to the pornographer's purpose that the girl be possessed of these or similar qualities, since he is engaged in the process of degrading her, and it is this *process* which the reader is invited to enjoy. This is, perhaps, an appropriate place to consider why a picture of a partially clothed woman (or a woman in undergarments) will often provide a more "obscene effect" than one of a woman totally nude. The former can serve to remind us that this is a woman (in the social and moral sense) who is about to become something less than that.

and manipulated by another. When scenes like this are presented in such a manner as to arouse sexual passion, one is undoubtedly in the presence of something approaching pornography in its pure form.

There are varying degrees of pornography. *Fanny Hill* is not as pornographic as is that kind of literature represented here by *The Lustful Turk*. Pornography, then, is a certain kind of obscenity—it is sexual obscenity in which the debasement of the human element is heavily accentuated, is depicted in great physiological detail, and is carried very far toward its utmost logical conclusion.

I have approached obscenity in such a way as to render moral considerations highly relevant to the definition and application of the term. To state the matter in its broadest ethical terms: obscenity is a way of looking at man which dehumanizes human purposes and human beings. It is, after all, what the dictionary says it is and what the etymology of the word implies: it is "the filthy," and it is that which ought to be "off the scene," off the public stage of life.

There are those who would regard the interpretation of obscenity set forth here as arbitrary and politically irrelevant. But there is a burden of proof on them to show that the moral perspectives from which this definition is derived are not those of Western civilization, and that the attitudes implicit in what I have called "obscenity" are not destructive of values with which this civilization is identified. In this author's view, civilized society cannot afford to be neutral toward a perception of life which undermines its efforts to make of man something more than a creature of elemental passions and sensations. And the political community cannot afford to be neutral toward a way of looking at man which undermines its efforts to promote decent human relations.

This is not to say that the law can stamp out all obscenity in human affairs or that the criteria elaborated in this chapter can be simply embodied in legal formulas. These criteria are the result of an inquiry into the nature of the obscene. It remains to be determined how much of what is by nature obscene can and ought to be proscribed by law and to be shown how moral and aesthetic standards can be translated into legal standards. These concluding remarks are designed to be contributory to deliberation about these problems.

Consider the definition according to which obscenity consists in making a gross public display of physical intimacies and that according to which it consists in presenting, graphically and in detail, a degrading (or reductive) picture of human life and inviting the reader to wallow in it to the accompaniment of desire or loathing. Our law cannot embody all that is implicit in these formulations. There are several reasons for this: Liberal democracy tolerates (perhaps paradoxically) a great deal of *social* intrusion upon privacy. That is, liberal democracy restricts the power of government to prevent men's activities in society from making a public display of private intimacies. Second, even if men agree that obscenity is what these formulations assert it to be, they will differ, often sharply, in the application of them to specific cases. Judges and juries will require criteria less complicated and more precisely delimited than these. Finally, these terms are not sufficiently simple and precise to provide that certitude of what constitutes crime which is a requisite of due process of law.

Nonetheless, such formulations as these can have practical import in two ways. First, they can serve as a guide to reflection and judgment, both public and private, about what constitutes obscenity and what is the moral evil connected with it. Second, they can provide a basis for interpretation and modification of existing laws.

Public policy toward obscenity will be rationally made and supported to the extent that judges, scholars, and citizens address themselves to those considerations which underlie the ordinary common-sense or legal definitions of obscenity. The ordinary notions and legal formulas do not sufficiently clarify the essential ingredients of obscenity; they do not sufficiently explain what is wrong about obscenity; and they do not provide a firm basis for the distinction between obscene literature and the literary treatment of the obscene. Reflection about these things can clarify the purposes of the law, encourage proper censorship, and discourage improper censorship.

But the overall definition of obscenity advanced in this chapter can be more directly related to prevailing legal definitions and criteria. It is submitted that some of the elements of this definition are already implicit (if not explicit) in the law of obscenity and that legal standards can be framed which will incorporate some additional elements.

The law defines obscenity in terms of prurient interests and the stimulation of lust. As has been observed, the term "lust" can have various gradations of meaning.[41] It can signify "sexual desire," or it can designate some kind of extreme or warped desire. It can also mean sexual passion in the absence of love or affection; that is, it can mean *depersonalized* sexual desire. I suggest that depersonalized sexual desire is one of the most prevalent meanings conveyed to average persons by the terms "lust" and "prurience." Indeed, this is what these terms primarily signify to most persons most of the time, however they would frame explicit definitions of them. The ordinary man does not ordinarily speak of lust in connection with marriage, or love, or those sexual relations in which persons are concerned about each other as persons.

If this is correct, then the law already embodies some of the perspectives and concepts on the basis of which obscenity has been defined here. Implicit in the law's terminology is a condemnation of that kind of sexual appeal which tends to reduce human beings to mere objects of sexual appetite. If the law is concerned about lust, this is not because it pronounces judgment upon sexual desire as such, or simply upon "venereal pleasure." What the law is concerned about is the systematic arousal of passions which are severed from the social, affectional, aesthetic, and moral considerations which make human relations human. This is precisely the kind of passion which must be promoted by obscene literature which stimulates desires that are unrelated to the human qualities of the persons portrayed. Obscenity arouses the desire for sex as such—not for sexual relations with a person for whom one cares. In the eyes of impersonal lust, human qualities are stripped away and a person becomes an instrument existing solely for the pleasure or manipulation of others.

Thus, the legal concepts of "lust" and "prurience" will serve to reach some of the evils which are associated with the obscene view of life. But the application of these terms would be rendered more effective if their implications were made more explicit.

The law of obscenity is largely concerned with literature that exploits sex. But some of its terms imply a recognition, however obscure, that sexual obscenity is not the only form of obscenity.

The American Law Institute's definition of prurient interest (which is, in some degree, incorporated in *Roth*) refers to "a shameful or morbid interest in *nudity, sex,* or *excretion"* (italics mine).[42] And when violence is combined with sex in such proportions that it is recognizable as "sadism," courts will often act as if they believe that the violence is an ingredient of the obscenity.

These insights should be elaborated and clarified, and standards should be framed which will permit the law to reach some obscene portrayals of brutality, death, and the human body. The following is offered as an indication of some of the elements which might be included in a legal definition of obscenity.

An obscene book, story, magazine, motion picture, or play is one which tends predominantly to:

1. Arouse lust or appeal to prurient interests.

2. Arouse sexual passion in connection with scenes of extreme violence, cruelty, or brutality.

3. Visually portray in detail, or graphically describe in lurid detail, the violent physical destruction, torture, or dismemberment of a human being, provided this is done to exploit morbid or shameful interest in these matters and not for genuine scientific, educational, or artistic purposes.

4. Visually portray, or graphically describe, in lurid physical detail the death or the dead body of a human being, provided this is done to exploit morbid or shameful interest in these matters and not for genuine scientific, educational, or artistic purposes.

Such a definition as this, properly elaborated to provide for strict interpretation of its key terms, would leave much of what I have called "obscenity" untouched by the law. But, properly interpreted, it would provide a barrier against the worst intrusions upon intimacies of the body and against some of the most obscene portrayals of sex, brute violence, and death.*

The moral considerations which underlie this definition are not the only relevant considerations. It remains to be established that the principles and recommendations set forth in this chapter are consistent with our society's interest in the circulation of literature and in the protection of community standards or beliefs.

---

* For example, a legal definition of obscenity framed in these terms could and should reach *Fanny Hill,* some of the more lurid sensationalist tabloids, and "exploitation films." Some of the writings of Mickey Spillane would also be affected.

7

Literary Values and
Contemporary Community Standards

Can a system of censorship be established which will protect the moral values of the community without infringing upon literary values? Can the law reconcile the moral demands of public opinion and the demands of art? These questions suggest a tension between moral and aesthetic values, or, at least, between moral and aesthetic opinions.

In his dissenting opinion in the *Roth* case, Justice Douglas refers to "the battle between the literati and the Philistines."[1] He does not explain why there must be such a battle. Henry Miller provides this explanation:

> There will always be a gulf between the creative artist and the public because the latter is immune to the mystery inherent in and surrounding all creation. . . . The very depth of [the artist's] interpretations naturally makes them unpalatable and unacceptable to the vast body which constitutes the unthinking public.[2]

These remarks, made from the perspective of the "literati," do not constitute an adequate statement of what the battle is about. And it may be questioned whether this conflict always rages with the same degree of intensity and whether it exists here and now in the same way or to the same extent as it has in other times and places. But the existence of such a conflict has been attested by artists and citizens in various times and places, and, indeed, it is attested by the censorship controversy of our own day.

The battle between the literati and the philistines arises, ultimately, from the tension between two divergent moral perspectives—two ways of apprehending the values and beliefs which may prevail in society at any given time. The literary artist does not accept these beliefs, or is not committed to them, in the same way that the average man accepts or is committed to them. The literary artist does not take them for granted. His work explores or questions the opinions by reference to which the majority in society act or claim to act. He is often a critic or an innovator or a liberator. As a critic he seeks to expose false values and to force men to look at themselves—to confront the disparity between their principles and their practice. As an innovator he seeks new ways of looking at man, new ways of experiencing the ends and values of life. As a liberator he seeks to destroy prevailing social forms and ethics in order to create new ones or simply in order to free men from old constraints.*

Frequently and increasingly, the modern artist takes the role of innovator and liberator. He sees it as his function to expose and to destroy what he regards as the irrational prejudices and taboos which make up contemporary community standards. Persons committed to these standards will often condemn this artist and his work as irresponsible, licentious, and destructive. The artist does not defend himself by disclaiming any capacity to undermine the standards he attacks. The artist and his opponents agree that literature can have significant effects upon community norms. To a large extent the controversy between them rests upon this agreement.

Where should the law stand with regard to this controversy? Where does the public interest lie, and what resources are available for judges and legislators to enable them to discern it and serve it?

In the recent history of judicial efforts to answer these questions one may discern a pronounced trend. The older view is expressed (though in extreme form) in the following judicial pronouncements:

> The defendant's brief refers the Court to eminent men of

---

* I do not mean to imply by these remarks that literary art is designed to be simply didactic, or that the artist approaches his subjects as does a philosopher, psychologist, or social scientist. These remarks refer only to some of the attitudes and ends which are associated with literary activity and particularly with modern literary activity.

letters, critics, artists and publishers who have praised *The Well of Loneliness*. . . . However, the book's literary merits are not challenged, and the Court may not conjecture as to the loss that its condemnation may entail to our general literature, when it is plainly subversive of public morals and public decency, which the statute is designed to safeguard. (From *People* v. *Friede, 1929*.)[3]

The Court cannot indulge any instinct it may have to foster letters. The statute is designed to protect society at large, of that there can be no dispute; notwithstanding the deprivation of benefits to a few, a work must be condemned if it has a depraving influence. (From the dissenting opinion of Judge Manton in *United States* v. *Ulysses, 1934*.)[4]

Thus, the older view assumes that society's interest in the maintenance of moral standards far outweighs any interest it may have in the promotion of literature. In fact, in the pronouncements just cited, the values associated with literature are not regarded as belonging to or serving the public interests at all. Encroachments upon public morality constitute deprivation inflicted upon "society at large"; restrictions upon literature will deprive only "a few."

In the major decisions from the *Ulysses* case to the present it has been the tendency of our courts to weigh literary values more and more heavily in the judicial scales. The most influential trend in contemporary thinking is expressed in this statement quoted by Justice Douglas from Lockhart and McClure: "The danger of influencing a change in current moral standards . . . can never justify the losses to society that result from interference with literary freedom."[5] Justice Douglas' *Roth* opinion contains frequent references to "society's interest in literature" or "society's values in literary freedom." As this attitude becomes the dominant one and is, more or less officially, incorporated into the First Amendment, courts tend increasingly to rely upon the testimony or views of literary critics and men of letters for the determination of obscenity cases. In some cases the status of a work in the eyes of literary critics appears to be the determining consideration for judicial judgment.

Has the older view been completely overthrown in favor of one exactly opposite it? Do the higher courts now hold that society's interest in literature far outweighs any interest it may have in the maintenance of prevailing morality? Do we now believe that restrictions upon literature injure society at large, while encroachments upon morality are deprivational only to a few?

Heavy reliance upon literary considerations and aesthetic judgments in obscenity cases can, conceivably, be justified on two grounds: (1) Literature and the values associated with it perform indispensable functions for society and its members. (2) The presence of literary qualities in a work nullifies such evil effects as may flow from it in the absence of these qualities.

In contemporary writings in this area there is very little systematic effort to explore the nature and relative importance of "society's interest in literature." Lockhart and McClure make an argument which addresses itself to some aspects of the problem. They assert: "Fiction and poetry, like all other forms of art and expression, are vehicles for the conveyance of ideas. They differ from other forms of art and expression in the use of their own peculiar means of communication."[6] Imaginative literature is, then, a vehicle of learning, and it promotes a kind of learning which it is most difficult for many to attain in any other way. In explication of the unique contribution which literature can make to the human mind, Lockhart and McClure summarize the views of a contemporary philosopher:

> Erwin Edman also tells us how the reader learns from fiction and poetry. The chief functions of art, he says, are the intensification, clarification and interpretation of experience. Experience is intensified by arresting the reader's sensations, focusing his attention upon his own emotions so that he can know them for what they are. Experience is clarified by setting emotions and random impressions in a pattern so as to make their meaning clear to the reader. And experience is interpreted, simply because any work of art necessarily carries in it the artist's view of life and his criticism of that phase of experience he has selected for treatment.[7]

Further, fiction enables us to share imaginatively in experiences and activities to which we can have no direct access. Thus, it enlarges our horizons and deepens our sensibilities. And it promotes "an understanding of unfamiliar problems and modes of life."[8]

These observations are surely true of the educative effects of good literature upon those who are able to appreciate and benefit from it. But how would they apply to the "learning" which results from such materials as *Fanny Hill,* the lurid tabloid, or the writings of Mickey Spillane? The "intensification," "clarification," and "interpretation" of experience promoted by such materials has been discussed in the preceding chapter. It will not be denied that these writings, as well as those of Swift, Shakespeare, and D. H. Lawrence, stimulate some kind of imaginative sharing in action, events, and lives unfamiliar to us. But Lockhart and McClure do not say (and probably would not say) that the imaginative experiences promoted by these various writings are all equally valuable and that they all promote an *understanding* of unfamiliar problems and ways of life. It is evident that if some kinds of intensification and interpretation of experience are educative, other kinds are dis-educative, and that, if some works can clarify experience, others can obscure it.

Lockhart and McClure's argument does not really establish "society's interest in literature," it establishes, at most, society's interest in a certain kind of literature. If an attempt would be made to weigh the value to society of literature as such, one would have to take account of various considerations concerning the circulation and consumption of literary materials which do not appear in Lockhart and McClure's discussion of the matter. One would want to consider, for instance, what is the circulation in our society of such works as those of D. H. Lawrence or James Joyce compared to that of materials much less worthy and less educative. How many persons are attracted to the former and how many to the latter? One would also have to consider the disparity between the literary objectives of some good works and their actual effects upon many of those who read them. It is not necessarily the case that all of those who read D. H. Lawrence or *The Well of Loneliness* (to take a lesser example) are able to do so in the right way or are going to do so for the right reasons. There is, inevitably, a gap between the profundity of great authors and the capacity or motives of many readers.

It is true that "there is a high breathlessness about beauty that cancels lust,"[9] and that, as argued in the last chapter, the "aesthetic distance" which characterizes genuine art is incompatible with obscenity. The appropriate reader, who is attuned to the artistic dimensions of a work, will not receive from that work an obscene experience of life. But it is also true that not all readers are the appropriate readers. Of those who do read Lawrence (instead of *Fanny Hill*), not all are capable of the contemplative experience which the work is designed to promote.[10]

Any balanced effort to assess the nature of "society's values in literary freedom," should involve the consideration of such questions as this: If one million Americans are exposed to literature of the caliber of *Lady Chatterley* and *Ulysses* and twenty million are exposed to Mickey Spillane, the tabloids or exposé publications, and sordid motion pictures, what is the net social value? It is needless to say that there can be no research leading to definitive answers to such questions, but there can be some thinking about them.

I am convinced that our society can afford to tolerate such evils as may result when people read Lawrence and Joyce in the wrong way or for the wrong reasons. Some people (an appreciable number) will receive such benefits as are described by Lockhart and McClure. It is not necessary that all, or a majority, of persons in this society develop the peculiar insights and sensitivities which such works can promote. But it is necessary, particularly in a commercial and in a democratic society, that some persons be in a position to do so.

As Tocqueville observed, commercial democracy tends to promote a kind of "virtuous materialism" which unduly restricts the aspirations and the intellectual horizons of men and which can lead to spiritual enervation.[11] Tocqueville explained how, in relatively egalitarian and affluent times, the energies of the vast majority are inevitably devoted to the private pursuit of physical comfort and security. The strivings of most men are confined to a series of small, incremental efforts to improve the material conditions of their existence. Life is more orderly and secure, but there is little in our daily routines to inspire the mind with lofty aspirations. This Tocquevillian prediction may be unflattering to us, but it is hard to deny its relevance to us.

Tocqueville insisted on the urgent need, in times such as these, that men be presented with visions of life broader, more elevated, and more inspiring than those which arise from our ordinary pursuit of material well-being. For the performance of this indispensable function he looked (though more in hope than in confidence) to religion.

But a case can be made for the vital role of imaginative literature as an antidote to the materialism and the moral mediocrity which commercial civilization often engenders. Literature and the arts can uplift the minds, develop the moral sensibilities, and enlarge the vision of those susceptible to its influence. Creative works may suggest to the mind ideas, aspirations, duties, and goals which our ordinary routines must generally fail to suggest. Such works can present visions of excellence, humanity, or tragedy, thus reminding us that there is more to life than comfortable self-preservation and that man is (or can become) something more than a pleasure-seeking calculator of enlightened self-interest.

If liberal democracy needs citizens who are reminded of such realities; if we need imaginative men and men with a capacity for independent thought, then literary and aesthetic values cannot be excluded from the realm of the *public interest*. For great works of art touch the feelings and promote those finer sentiments which are the basis of sound ethical judgment and humane purpose.

But this way of stating a First Amendment case for literary and artistic expression serves to remind us that we have a problem. For, if there is a public interest in good literature which stimulates the imagination and enlarges the moral horizons of citizens; correspondingly, there is a public interest in the restriction of certain materials which corrupt imagination and contract moral horizons. When liberal society seeks to prevent the circulation of corrupting literature, it must constantly strive to do so in such a way that all good literature remains free of restrictions. This means that the liberal community will have to tolerate much of what is bad in order to insure the protection of what is good. From these very general principles two propositions of more practical import follow. (1) The law must strive to protect not only works of acknowledged *excellence,* but also works of acknowledged *seriousness.* (2) In doubtful cases the benefit of the doubt should usually be given to work which can lay claim to genuine moral, intellectual, or aesthetic purposes. It should be the policy of liberal democracy to strike a balance in favor of the free circulation of serious literature.

In most cases, it will not be impossible to make the reasonable distinctions which such a policy requires. But there is a form of literature prevalent in our society which does pose grave practical difficulties for this policy. This is the literature of "liberation," to which I have referred. This literature is designed to free men from the constraints and the values of conventional society. Very often it takes the form of a direct attack upon morality as such and upon organized society as such. And very often obscenity is one of the major devices by which this attack is conducted.

The writing of Henry Miller may stand as an example of that literature of liberation which is designed to assault and, if possible, to destroy the moral and aesthetic taboos of civil society. Miller is quite clear about his purpose. At the beginning of *Tropic of Cancer* he tells us:

> This is not a book. This is libel, slander, defamation of character. This is not a book in the ordinary sense of the word. NO, this is a prolonged insult, a gob of spit in the face of art, a kick in the pants to God, Man, Destiny, Time, Love, Beauty . . . what you will.[12]

There follows after this introduction five pages of systematic obscenity concerning the sexual act and the sexual organs of men and women. The author is not concerned with arousing sexual desire. He seeks to profane the sacred, to break down those barriers of propriety and sensibility with which social man surrounds certain intimacies, and to assault the most deeply held moral and aesthetic convictions.

The purpose for which this is done may be variably described in terms of "truth" or "freedom." Each man must discover truth, which is an utterly personal truth at war with social forms and moralities. And each man must be utterly free from all restraints which inhibit his experience of "the gamut of human passions." Says Miller: "If we are denied the smallest measure of freedom we are spiritually thwarted and crippled."[13] And the way to freedom is via the release of elemental passions.

Thus, Miller is not simply a critic of contemporary society. He does not simply condemn certain moral taboos and certain social corruptions. He condemns all externally imposed restraints, and he attacks such standards as might be the basis for restraints, either externally or voluntarily imposed. His attack is upon society as such. Speaking of *Tropic of Cancer,* George Elliott says: "It does have an unmistakable message: Society is intrinsically vile, let us return to the natural man. In effect, this means as little work as possible and lots of loveless sex."[14] Miller suggests that if his end is to be achieved "the whole structure must topple."[15] By the skillful use of obscenity, he seeks to assault "the structure"— to desecrate the things that are revered within it.

Is Miller's work obscene? It certainly does embody some of the properties laid down in the previous chapter as identifying marks of the obscene. But it cannot be denied that Miller's work is *serious* literature. He uses obscenity for a serious literary, intellectual, and "moral" purpose. The anomaly lies in the fact that that purpose itself tends to be obscene. In the light of the criteria I have offered (those defining obscenity and those concerned with the protection of genuine literature), Miller is clearly a borderline case. Since Miller's work is typical of a prominent movement in modern literature, it follows that there is a large number of borderline cases.

What should the law undertake to do about them? For practical reasons it may be wisest to leave them alone. This is a matter for prudential judgment in the light of times and circumstances. But if those who represent society choose to leave such materials uncensored, the grounds upon which they do so would be of some importance; for it is important to determine what the posture of organized society should be toward literature of this kind. Society could leave these works uncensored on the assumption that they are works of social value; or it could strongly disapprove of them and leave them uncensored out of practical necessity. By the adoption of the former alternative, the community announces that it regards as socially valuable materials which are designed to attack and undermine it. By the adoption of the second alternative, the community announces that it is well aware of what "society's interest in literature" really is and places itself in a position to observe carefully the development and the effects of a literary movement deeply hostile to it.

It may be observed that those who represent the interests of organized society cannot afford to be so libertarian that they are unable to recognize its avowed enemies when confronted by them. And they cannot afford to assume that whatever various artists and authors choose to do must necessarily benefit society. These propositions would be vigorously contested by a certain segment of the literati which appears to believe that the products of literary expression must necessarily be beneficial to human beings and human societies. This view of the matter deserves some attention here.

It is sometimes affirmed that "what is good for literature and the arts is good for mankind"; the interests of the former are identical with those of the latter. This idea has a rather long history. Some thinkers of the Enlightenment tended to view the contribution of the arts to human well-being in terms of a softening or mellowing of primary natural impulses. Through the influence of the arts, brutish or potentially violent passions of the natural man are tempered, modified, and eventually transformed into more subtle and refined sentiments.[16]

This way of describing the contribution of artistic expression to mankind is seldom heard today. Today the argument on behalf of the artist takes a different form. He is more often presented as an uncompromising "realist," a teller of harsh truths, the man who confronts us with the brute realities which lie beneath the surface of deceptive convention. Among these realities are passions, normal or abnormal, moderate or extreme, loving or brutal, which social forms and restraints inhibit and hide from view. Art, particularly literary art, performs a service when it strips off the masks, compelling us to see and experience realities which our conventional social relations keep "underground." Thus, art does not "soothe the savage breast" as much as it reveals the savagery within and around us. To be fully human is to understand what we are and to be able to experience the full range of human possibilities. We are less than fully human to the extent that we deny some part of what we are and cut ourselves off from some part of human experience.

It will be noted that this view can provide the basis for a defense of obscenity and even pornography. It can be argued that the wide circulation of pornography is positively desirable in a society such as ours. The pornography represents and conveys precisely those dimensions of experience which are repressed by our conventional patterns of thought and conduct. If the pornography is shocking to many people, perhaps these are just the ones who need to be shocked into awareness. After all, sexuality of diverse kinds, brutish passions, and the association of sensuality and violence are realities of human existence, are they not? At any rate, obscenity can be useful to those who have the capacity to face realities and who need some help in their struggle for liberation from oppressive "establishments." Obscenity can be a means of breaking through to the vital forces of life.

This is the most radical argument for unlimited freedom of expression. Beginning with a certain view of the nature of art and the role of the artist, it concludes with a positive sanction for the most extreme forms of obscenity.

It cannot be denied that some artists are tellers of harsh truths and that they can serve us by compelling us to confront ugly realities. But we should not forget the importance and dignity of that art which is a creation of beauty and form and which serves us by elevating our thoughts and cultivating our emotions. The radical argument for obscenity rests on some assumptions about what is human which should not, because of the partial truths they embody, go unchallenged.

Traditional philosophy does indeed identify human dignity with man's capacity for understanding, and this includes self-understanding. But it does not conclude from this that all realities should be presented to all men at all times, by any means which, in the opinion of an author or film-maker are likely to be effective. The greatest educators have known that the understanding of reality is a complicated matter, that some realities pose delicate problems and must be approached with some care at an appropriate time, and that awareness of some truths must involve awareness of them in relation to other and, perhaps, more important truths. The assumption that self-knowledge or awareness results from indiscriminate exposure to all (and especially the most ugly and pornographic) realities has yet to be formulated into a coherent, defensible theory.

The viewpoint that, to be fully human, we must be open to all passions and experiences has something in common with the Miltonian condemnation of a "cloistered virtue." But Milton would have us be aware of vice in order that virtue may be freely chosen. The radical argument under consideration is not concerned with virtue, but, it seems, with experience for its own sake.

To take issue with this view is not to hold that human experiences should be narrow and passions nonexistent; it is to affirm that, with regard to experiences, the distinctively human element is that of evaluation, and with regard to passions, the distinctively human element is that of control or direction. It is a premise of this whole essay that *human* existence requires that experiences be judged and that some be ranked as base or degrading.

But the proponents of pornography do not really regard all experiences as equal; they seem to have a decided animus against those which result from restraints imposed by custom and convention. At the bottom of their argument is an identification of our humanity with our elemental, pre-civil passions. But our humanity ought to be identified with the *cultivation* of elemental feelings and dispositions. It is another premise of this essay that some customary and conventional restraint of raw passion is a necessary precondition for such capacity as reason may have to direct conduct. Some establishments are necessary and desirable.

Yet, after these refutations have been made, we must acknowledge the kernel of truth in the radical view. Modern civilized life insulates most of us to a considerable degree from certain basic facts of existence; from, for instance, violence, pain, and death. Perhaps it is possible for men to become overcivilized and unduly tamed. Surely we should have some opportunity to experience vicariously the primal facts of violence, pain, and death.

Obscenity can be seen, in part, as an effort to escape from the tensions and burdens of civilization. Obscenity can be seen as the endeavor to throw off, for a time, the restraints and refinements of our higher humanity and return to things primal and elemental. Should men be denied such an opportunity to escape? Should we be compelled to be always civilized and humane?

The case against obscenity would be one-sided if it did not acknowledge this human need for temporary relief from humanity and this possible function of obscenity. It would seem that large numbers of civilized men will continue to require of literature, the arts, and the mass media some portrayal of raw passions and brutality. The rationale I have presented for legal control certainly does not require that there be an end to all this, and it does not require the censorship of all literary materials that fall clearly within the broad definition of obscenity. It is unnecessary to say that this would be impossible, and the attempt to bring it about under modern conditions could only be tyrannical.

There is little danger, in this day and age, that people who need it will be denied all access to the escape mechanism of obscenity. But it is one thing for ethical theory and public policy to make this concession to a human frailty and quite another for them to adopt the doctrines by which pornography is declared a positive good and the artist is taught that he can do no wrong. Obscenity, while ineradicable from human affairs, is an evil of sufficient magnitude to require the attention of organized society. Representatives of the community have the task of ensuring that this ineradicable evil does not grow to undue proportions and get out of hand. Thus, it is not true that authors and artists can do no wrong as long as they are "creative."

The philistine, unappreciative of genuine creative work, fails to distinguish between art and obscenity. But some of the literati are given to a facile identification of literary sincerity or self-expression with human excellence or progress. The law cannot afford to adopt either of these postures.

The foregoing discussion is relevant to the problem of the proper employment of literary critics in the determination of obscenity cases. Literary critics are experts in literary matters and in questions of aesthetics, but they are not quite experts on the question of society's interest in literary values. With regard to the latter question, the literary critic can be said to be a partisan of the literati. To recognize this fact is not to depreciate the critic and his function. It is not his task to weigh carefully those elements of the public interest which may be found on the philistines' side of the controversy. If a work attacks contemporary moral standards, a critic may or may not defend these standards, but they are not his primary concern. He is primarily concerned with a work's contribution to the literary world—to aesthetic interests and to the literary communication of ideas.

Thus, eminent critics have testified that *Tropic of Cancer* is a work of literary and intellectual interest. They are interested in Miller's work as writing. It represents an innovation in literary styles and techniques; and it represents a new mode of expression. Some critics might find in it a contribution to the art of the novel. Critics have been found who were willing to testify that *Fanny Hill* is a work of some literary merit.[17] They found in it certain stylistic merits, and they proclaimed interest in it as an example of a certain kind of English novel of the eighteenth century. These considerations are not without significance, but they do not express the public interest. And they should not wholly determine whether, for the purposes of the law, a book is obscene or is of redeeming social importance. A judge, or a jury under a judge's guidance, must assume responsibility for deciding these matters.

This poses for the judge a serious problem. He must take account of literary values, but he cannot rely simply upon the judgment of literary men. This problem cannot be completely resolved; but it is not impossible to live with. Judges are readers and they are intelligent men. And, under proper laws, they will not often be required to make the most delicate kinds of literary judgments. In most obscenity cases the only literary judgment to be made will concern the distinctions between seriousness and the pretense of seriousness in literary works. Judges need not be total strangers to the criteria by which the evidences of seriousness—intellectual content, character development, stylistic excellence, and aesthetic distance—are discovered. It should not be too difficult to apply these criteria so as to distinguish between the treatment of death in "men's action" magazines and in the Sherlock Holmes stories of Arthur Conan Doyle.

Judges can, of course, invite the testimony of literary critics, and in difficult cases they should give considerable weight to that testimony. But the critic should not be asked simply whether he finds *any* literary merit in the work; it is very likely that he can find some. And he should not be asked simply about the stylistic qualities of a work. He should be invited to render his critical judgment of the work, including his judgment of its intellectual content, the depth of its characterization, and the literary purposes for which allegedly obscene passages are employed.

But, in the final analysis, it is the judge who must decide or who must guide the decision. For he has in view the public interest which includes the maintenance of moral standards and, in some degree, the protection of contemporary community standards.

The literati, like their supporters, the libertarians, do not see why community beliefs should receive any legal protection at all. Their views imply that the public good is always served by the questioning and criticism of prevailing standards. Their views sometimes imply that the public good is necessarily served when old standards are abandoned for new ones.

Chapter 5 presents arguments justifying some legal support for community standards—for a community's particular conceptions of virtue—when these are reasonably related to standards of virtue which are more universally recognized.[18] Common beliefs or moral consensus may not be an indispensable requisite of all society, but it is an indispensable requisite of decent civil society. It is possible to conceive of a large body of men held together solely by economic interests or by force, but it is not possible to conceive of a good society so governed.

There are some literati who would not quarrel with these propositions. They would disclaim any intention of attacking moral consensus as such. They seek to undermine only false or corrupt beliefs. They envision, not a society without common beliefs, but one whose common beliefs are based on truth and right.

This argument is most appropriately addressed to a situation in which the artist confronts a false and corrupt public consensus. It is with regard to such a consensus that the artist as critic, as innovator, or as liberator performs his most valuable social function. He is a gadfly. But what of that situation in which the artist confronts a social ethic which approximates moral decency, though that ethic is supported by beliefs which are a mixture of truths, half-truths, and prejudices? It is not clear that the public interest would be served by any and all attacks (no matter how conducted) upon that part of the community ethic which is not simply true or simply good.

I submit that no community ethic can be simply true or simply good. Certain individuals can discern wisdom and virtue and make them predominate in their lives. Man in society will, for the most part, have to live on a lower level.[19] Thus, assaults upon the imperfect "virtues" of a community may have results other than those intended. The artist may succeed in undermining these virtues, but he may not be able to replace them with something better. It is usually easier to undermine faith than it is to replace faith with knowledge.

There are those who would deny that moral consensus can be dissolved or that its dissolution could constitute a serious social problem.[20] They assume, without evidence, that moral decency will always prevail. Or they assume, against evidence, that society is a morally self-regulating organism which will always succeed in producing spontaneously the values and the beliefs which it requires.

There is, then, in some times and places, a public interest in the protection of the moral consensus. I would contend that our contemporary community standards concerning sex and concerning obscenity still embody much that, in Western civilization at least, has been recognized as good. These standards also embody some prejudices and much that falls short of excellence. The law cannot simply separate the good from the bad, the true from the false, though it should endeavor to do so.

These arguments have been designed to constitute a rationale for the recognition of contemporary community standards in the determination of obscenity cases. This is, however, a rationale for the *recognition* of community standards—and not for their blanket imposition regardless of all competing considerations. The law should undertake to give them their due. But how is this to be done? How are the relevant community standards to be discerned and applied?

Any serious effort to answer these questions must confront the fact that multiplicity and variety are characteristic of our society. Some observers are so impressed with the ethical diversity which they find in American life that they deny the very existence of community standards on sex and related matters. The Kronhausens assert: "As to 'contemporary community standards': We have demonstrated that there is such an enormously wide variation in what is more commonly practiced that in effect there is no such thing as a contemporary community standard to relate to erotic writings."[21]

The Kronhausens' "demonstration" consists almost wholly of citations from the Kinsey Reports and their own commentaries thereon. They find that "as to extramarital sex activity, Kinsey *et al.* report that by age forty, 26 percent of American females *had had coitus* with males whom they could not call their husbands" (italics in the original).* They also cite Kinsey's estimate that approximately half of all married men have extramarital intercourse at some time during their married lives. Further, they find that the sexual conduct of persons in the lower socioeconomic classes differs widely from that of persons in the upper economic and educational groups. In the former, "premarital

---

* Eberhard and Phyllis Kronhausen, *Pornography and the Law,* p. 176. The quotations which follow on pp. 261–63 are all taken from the Kronhausens' discussion of the Kinsey Reports, pp. 175–94 of *Pornography and the Law.*

intercourse is . . . nearly universal"; while "with upper-class men things work out quite differently." As for sexual perversions, such as incest, "by methods of indirect proof one can only arrive at the conclusion that it is not nearly as uncommon as is usually assumed."

With regard to the problem of contemporary community standards, the Kinsey statistics presented by the Kronhausens are susceptible of more than one interpretation. The only certain and unambiguous conclusion which can be reasonably drawn from them is that the sexual behavior of the American people is neither as homogeneous nor as virtuous as it has often been thought to be. There are considerable variations in our patterns of sexual conduct. This does not yet prove that there are no community standards. To demonstrate this one would have to investigate more searchingly than do the Kronhausens the *attitudes* and *beliefs* of the American people.

The Kronhausens do make some effort to consider attitudes, though they grant that "we have to rely here on anecdotal material, and—to make things more difficult—sometimes we have to *infer* attitudes from what people tell us" (italics in original). They find that "as to premarital coitus, the Kinsey study suggests that between 69 to 77 percent of the women in their sample did not have the slightest regret about their experience." This is to say that 69 to 77 percent of those women interviewed who have had such experiences are willing to report that they have no regrets about their particular experiences. This does not establish the character of their beliefs or standards about sexual conduct and sexual life as such. For instance, would they advocate sexual promiscuity as a way of life (and teach it to their children), and if not, why not?

The Kronhausens find that attitudes about premarital sex vary considerably in accordance with economic and educational factors. This is not to be denied, but the authors' handling of these facts and their inferences from them are highly questionable. They tell us that young men who attend or have attended college usually have "certain convictions" against premarital intercourse, while the rest of the male population "takes premarital intercourse for granted as the most normal and natural thing in the world." They cite Kinsey as insisting "that for this group there just is no question of right or wrong involved." But later in the text we are told:

> This does not mean that the majority of such men (and women) [the lower or less-educated classes] are without any sexual guilt. Quite the contrary! Even for them puritanical inhibitions and qualms cast a shadow over their "happiest moments." Says Kinsey: "They 'know that intercourse is wrong' but 'they expect to have it anyway, because it is human and natural to have it.'"

There is evidently some confusion here about what the attitudes and beliefs of these people really are. And it does not constitute an adequate inquiry into attitudes and beliefs simply to dismiss some of them as mere "guilt" or "puritanical inhibitions."

In fact, the Kronhausens' data does not support their sweeping conclusion that there are no generally shared or common moral standards. For instance, they report that when an upper-class male has premarital intercourse, "he rationalizes, 'it's all right because we love each other.'" But when a lower-class male has premarital intercourse, he rationalizes in this manner: "I didn't think much of her so I went ahead and had intercourse with her. But when I find the 'right' girl, the one I really love and want to marry, I won't touch her until we're married." If this is an adequate account, it does obviously suggest two different sets of moral attitudes. But these two attitudes are quite clearly embraced within a common moral framework which requires that sex outside of marriage be justified, which respects love, and which attaches special importance to the relation between sex and love.

The Kronhausens' failure to note this common moral framework indicates that they are not really concerned with an investigation of moral standards. They are concerned with conduct. And when conduct falls short of standards, they tend to regard the latter as mere rationalization and to investigate them no further. It is an underlying assumption of this approach that the real standards are only those upon which people are in fact acting. Standards are identified with and reduced to conduct. Since the sex conduct of Americans is diversified, it follows that there are no community standards concerning sex. This is a simplistic view of what is meant by "contemporary community standards."

The evidence gathered by such studies as those of Kinsey and the Kronhausens must be weighed against other forms of evidence. It is still the case in this country that political candidates who would have any hope of attaining high office must avoid a reputation for sexual impropriety. In some cases a candidate who is divorced becomes "unavailable" for high national office. And it is still the case that great numbers of Americans disapprove of obscenity and that majorities in state legislatures and in Congress continue to support statutes which control it. It is an assumption of our political system that existing laws reflect community or majority opinion. This is perhaps not true of laws which are unenforced or sporadically enforced. But the obscenity laws continue to be the subject of a great deal of enforcement activity as well as legislative activity. In recent decades state and congressional legislative committees have devoted much attention to gathering evidence concerning obscenity and reviewing the operation of statutes. The statutes are very much alive. Should we conclude that such laws and such activity are no indication whatever of public opinion and community standards?

Judges are not entitled to assume that the standards of the community are nothing more than what can be discovered in statistical surveys of personal behavior. The judicial process requires a more subtle concept than this. Reflection upon judicial decisions and the judicial process suggests four ways in which the concept "contemporary community standards" can be understood.

1. It can be understood as the lowest common denominator of shared attitudes and proscriptions. These are a society's "taboos." A legal criterion based upon them could be stated in terms of outer limits of tolerance. The only things which are beyond the pale of community standards are those things which the vast majority habitually refuses to tolerate.

2. Community standards can be identified with the actual behavior of most people here and now. This identification rests upon the premise that conduct is the only meaningful indicator of belief.

3. The standards of the community can be understood in terms of its common conscience—the beliefs of the people concerning what is right and desirable. The common conscience is not adequately revealed by questionnaires addressed to isolated individuals and eliciting their attitudes about their private affairs. It is more adequately manifested in what the people would be willing to vote for in a solemn referendum or what they would be willing to argue for as public policy—after debate and deliberation. This is what *The Federalists* called the "deliberate sense of the community."[22]

4. Community standards can be identified with the common conscience as this is interpreted by recognized national leaders and by leaders of various communities within the nation.

These are four dimensions of contemporary community standards. Judges and others concerned with the control of obscenity must take account of them all. For the determination of outer limits of tolerance, trends appearing in the mass media of communication can be a useful guide. For the determination of patterns of behavior, statistical studies and carefully conducted interviews can be a useful guide. The proper determination of the "deliberate sense" of the people requires experience and insight or practical wisdom, as well as specific knowledge. Finally, judges must be able to identify relevant and responsible leaders and to interpret their pronouncements.

The four dimensions of community belief are all important, but they are not equally relevant to the moral and political purposes of the law. These four "public opinions" reflect varying degrees of moral consciousness and political virtue. The first public opinion on the list is likely to embody the community's most minimal ethical requirements. The *conduct* of its members may, but will not necessarily, reflect standards somewhat higher. The third and fourth public opinions will tend to reflect the community's highest moral ideals and political principles.*

In the determination of community standards, judges should take their bearings primarily from the "deliberate sense" of the people and from the common conscience as interpreted by the community's most responsible leaders. They will take account of all four public opinions, but they should have a standing bias (an official bias) towards the latter two. In this way the higher ends of the law will be observed while the beliefs of the people will be respected. The law will not simply impose ethical commandments upon the people—it will recognize and reflect their ethical beliefs. But it will tend to recognize and reflect their higher ethical beliefs.

* This generalization is subject to some limiting conditions. It is true that large majorities can become corrupt and can solemnly vote for vicious public policies. My proposition presupposes a society whose institutions and customs tend to promote a fair degree of decency and humanity. But then, it is also true that, even in such a society, there will be individuals whose ethical consciousness transcends that of the community. The third and fourth "public opinions" will represent the highest standards which the community as such is habitually capable of envisioning—but not the highest standards which the community may embody within it.

This judicial policy encounters difficulties in a society as diversified and as subject to change as ours. One of the difficulties arises from the fact that various groups in society proclaim diverse values, often identifying their values with the standards of the community. Another difficulty arises from the fact that patterns of behavior and personal attitudes can be highly volatile under modern conditions.

The policy suggested allows for (and indeed requires) the consideration of the moral claims of groups and the consideration of changing patterns of conduct. The judge will often have to make concessions to opinions which fall short of the community's best opinions. And if the conduct of large numbers of people falls below standards of decency which have previously governed conduct, the judge will have to weigh this fact in his determination of what "community standards" are. But he will endeavor at all times to insure that the most carefully formed opinions and the best patterns of conduct will weigh heavily in the balance. This has been the posture of many judges, and it is the posture recommended by some eminent interpreters of the judicial process. In a passage often quoted (but seldom quoted in its entirety), Benjamin Cardozo says:

> Law accepts as the pattern of its justice the morality of the community whose conduct it assumes to regulate. In saying this, we are not to blind ourselves to the truth that uncertainty is far from banished. Morality is not merely different in different communities. Its level is not the same for all the component groups within the same community. A choice must still be made between one group standard and another. . . . All that we can say is that the line will be higher than the lowest level of moral principle and practice, and lower than the highest. The law will not hold the crowd to the morality of saints and seers. It will follow, or strive to follow, the principle and practice of the men and women of the community whom the social mind would rank as intelligent and virtuous.[23]

The law aims higher than the lowest common denominator of communal morality. The judge should strive to embody in the law the morality of the community's intelligent and virtuous people. But how are these to be identified? The judge must have access to criteria by reference to which he can determine who are the intelligent and virtuous men. Thus, it would seem that he must have access to ethical standards which transcend contemporary opinions and practices. Cardozo recognizes the need for some kind of transcendent standard, but he locates this in the "social mind"—a concept which his writings do not completely clarify.[24]

The problem which this discussion has now reached—the problem of the source of the law's moral guidance—has received the sustained attention of Lord Devlin. Devlin appears to locate this source unqualifiedly in prevailing popular opinion and moral feeling. He insists that "the morality which the law enforces must be popular morality."[25] He argues that the democratic lawmaker does not (and must not) make an independent judgment about what is good and what is bad.

> The morals which he enforces are those ideas about right and wrong which are already accepted by the society for which he is legislating. . . . He does not therefore need the assistance of moral philosophers nor does he have to study the arguments on peripheral questions. He is concerned with what is acceptable to the ordinary man, the man in the jury box, who might also be called the reasonable man or the rightminded man.[26]

Thus, the question for the lawmaker or judge is not really a *moral* question at all; it is a question of fact—what, in fact, do our people believe, or what would the man in the jury-box think? Devlin rejects moral philosophy and the opinions of the most educated citizens as sources of the law's ethical standards, because moral philosophers continue to disagree and because the dictation of an intellectual elite is incompatible with democracy.

Justice Devlin is surely one of the greatest living exponents of the view that law and ethics cannot be simply separated; that the law has, inevitably, a moral function. But his populistic view of the law's morality appears to stand in sharp contradiction to the position which I have sought to develop in this essay. For it is implicit in the arguments made here that the law is, in some degree, an educator; it educates by setting standards for the guidance of public opinion and feeling. The judge relies on contemporary community standards, but he is to identify and emphasize the best public opinions, thus encouraging what is best in public opinion. To do this he must have some notions of what is good which are not simply the reflection of transient popular views. Devlin's understanding of the matter would seem to deprive the law of this educative function. Devlin's law does not guide the popular sense of what is good; it reflects and follows that popular sense.

But it is necessary to look more closely at Devlin's view. He calls the man in the jury box "the reasonable man" because this man's official function requires him to deliberate, to *think* about communal morality. Further, in the same essay in which he asserts the populistic origin of the law's morality, Devlin also grants to the legislator "a wide discretion in determining how far he will go in the direction of the law as he thinks it ought to be." He continues: "The restraint upon him is that if he moves too far from the common sense of his society, he will forfeit the popular goodwill and risk seeing his work undone by his successor."[27] Devlin does concede to the legislator (and, to a lesser extent, to the judge) some opportunity to exercise initiative in the setting of standards. But he reminds the legislator that he cannot "move too far"; he is confined within the outer limits of his community's common sense.

This is not wholly incompatible with the position I have endeavored to establish, though it is not quite the same position. It is one thing to assert (as I have) that the law has a standard-setting function, though this must be exercised within the confines of contemporary community opinion. It is another thing to assert (as Devlin does) that the law is a reflector of community beliefs, though some concession may be made to the desire of some legislators to improve upon that belief. Nonetheless, Devlin's concessions are not without significance. Evidently, this serious legal thinker does not find it easy to abide rigorously by a view which relegates law to such a secondary and passive role in human affairs.*

To maintain a more significant and active role for the law it is not necessary to say that legislators should ignore public opinion, appealing instead to the abstract doctrines of some moral philosopher or to the views of some educated elite. Though the law is, in significant respects, the product of popular opinion and demands, it is also a result of the *deliberations* of legislatures, courts, and

---

* I have already suggested that what is here called Devlin's "populistic" view is not quite compatible with the argument he makes in his essay "Mill on Liberty in Morals." In that essay (originally delivered as a lecture in 1964 and reprinted in *The Enforcement of Morals*), the law's concern with morality is attributed to a public interest in the restriction of vice, not simply to a public interest in the protection of prevailing opinion. *Supra*, pp. 186–87.

juries. Legislatures, courts, and juries, while reflecting prevailing community beliefs, are also deliberative bodies, required by their traditions, their institutional structures, and their guiding principles to *reason* about the public good. The reasoning of some particular legislative body may be grossly defective, but its members are compelled to debate according to established forms and by reference to some standards of public interest. The legislative output, then, is a "refinement" of popular views as well as a reflection of popular views.[28]

Juries are supposed to represent the attitudes and standards of the average man, but they do not simply reflect these attitudes and standards in their raw or original condition. As Devlin points out, the jury deliberates within a system of law and under the guidance of a judge. The judge, in his guidance of the jury and in his interpretation of statutes, is himself guided by rules and traditions which embody standards of justice and ethics.*

The legislative and judicial processes by which public policy is determined involve judgment upon standards of right, implicit if not explicit. These principles may be embodied in a constitution, written or unwritten, or national doctrine which has been influenced by political and moral philosophy. The legislator and the judge do not have to appeal directly to such philosophy in order to be under its influence. And, in difficult cases—those raising fundamental questions—judges will sometimes appeal explicitly to philosophic doctrine.

Thus, the public processes and deliberations which are called "the law" provide ample opportunity for public education. Indeed, they are inevitably a form of public education. The law derives from the desires and values of the people, but it also affects those desires and shapes those values. The pronouncements and decisions of judges do in fact set standards and provide moral guidance.

Therefore, when judges have to decide upon the character of contemporary community standards, it cannot be said that they are merely making a judgment of "fact," wholly separable from any judgment of "value." This decision must involve considera-

---

* Needless to say, this view of the subject is at odds with some fashionable theories which regard legislative decisions as simply the result of interest-group pressures and judicial decisions as simply the result of the personal opinions of the judges.

tions of both fact and value; the determination of what community standards are is not wholly separable from consideration of what they ought to be or could be.[29] A judgment about what the law *is* generally includes some interpretation of what it *ought* to be or can be, and "contemporary community standards" is a legal concept as well as a sociological concept.

In obscenity cases the judge can legitimately strive (whenever possible) to identify contemporary community standards with the highest or most worthy public opinions. Correspondingly, he should avoid (whenever possible) identifying them with the lowest or least worthy opinions. These propositions have certain implications for the strategy and rhetoric, as well as the substance, of judicial decisions.

The judge should not frame his decisions in such a way as to imply that the public has a broad tolerance for a great deal of obscenity. For instance, he should avoid saying that a novel such as *Fanny Hill* does not offend the common conscience of the community or that the contemporary public would not regard it as pornography. He should not, in order to free a book from censorship, heavily emphasize those trends in modern life which imply a general relaxation of moral standards. Of course, it is often necessary to invalidate a statute or a lower court judgment on First Amendment or due process grounds. But when this is necessary, the judge should make sure that the rhetoric of his decisions does not frustrate the moral purpose of the law by appearing to sanction obscenity or by emphasizing the relativity of moral standards. He should not announce from the bench that the ethical principles which condemn obscenity are nothing more than the mores of the day, relative to our time and place and destined to disappear. He should, if possible, reaffirm these principles.

These are some of the ways in which courts can give public opinion and public morality their due. They must also give the literati their due and recognize the community's interest in literature. The broad concept of contemporary community standards offered here will serve in some ways to protect literature. Those higher public opinions upon which the judges should primarily rely are not, as a rule, hostile to literature or unaware of its values. National leaders and eminent leaders of communities within the nation are usually men with some appreciation for literature or, at least, men who are aware of a distinction between good literature and obscenity. And the courts can reasonably interpret the "deliberate sense" of the community in such a way that a tolerable distinction between obscenity and good literature emerges. These sources of contemporary community standards can serve to guide the judge, not only in his identification and condemnation of obscenity, but also in his effort to separate art from obscenity.

Further, the concept of community standards offered here allows for a considerable degree of flexibility. If the "deliberate sense" of the community changes in a permissive direction, this change will have to be incorporated into the law of obscenity. If society extends its outer limits of tolerance; if patterns of conduct change radically in the direction of permissiveness or sensualism, then the law will have to make some accommodation to these changes, and its judgments of literature will reflect that accommodation.

But the posture of the law should remain fundamentally conservative. Tendenacies in society toward a permissive morality or toward a relaxation of ethical standards should not be incorporated into the law without resistance. The law is something more than a device for registering "social change"; it is also a primary agent in the definition and protection of the way of life of a people. As such it endeavors to remind the people of their common conscience. The judge should make sure that the new opinions are widely held and well-considered opinions before he permits them to determine legal standards. Radical changes in morality should encounter, at least, the initial resistance of the law.

8

Morality, Freedom, and Moderation

> *The education of a citizen in the spirit of his constitution does not consist in his doing the actions in which the partisans of oligarchy, or the adherents of democracy, delight. It consists in his doing the actions by which an oligarchy or a democracy will be enabled to survive.*
>
> Aristotle[1]

In the ideal system of legal control, that perfectly suited to the needs of modern society, wise men would solemnly weigh three considerations: the moral evils of obscenity, the virtues of art, and the requirements of public consensus in a regime of rational liberty. Each consideration would be given its full weight in the light of the common good. No work which is grossly obscene would ever be publicly circulated in society. No work which is not obscene would ever be censored. Good or useful literature would always be free to circulate and, encouraged by an organized community aware of distinctions between the noble and the base, it would flourish. Public opinion would be fully respected, but it would also be elevated, both morally and aesthetically.

This perfection cannot be achieved among us. But is can serve us as a model; it can serve to indicate what are the considerations which must be involved in a justifiable system of censorship. The effort to approximate in reality what this model sets forth in ideal terms must involve us in certain compromises. Our lawmakers and courts should not be confronted with unmanageable tasks.

But, in the endeavor to make their tasks manageable, we should not surrender to solutions of the problem which are in fact evasions of the problem.

I could not attempt an exhaustive description of the various compromises which might be devised by legislative or judicial wisdom. But it is submitted that, in the two alternative censorship policies outlined below, the various ends of the community could be served to a satisfactory degree, while the difficulties of judgment could be reduced to tolerable proportions.

1. A work shall be considered obscene if it is predominantly characterized by any of the four properties which are included in the definition of obscenity proposed at the end of chapter 6.[2] If a work embodying these properties to a high degree be also found to embody any literary, aesthetic, or other values, these must be weighed and balanced against its obscene elements. A *legally* obscene work is one in which the former (obscene) properties outweigh the latter (redeeming) qualities. The criterion of contemporary community standards (as defined in the preceding chapter) will serve as a guide to the interpretation of the four aspects of obscenity. For instance, if some literary material is alleged to be obscene by virtue of its appeal to prurient interests, one of the determinations to be made will be whether or not such material is regarded as prurient by the contemparory common conscience. Likewise, if a work is alleged to be obscene by virtue of its lurid portrayal of the violent destruction of a human being, it will have to be determined that such portrayal is, or is not, lurid in the light of contemporary community standards.

The policy proposed may be summarized as follows. To be legally censorable a work must be *predominantly* obscene; that is, prurient or other obscene elements must be characteristic of the work, and these elements must preponderate over any literary values it may have.[3] In order to preclude certain misunderstandings or misapplications of this principle, it is desirable that three provisos be made explicit. First, literary classics and works of acknowledged excellence should not be subject to censorship. Second, works indicating serious literary purpose, though of dubious literary excellence, should be given the benefit of any doubt. Third, works lacking in artistic worth or seriousness should not be censored unless the obscenity they contain be considerable and pronounced.

2. The obscene properties of a work will be weighed against its redeeming qualities. But, should the results of such weighing be indeterminate—should the two sets of considerations appear to be equally balanced—a separate judgment shall be made concerning the status of the work in the light of contemporary community standards. Thus, in very doubtful or very difficult cases (and only in such cases), an assessment of the "deliberate sense" of the community will determine the issue. This approach should also embody the provisos that literature of acknowledged excellence should not be censored and that works of mere entertainment value should be left alone unless obscenity be highly prevalent. As for serious works on the borderline, these would be censorable only when they are beyond the community's outer limits of tolerance.

These two alternative censorship policies are not equally liberal. The latter is designed to be somewhat more restrictive or conservative than the former. The selection of one or the other would depend upon the times and circumstances and upon the character of the community's liberalism.* It is stressed that these

---

* In a work recently published, which has only lately come to my attention, Richard Kuh advocates a policy which differs in some significant respects from those I suggest here. See Richard H. Kuh, *Foolish Figleaves?* pp. 215–334. This worthy book deserves much more attention than can be devoted to it here. To satisfy one of the liberal's major objections to censorship, Kuh would studiously avoid any explicit control of adults' access to written materials as such. But he would place very rigorous restrictions upon commercial sales of erotica to the young, quite rigorous restrictions upon pandering, and moderate restrictions upon offensive public advertising and upon indecent films, plays, and pictorial materials. Another objection to censorship is to be dealt with by provision of fixed criteria designed to avoid the vagueness and subjectivity which usually infect this subject. To this end Kuh presents three elaborate model statutes which undertake to define, specifically and in detail, just what constitutes the forbidden portrayals of "nudity," "sado-masochistic abuse," "sexual conduct," and "sexual excitement" (see pp. 249–68, 275–79, 295–316), and the forbidden "commercial exploitation of morbid interest" in these things (pp. 297–98). Since the statutes describe, with a high degree of exactitude, just what is forbidden, those applying them would not have to weigh prurient appeal against redeeming values. Kuh's plan, if it could be adopted in its entirety, would partially satisfy (but only partially) the public interests in obscenity control as these are described in the rationale for censorship I have presented. It would be, perhaps, a tolerable compromise. Concerning sexual obscenity, this policy would maintain high public standards with regard to children and moderate standards with regard to prurient huckstering, public performances, and motion pictures. But it would allow the free circulation of the most extreme forms of pornography, as long as the purveyor can find ways to sell the pornography without pandering. It is likely that he can find the ways. For further discussion of Kuh's position, see pp. 300–301, n. 6.

are *policies*—not statutes or detailed rules. For their proper implementation, careful legal draftsmanship and sensitive judicial interpretation would be required.

In the application of these, or any, censorship policies, special attention must be given to the peculiar character and effects of visual and public performances, such as films, plays, and shows. Perhaps these require special statutory provisions or legal rules. But whether or not we should have separate rules for motion pictures (like Chief Judge Conway's formulation of the "alluring portrayal" in the *Kingsley Pictures* case),[4] there are several factors which must be kept in mind. A visual portrayal of prurient, bestial, or indecent things, viewed in public by multitudes of strangers, is not as easily redeemed as is the same portrayal written in a book and read in private. Consider what is likely to be the dominant effect of a motion picture of *Tropic of Cancer* which would endeavor to be scrupulously faithful to the original text. It is hard to envision how the author's presentation of his ideas in some scenes could outweight the impact of certain other scenes. And it should be remembered that what is done in public—and allowed to be done—has a particular effect on the popular sense of what is right.

Thus, there is also a justification for legislation against pandering, a justification which does not rest simply upon the offensiveness of the panderer's conduct. For the panderer is usually engaged in some public defiance or violation of moral standards. If he can blatantly violate the moral code in public, then why should we, the citizens, respect it in private? Of course, the offensiveness of the panderer's conduct can serve as an indicator of its harmfulness. Pandering should be a statutory offense, but it should consist only in the solicitation of prurient interest in materials which really are obscene or in grossly offensive public conduct. In certain borderline obscenity cases the conduct of the purveyor might be considered, but no one should go to jail for merely emphasizing, in a non-obnoxious manner, the sexual aspects of material which is clearly not obscene.

There should be special legislation addressed to the protection of children and adolescents, embodying censorship provisions more restrictive than what would be allowable for legislation concerning adults. These laws can legitimately reach, not only the "girly" picture magazines at issue in *Ginsberg* v. *New York*,[5] but also certain kinds of serious works, such as those of Henry Miller.

Necessarily, parents would remain at liberty to expose their children to literary works of this, or any other, kind.

But legislation designed to protect children and prevent the worst forms of pandering is not a sufficient answer to the larger social issues. Children will not be protected and the panderer will not be deterred if adult standards of decency are corroded.

It is hardly to be expected that the policies I have discussed would resolve all the dilemmas involved in the effort to conduct moral censorship in modern and liberal times. Any system of censorship must confront certain conditions which are endemic to a pluralistic and egalitarian society. Such a society does not readily engender (if it engenders at all) a clear and stable hierarchy of values. It does not establish and recognize a superior social class as the official custodian of its public virtues. It recognizes various sources of values, and it consciously allows for change. Therefore, it will always be difficult for those charged with the protection of its public morality to determine just what values to recognize, when to apply them, and how to apply them.

General principles can be established which will identify the relevant public interests, which will require the decision maker to take account of them, and which will guide him in his efforts to do so. General principles can be established which will promote the just consideration of the community's interest in freedom and in virtue, in the innovative role of literature and in the socializing role of common belief. But the formulation of rules and their application to particular cases must necessarily involve compromises and provisional formulations which will remain open to some criticism from some points of view.[6]

This state of affairs is unacceptable to the extreme moralist and the extreme libertarian. In the eyes of the former, it allows for too many concessions to evil—it compromises with virtue. In the eyes of the latter, it allows for too many concessions to public authority —it compromises with individual liberty.

Neither the extreme moralist nor the extreme libertarian will compromise, because each is, in his own way, a purist or an absolutist. The moralist dreams of the "purification" of a vast industrial and a commercial society; he dreams of a modern society from which the moral evils generated by modern life have been removed. The libertarian dreams of total freedom; he dreams of a society so "free" that in it morality is a private matter and sexual life is spontaneous and unregulated.

The libertarian, like the moralist, tends to be a man of one principle and one purpose. But, unlike the moralist, he can claim that his principle is the ruling principle of liberal democracy. Freedom, he observes, is what liberal democracy stands for. Therefore he is inclined to regard any restriction of individual liberty as an intolerable violation of first principles, and he is inclined to regard any form of censorship as a dangerous first step down the road to totalitarianism.

The libertarian cannot tolerate "hypocrisy." He condemns the hypocrisy of a society which proclaims by law its commitment to moral standards which do not perfectly govern the conduct of its members. Likewise, he condemns the hypocrisy of a liberal society which preaches freedom while allowing for restraints upon speech and press. If our society stands for freedom, it is not sufficient that essential liberties be protected—liberty as such must be constantly enlarged and extended in every area of political and social life.

But, if it is the case that the good society cannot be a society devoted wholly to one principle and one purpose, then it follows that the good society will make compromises. And it will tolerate some "hypocrisy" as an inevitable concomitant of the complexities of ethical and civil life. In modern times the good society will proclaim its commitment to both freedom and morality, but it will not undertake to carry the demands of either to their utmost extreme. Laws can be made to support moral standards, but they will not always be rigorously enforced. Laws will be made to protect individual liberty, but individual liberty will sometimes be sacrificed to other interests of social man.

The confrontation between the moralist and the libertarian can be productive. Some moralists may learn from this confrontation how to develop a broader and more subtle concept of the ethical. Some libertarians may learn how to develop a more subtle concept of freedom and its relation to the other human ends of a community.

And perhaps these protagonists of the obscenity controversy have something to learn from a point of view which is older than theirs. It is a tenet of the oldest political philosophy that purity is unattainable in the civil life of man. The best civil society for most men most of the time will be one embodying a mixture of various principles or ideas. When one of these ideas is pushed too far, when the realization of one purpose is sought at the expense of all others, the social order may be undermined. Aristotle, reminding us of "the value of the mean," asserts: "Many of the measures which are reckoned democratic really undermine democracies; many which are reckoned oligarchic really undermine oligarchies. The partisans of either of these forms of government, each thinking their own the only right form, push matters to an extreme."[7]

What the partisans forget is the necessity of "proportion." Thus, the democrat is likely to insist that public policy embody *only* democratic measures and that it embody only the *most* democratic measures. But "it is the duty of legislators and statesmen to know which democratic measures preserve and which destroy a democracy."[8] Likewise, it is the duty of the statesman to know what nondemocratic measures may be necessary to preserve a democracy and how these may be safely incorporated into the political regime.

The censorship of obscenity is not (as some assert) diametrically and dangerously opposed to all the purposes of democracy. But it is not a liberal-democratic measure. It is a nondemocratic measure which can serve democracy by helping it to maintain ethical and political proportion. Censorship, properly conducted and confined, can serve liberal democracy as a counterweight to those evils or excesses which are a by-product of its virtues.

The libertarian, who demands *only* freedom, can offer no such counterweight. Indeed, where the libertarian mentality prevails, no countervailing considerations can stand against increasing demands that laws and restraints be relaxed.

The moderate democrat knows that the maintenance of genuine liberty is not a simple task, for it involves the maintenance, in health and strength, of a *regime* conducive to liberty. He knows that a regime of liberty has certain ethical and political prerequisites and that for its preservation more is required than the mere extension of individual rights and privileges. The moderate democrat does not delight in censorship. But he can learn how to use it, intelligently and with restraint, for the promotion of public standards of civility which our democracy needs.

Epilogue

Friendly critics have observed that, since the trend of recent developments seems to be so contrary to the thesis of this book, its author should face the fact that the thesis may be unrealistic or impractical. I have not thought it likely that the policies suggested in the concluding chapter, or any similar policies, would be adopted in the near future, and I did not write with any such expectation in view. It was my hope and intention to contribute to serious thinking about this subject and particularly to the thinking of those who might be dissatisfied with some of the prevailing trends. These developments need not be regarded, in the long run, as wholly irresistible, unmodifiable, and irreversible. When moderate men—both liberal and conservative—become aware of their basic agreement on certain principles and values, they can have an effect on events.

But readers will know that the author of this book has had various ends in view. The problem of obscenity can be seen as a prototype of a certain kind of political issue; as such it has much in common with many of the issues that we face, and it is quite different from others. The dilemma of Vietnam will be resolved, one way or another; someday we will be free of it. But the dilemma of free expression, public morality, and the law will not be resolved; we will not be free of it someday. This is a pervasive and permanent problem of civilized society. The controversies and opposing attitudes which are associated with this problem reflect fundamental controversies of political life and typical alternative political postures within liberal democracy. Do we not see how the libertarian and the moderate democrat confront each other today on so many battlefronts, present and potential? Do we not see reflected in so many of these battles those underlying issues concerning the functions of law, the importance of public standards, and the prerequisites and limits of liberty? Serious exploration of the problem of obscenity and the law can contribute to our understanding of much more than that problem.

Notes

Introduction

1. The Gathings Committee: U.S., Congress, House, Select Committee on Current Pornographic Materials, *Hearings before Select Committee,* and *Report of Select Committee to the House,* 83d Cong., 2d sess., 1952, H. Rept. 2510. The Kefauver Committee: U.S., Congress, Senate, Committee on the Judiciary, Subcommittee to Investigate Juvenile Delinquency, *Hearings before Subcommittee,* 83d Cong., 2d sess., 1954; 84th Cong., 1st sess., 1955 (subtitled *Obscene and Pornographic Materials*); 84th Cong., 2d sess., 1956, H. Rept. 2381 (hereafter cited as *Kefauver Hearings, 1956*). The Granahan Committee: U.S., Congress, House, Committee on Post Office and Civil Service, Subcommittee on Postal Operations, *Hearings before Subcommittee,* and *Report of Subcommittee to Committee,* 86th Cong., 1st sess., 1959 (hereafter cited as *Granahan Hearings, 1959,* and *Granahan Report, 1959,* respectively); *Hearings before Subcommittee,* 86th Cong., 2d sess., 1960 (hereafter cited as *Granahan Hearings, 1960*); and *Hearings before Subcommittee,* 87th Cong., 1st sess., 1961 (hereafter cited as *Granahan Hearings, 1961*).

2. *Kefauver Hearings, 1956,* pp. 3, 61.

3. *Granahan Report, 1959,* p. 3.

4. Ibid., pp. 8–9.

5. Ibid., pp. 42–43.

6. Ibid.

7. Morris L. Ernst and Alexander Lindey, *The Censor Marches On,* pp. 258–59.

8. "American Civil Liberties Union Statement on Censorship Activity by Private Organizations and the National Organization for Decent Literature"; quoted in Harold C. Gardiner, S.J., *Catholic Viewpoint on Censorship,* p. 180. This text contains the ACLU statement in its entirety.

9. For an explicit denial that freedom is, or can be, the first principle of our political order, see Walter Berns, *Freedom, Virtue and the First Amendment.*

10. Quoted in Gardiner, *Catholic Viewpoint on Censorship,* pp. 187–88.

281

Notes

11. St. John-Stevas, *Obscenity and the Law*, p. 196.

12. Act 3, scene 2, lines 258–60.

13. Jack Kahler, *Passion Psycho* (San Diego: Satan Press, 1965).

14. E.g., *The Big Kill* (New York: New American Library, 1952) or *Kiss Me, Deadly* (New York: New American Library, 1952).

15. There are many dozens of these publications, differing in degrees of lewdness. Among those most frequently displayed are: *Man's Adventure, Spree, Caper, Gent, Rogue, Knight,* and *Adam.*

16. From John Milton, "Areopagitica," *Areopagitica and Of Education,* ed. George H. Sabine, p. 25.

Chapter 1

1. *Roth* v. *United States,* 354 U.S. 476 (1957).

2. The federal obscenity statute, 18 U.S. Code, Section 1461, provides in pertinent part:
"Every obscene, lewd, lascivious or filthy book, pamphlet, picture, paper, letter, writing, print or other publication of an indecent character; and . . .
"Every written or printed card, letter, circular, book, pamphlet, advertisement, or notice of any kind giving information, directly or indirectly, where, or how, or from whom, or by what means any of such mentioned matters, articles, or things may be obtained or made, . . . whether sealed or unsealed . . .
"Is declared to be nonmailable matter and shall not be conveyed in the mails or delivered from any post office or by any letter carrier.
"Who ever knowingly deposits for mailing or delivery, anything declared by this section to be nonmailable, . . . shall be fined not more than $5,000 or imprisoned not more than 5 years, or both." Cited in *Roth* v. *United States,* at p. 479.
The statute was passed in 1873. Since then it has been amended or expanded many times. In 1888 obscene letters were added to the list of nonmailable materials. In 1909 the term "filthy" was added to the statutory language.

3. 354 U.S. 476 (1957) at 485–87.

4. 96 U.S. 727 (1878). The statute was again upheld in *Rosen* v. *United States,* 161 U.S. 29 (1896).

5. 24 Fed. Cas. 1093 (N.Y. S.D. 1879); also found under, 16 Blatchford 338 (N.Y. S.D. 1879), (U.S., *Blatchford's Circuit Court Reports*).

6. Idem at 360.

7. 45 Fed. 414 (D.C. Kan. 1891).

8. Idem at 415.

9. Idem at 416.

10. 16 Blatchford 338 (N.Y. S.D. 1879) at 355.

11. *Queen* v. *Hicklin,* L.R. 3 QB 360, 371 (1868).

12. Ibid.

13. 16 Blatchford 338 (N.Y. S.D. 1879) at 365.

14. Idem at 361.

15. 161 U.S. 446 (1896) at 451.

16. 188 N.Y. 478 (1907).

17. *People* v. *Seltzer,* 122 N.Y. Misc. 329 (1924).

18. Idem at 335.

19. *People* v. *Friede,* 133 N.Y. Misc. 612 (Mag. Ct. 1929) at 613.

20. Ibid. This decision was overruled by the appellate court in a very brief opinion.

21. 272 N.Y. Supp. 586 (1934) at 588.

22. *People* v. *Dial Press,* 182 N.Y. Misc. 416 (1944) at 417.

23. 209 Fed. 119 (S.D. N.Y. 1913).

24. Idem at 121.

25. Ibid. The *Kennerley* opinion has been made use of by both sides in the obscenity debate, and it appears in judicial opinions in support of conservative as well as liberal rulings. See *Besig* v. *United States,* 208 F. 2d 142 (9th Cir. 1953), in which *Kennerley* is quoted in support of a ruling against Henry Miller's *Tropic of Cancer* and *Tropic of Capricorn.*

26. *U.S.* v. *Dennett,* 39 F. 2d 564 (2d Cir. 1930).

27. Idem at 569.

28. *United States* v. *One Book Called "Ulysses,"* 5 F. Supp. 182 (S.D. N.Y. 1933).

29. Idem at 184.

30. Ibid.

31. *United States* v. *One Book Entitled "Ulysses,"* 72 F. 2d 705 (2d Cir. 1934).

32. Idem at 707.

33. 83 F. 2d 156 (2d Cir. 1936).

34. Idem at 158.

35. Idem at 157.

36. 113 F. 2d 729 (D.C. Cir. 1940).

37. *Doubleday & Co.* v. *New York,* 335 U.S. 848 (1948).

38. See "Brief for Petitioner" and "Reply Brief for Petitioner," *U.S. Supreme Court Records and Briefs,* 354 U.S. 476–514, Vol. 1 (Oct. Term, 1956). (Hereafter cited as *Roth Briefs.*)

39. *Roth Briefs,* "Brief of American Book Publishers Council as *amicus curiae,*" p. 5.

40. *Roth Briefs,* "Brief for the United States," p. 20.

41. Idem at 29.

42. See *Roth Briefs,* "Brief of Morris L. Ernst, *amicus curiae,*" pp. 10–23.

43. 354 U.S. 476 (1957) at 484.

44. Idem at 484–85.

45. *Chaplinski* v. *New Hampshire,* 315 U.S. 568 (1942) at 571–72.

46. *Beauharnais* v. *Illinois,* 343 U.S. 250 (1952) at 266. It may be that the Court has taken note of and rejected the Lockhart and McClure interpretation of these passages. See William B. Lockhart and Robert C. McClure, "Literature, the Law of Obscenity, and the Constitution," *Minnesota Law Review* 38 (March, 1954): 353–56. These authors contend that the passages cited from *Chaplinski* and *Beauharnais* must refer only to *conversational* or *public* speech of an expletive nature. Justice Brennan cites this article in

the notes appended to his opinion, as does Justice Douglas in the text of his dissent.

47. 315 U.S. 586 (1942) at 571–72.

48. 333 U.S. 507 (1948) at 510.

49. 310 U.S. 88 (1940) at 101–2.

50. In this section of its opinion the Court appears to adopt both the argument and the precise language employed by Lockhart and McClure in their advocacy of First Amendment protection for this kind of literature. (See "Law of Obscenity," pp. 358–60.) But the Court did not adopt the legal standards urged by these authors for the protection of such literature.

51. 354 U.S. 476 (1957) at 489.

52. Idem at 487, n. 20. See A.L.I., Model Penal Code No. 207.10 (Test Draft No. 6, 1957), pp. 29–46.

53. Model Penal Code No. 207.10 at 10.

54. Idem at 29.

55. *Webster's Collegiate Dictionary,* 5th ed., s.v. "lust."

56. William B. Lockhart and Robert C. McClure, "Why Obscene?" *"To Deprave and Corrupt . . . ,"* ed. John Chandos, pp. 59–60.

57. *Roth Briefs,* "Brief for the United States," pp. 35–39.

58. 318 Mass. 543 (1945) at 550. Although this opinion is generally considered a more conservative one, its text can be highly instructive concerning the problems that arise under the more liberal rules. The *Isenstadt* opinion may be regarded as an intermediate or transition opinion, and, as such, an illuminating one.

59. 354 U.S. 476 (1957) at 490.

60. See *supra,* p. 19.

61. This aspect of the *Roth* rule was a source of considerable confusion or misconception in the years immediately following the decision. A number of persons appeared to be under the impression that the *Roth* decision had set up prevailing community norms as the sole test, or the predominant test, of obscenity. See *Granahan Report, 1959* and James Jackson Kilpatrick, *The Smut Peddlers.*

62. 354 U.S. 476 (1957) at 503–06.

63. Idem at 511–12.

Chapter 2

1. *Kingsley International Pictures Corp.* v. *Regents,* 360 U.S. 684 (1959).

2. *McKinney's N.Y. Laws,* 1953 (cum. supp. 1958), Education Law, No. 122a. Cited in 360 U.S. 684 (1959) at 685.

3. *Kingsley International Pictures Corp.* v. *Regents,* 175 N.Y.S. 2d 39 (Ct. App., N.Y., 1958) at 45.

4. 360 U.S. 684 (1959) at 688.

5. Idem at 689.

6. Idem at 693.

7. Cited by Justice Harlan, 360 U.S. 684 (1959) at 706.

8. Idem at 702.

Notes

9. 175 N.Y.S. 2d 39 (Ct. App., N.Y., 1958) at 42.

10. Section 122 of the Act proclaims that a license shall issue unless a film is "obscene, indecent [or] immoral . . ." Section 122 A explicitly defines "immoral" as a special category of the offense.

11. 175 N.Y.S. 2d 39 (Ct. App., N.Y., 1958) at 41.

12. Idem at 48–49.

13. Idem at 46.

14. *Supra,* p. 45.

15. 360 U.S. 684 (1958) at 688.

16. 343 U.S. 495 (1952).

17. Idem at 500.

18. *Mutual Film Corp.* v. *Industrial Commission of Ohio,* 236 U.S. 230 (1915) at 244.

19. Idem at 242.

20. *Pathe Exch., Inc.* v. *Cobb,* 202 App. Div. 450 (1922).

21. 343 U.S. 495 (1952) at 503. This passage is quoted by Chief Judge Conway as support for his ruling in *Kingsley Pictures,* 175 N.Y.S. 2d 39 (Ct. App., N.Y., 1958) at 48.

22. In *Times Film Corp.* v. *City of Chicago,* 365 U.S. 43 (1961), the Court declined to rule unconstitutional the licensing of motion pictures in advance of exhibition.

23. 175 F. Supp. 488 (D.C. S.D. N.Y. 1959).

24. Idem at 500.

25. See 5 F. Supp. 182 (S.D. N.Y. 1933) at 183–84. See also *supra,* p. 21.

26. 175 F. Supp. 488 (D.C. S.D. N.Y. 1959) at 501.

27. *Grove Press* v. *Christenberry,* 276 F. 2d 433 (2d Cir., 1960) at 440.

28. Idem at 443.

29. Terry Southern and Mason Hoffenberg, *Candy* (New York: G. P. Putnam's Sons, 1963).

30. 175 F. Supp. 488 (S.D. N.Y., 1959) at 502.

31. 370 U.S. 478 (1961).

32. Idem at 481.

33. Idem at 482.

34. Idem at 490.

35. The Court's latest definitive ruling on the requirements of *scienter* appear in *Smith* v. *California,* 361 U.S. 147 (1959).

36. 370 U.S. 478 (1961) at 487.

37. See *ALI Model Penal Code No. 207.10 (2)* (Tent. Draft No. 6, 1957) at 32.

38. 370 U.S. 478 (1961) at 487.

39. Idem at 490.

40. *Jacobellis* v. *Ohio,* 378 U.S. 184 (1963).

41. Idem at 191.

42. *Attorney General* v. *The Book Named "Tropic of Cancer,"* 345 Mass. 11 (1962).

Notes

43. Idem at 20.

44. 378 U.S. 184 (1963) at 196.

45. *Attorney General* v. *"Tropic of Cancer"* reached this decision before the *Jacobellis* decision, adopting a "hard-core pornography" standard largely on the basis of *Manual Enterprises*. 354 Mass. 11 (1962) at 17–19.

46. 378 U.S. 184 (1963) at 199.

47. Idem at 203–04.

48. Says the Justice: "I would not prohibit them [the states] from barring any material which, taken as a whole, has been reasonably found in state judicial proceedings to treat with sex in a fundamentally offensive manner, under rationally established criteria for judging such material." Idem at 204.

49. See James C. N. Paul and Murray L. Schwartz, *Federal Censorship: Obscenity in the Mail*, pp. 222–23.

50. The following are only a few examples of the kind of publications which have become easily available in local bookstores in the past few years: *Lust Bosses* (sadism), *Always Wanton* (masochism-sadism), *Flesh Stud* (nymphomania), *Gay Vet* (homosexuality), *Another Way of Love* (lesbianism), *Stud Ship* (multiple orgies involving mass participation), *Sex Fever* (lesbianism, fetishism, and transvestitism). The *Sado-Swappers*, a novelette published in 1967, features the systematic torture and degradation of naked women who are vividly represented as inviting and enjoying this treatment. In recent years a large variety of pictorial magazines have appeared which cater to these and similar tastes, many of them specializing in one or another of the sexual perversions. The June 1967 issue of a magazine called *Ultra* presents a sequence of pictures in which a practically nude woman is bound, beaten, and otherwise tortured by a "hooded monster" who is equally unclothed. In another sequence a woman is progressively stripped, fondled, and then shot—presumably to death. In presentations of this kind the women are frequently portrayed in postures which alternate between agony and desire.

51. 209 Fed. 119 (S.D. N.Y. 1913) at 121.

52. See the discussion of *Dennett, Ulysses,* and *Levine* in chapter 1.

53. *Memoirs* v. *Massachusetts,* 383 U.S. 413 (1966). The case concerns John Cleland's *Memoirs of a Woman of Pleasure,* commonly known as *Fanny Hill.*

54. *Ginzburg* v. *United States,* 383 U.S. 463 (1966).

55. 383 U.S. 413 (1966) at 419–20.

56. 206 NE 2d 403 (1965) at 406. This passage is cited in Justice Brennan's opinion at page 419.

57. 383 U.S. 463 (1966) at 465–66.

58. See *Rebhuhn* v. *United States,* 109 F. 2d 512 (2d Cir., 1940). See also my discussion of Judge Bryan's opinion in *Grove Press* v. *Christenberry, supra.*

59. See notes to chapter 1, note 2.

60. Justice Brennan observes: "*Eros* [one of the Ginzburg publications] early sought mailing privileges from the postmasters of Intercourse and Blue Ball, Pennsylvania. The trial court found the obvious, that these hamlets were chosen only for the value their names would have in furthering petitioners' efforts to sell their publications on the basis of salacious appeal.

... Mailing privileges were [later] ... obtained from the postmaster of Middlesex, New Jersey" (at 467–68). For examples of Ginzburg's advertising see footnote 9 at pp. 468–69 of Justice Brennan's opinion.

61. 354 U.S. 476 (1957) at 495.

62. 383 U.S. 463 (1966) at 475. See also idem at 38.

63. *Redrup* v. *New York,* 18 L. ed. 2d 515 (1967) at 517.

64. *Ginsberg* v. *New York,* 20 L. ed. 2d 195 (1968) at 203–4.

65. Idem at 205–06.

66. Idem at 204.

67. See C. Peter Magrath, "The Obscenity Cases: Grapes of Roth," *1966 Supreme Court Review,* ed. Philip B. Kurland (Chicago: University of Chicago Press, 1966). Magrath urges that the Court adopt a "hard-core pornography" standard as the only reasonable way out of its present dilemmas.

Chapter 3

1. *Roth* v. *United States,* 354 U.S. 476 (1957) at 514.

2. *Smith* v. *California,* 361 U.S. 147 (1959) at 157–59.

3. See Justice Black's dissenting opinion in *Adamson* v. *California,* 332 U.S. 46 (1947), and his concurring opinion in *Rochin* v. *California,* 342 U.S. 165 (1952).

4. *Cox* v. *Louisiana,* 379 U.S. 559 (1965), opinion of Black, J., at 578.

5. Hugo L. Black, "The Bill of Rights," *New York University Law Review* 35 (1960): 865, at 867.

6. Ibid., p. 874.

7. Ibid., pp. 871–72.

8. Ibid., p. 873.

9. Dissenting in *Wilkinson* v. *United States,* 365 U.S. 399 (1960), Justice Black seems to deny that there is "any lack of precision" in the language of the First Amendment. He asserts that "the principles of the First Amendment are stated in precise and mandatory terms and unless they are applied in those terms, the freedoms of religion, speech, press, assembly and petition will have no effective protection" (at pp. 422–23).

10. Justice Black dissented from the decision in *Beauharnais* v. *Illinois,* 343 U.S. 250 (1952), which held "group libel" laws constitutional under the First Amendment.

11. *Reynolds* v. *United States,* 98 U.S. 145 (1879).

12. See *Braden* v. *United States,* 365 U.S. 431 at 444 (Black, J. dissenting).

13. 354 U.S. 476 (1957) at 512–13.

14. See particularly Judge Curtis Bok's opinion in *Commonwealth* v. *Gordon,* 66 Pa. D. & C. 101 (Philadelphia County, 1949), and the concurring opinion of Judge Jerome Frank in *United States* v. *Roth,* 237 F. 2d 796 (2d Cir., 1956). While these judges offer a rigorous "clear and present danger" standard, it is evident that they regard even this concession to censorship as a deviation from the original intention of such men as Madison and Jefferson.

15. James Madison, *The Writings of James Madison,* ed. Gaillard Hunt (New York: G. P. Putnam's Sons, 1906), 6: 389–92.

16. James Madison, *The Complete Madison,* ed. Saul K. Padover (New York: Harper & Brothers, 1953), p. 295.

17. Madison, *Writings of Madison,* 6: 334.

18. Thomas Jefferson, *The Complete Jefferson,* ed. Saul K. Padover (New York: Duel, Sloan & Pierce, 1943), p. 129.

19. Thomas Jefferson, *The Writings of Thomas Jefferson,* ed. Paul Leicester Ford (New York: G. P. Putnam's Sons, 1905), 10: 89–90.

20. See Leonard Levy, *Legacy of Suppression* (Cambridge, Mass.: Harvard University Press, 1960).

21. Thomas Jefferson, *The Living Thoughts of Thomas Jefferson,* ed. John Dewey, p. 114.

22. Jefferson, *The Complete Jefferson,* p. 889.

23. *Supra,* p. 94.

24. It is in a statement devoted to freedom of the press that Jefferson voices the expectation "that man may be governed by reason and truth." Jefferson, *Living Thoughts of Jefferson,* p. 120.

25. Levy, *Legacy of Suppression,* p. 236.

26. See *McCulloch* v. *Maryland,* 4 Wheat. 316 (1819).

27. Levy, *Legacy of Suppression,* p. 4.

28. This very broad and vague usage of the term "idea" appears frequently in Ernst's writings. In a recent discussion of the New York "Anti-Sadism" statute which made it a misdemeanor to publish magazines principally made up of "accounts of criminal deeds, or . . . deeds of bloodshed, lust or crime," Ernst characterized the statute thus: "All human beings were to be immunized from certain ideas in print." Morris L. Ernst and Alan U. Schwartz, *Censorship: The Search for the Obscene,* pp. 170–71.

29. Of course, it is not quite true that commercial speech is simply concerned with "things." It is also concerned with the livelihood and comforts of human beings.

30. Alexander Meiklejohn, *Political Freedom* (Copyright, 1948, 1960 by Harper & Brothers. All quotations from this work by permission of Harper & Row, Publishers, Inc.), p. 57.

31. Ibid., p. 27.

32. Ibid., p. 81.

33. Ibid., p. 20.

34. Ibid., pp. 26–27.

35. Ibid., p. 18.

36. Alexander Hamilton, James Madison, and John Jay, *The Federalist Papers,* pp. 226–27.

37. Alexander Meiklejohn, *Free Speech and Its Relation to Self-Government* (New York: Harper and Brothers, 1948).

38. Meiklejohn, *Political Freedom,* p. 79. This work contains the text of *Free Speech and Its Relation to Self-Government,* with certain minor changes and some additions.

39. Alexander Meiklejohn, "The First Amendment Is An Absolute," *1961 Supreme Court Review,* p. 257.

40. Ibid., p. 263.

Notes

41. Meiklejohn, *Political Freedom*, pp. 87–88.

42. Meiklejohn, "First Amendment Is Absolute," p. 262.

43. *Commonwealth* v. *Gordon*, 66 Pa. D. & C. 101 (1948) at 156.

44. *United States* v. *Roth*, 237 F. 2d 796 (1956) at 826.

45. Lockhart and McClure, "Literature, the Law of Obscenity, and the Constitution," 38 *Minn. L. Rev.* 295 (1954) at 391. (All quotations from this work by permission from the authors and from the *Minnesota Law Review*.)

46. 66 Pa. D. & C. 101 (1948) at 110.

47. See John Milton, "Areopagitica," *Areopagitica and Of Education*, ed. George H. Sabine, p. 18.

48. 237 F. 2d 796 (2d Cir. 1956) at 805.

49. Idem at 823.

50. Judge Frank, like so many of those holding his view, does not seem to be be able to take these kinds of distinctions seriously. He finds no way whatever to distinguish between the sexual thoughts stimulated by pornography and those stimulated by the daily press (237 F. 2d 796 [1956] at 805), between the sadism presented in some children's comic books and the sensational news reporting of the major newspapers (idem at 818), and between the obscenity of Roth's materials and the "obscenity" of Chaucer's *Canterbury Tales* (idem at 820). Indeed, he finds it incomprehensibly "irrational" that classics such as those of Chaucer, Aristophanes, and Rabelais have been exempted from the operation of obscenity statutes (idem at 820).

51. Lockhart and McClure, "Law of Obscenity," p. 320.

52. *Ginsberg* v. *New York*, 20 L. ed. 2d 195 (1968). Dissenting opinion of Douglas, J., at 213.

53. In *The Censor Marches On*, Morris Ernst and Alexander Lindey present a four-page list of works "banned" during the last three thousand years. The list is impressive, but its impressiveness diminishes upon analysis. It includes many works banned or restricted by the Catholic church. It includes many instances involving no "banning" whatsoever. We are told that "Shelley's 'Alastor' was attacked as indecent," that "the Rev. A. C. Coxe was outraged by Hawthorne's *The Scarlet Letter*," and that "Walt Whitman was discharged from the Department of the Interior because of *Leaves of Grass*." We are not told that *The Scarlet Letter* and *Leaves of Grass* flourished in most parts of the country. We are told of "prosecutions," but we are not told that they failed. This procedure is characteristic of many of these "lists" (pp. 228–31).

54. Heywood Broun seems to have made his case, or a large part of it, against Anthony Comstock. See Haywood Broun and Margaret Leech, *Anthony Comstock* (New York: A. & C. Boni, 1927). But he generalizes far beyond his data in assertions such as: "Once censorship is let loose, nothing is safe from the smirch of its exceeding dirtiness" (p. 275). Of course, such assertions are not validated by research, however intensive, into the life and mind of one man or group of men.

55. Lockhart and McClure are cited by Judge Frank, by Justice Douglas in his *Roth* dissent, by Justice Harlan in his *Manual Enterprise* opinion, and by the Massachusetts Supreme Court in the *Tropic of Cancer* case, and in many other cases too numerous to mention.

56. Lockhart and McClure, "Law of Obscenity," pp. 374–87.

57. *Supra*, p. 81, footnote.

Notes

58. Lockhart and McClure, "Censorship of Obscenity: The Developing Constitutional Standards," 45 *Minn. L. Rev.* 5 (1960) at 80.

59. William B. Lockhart and Robert C. McClure, "Why Obscene?" "*To Deprave and Corrupt . . . .*" ed. John Chandos, p. 68.

60. Ibid., pp. 69–70.

61. Lockhart and McClure, "Law of Obscenity," p. 378.

62. Ibid., p. 381.

63. Ibid., p. 382.

64. See Hamilton, Madison, and Jay, *Federalist Papers,* nos. 49, 63, 71, and 78.

65. Since *West Virginia* v. *Barnette,* 319 U.S. 624 (1934), the flag-salute may not be made compulsory. For the reason behind the ceremony see *Minersville School District* v. *Gobitis,* 310 U.S. 586 (1940).

66. In *Davis* v. *Beason,* 133 U.S. 333 (1890), however, the validity of a statute of the territory of Idaho denying the franchise to anyone who taught bigamy or polygamy was upheld against challenge on freedom of speech grounds.

67. Lockhart and McClure, "Law of Obscenity," pp. 374–75.

68. Lockhart and McClure never quite spell out what kinds of acts they have in mind. Presumably they would have to be serious violations, and, possibly, they would have to be acts which might have led to breaches of the peace.

69. Lockhart and McClure, "Law of Obscenity," p. 374.

70. In their article "Why Obscene?" Lockhart and McClure themselves indicate that this is impossible. *Supra,* p. 118.

71. Lockhart and McClure are willing to allow legal control of expression that directly promotes immoral conduct. But *why* are they willing to allow this form of censorship—because such conduct is destructive of morality, *or* because it may result in disturbance of peace and order? They do not answer this question, but their arguments, taken as a whole, point to the latter conclusion.

72. 354 U.S. 476 (1957) at 512–13.

73. Idem at 514.

74. 383 U.S. 463 (1966) at 489–90.

75. See Ernst and Schwartz, *Search for the Obscene,* particularly pp. 1–5, 78–79, 205, 243, and 245; and Morris L. Ernst and William Seagle, *To the Pure,* particularly pp. 250–62.

76. Ernst and Seagle, *To the Pure,* p. 262.

77. *Supra,* p. 110.

78. Meiklejohn, "First Amendment Is Absolute," p. 262.

79. Ibid., p. 263.

80. Meiklejohn, *Political Freedom,* p. 57.

81. Ibid.

82. Milton, "Areopagitica," pp. 18–19.

83. Ibid., p. 23.

84. Ibid., p. 52.

85. Edwin A. Burtt, ed., *The English Philosophers from Bacon to Mill,* p. 956.

86. Ibid., pp. 961–64.

87. Ibid., pp. 992–93.

88. In a typical passage Mill asserts: "It is not by wearing down into uniformity all that is individual in themselves, but by cultivating it . . . that human beings become a noble and beautiful object of contemplation, and as the works partake the character of those who do them, by the same process human life also becomes rich, diversified and animating, furnishing more abundant aliment to high thoughts and elevating feelings, and strengthening the tie which binds every inividual to the race, by making the race infinitely better worth belonging to. In proportion to the development of his individuality, each person becomes more valuable to himself, and is therefore capable of being more valuable to others." Ibid., p. 998.

89. Patrick Devlin, *The Enforcement of Morals,* p. 108.

90. Burtt, ed., *English Philosophers,* p. 956.

91. Ibid., p. 921.

Chapter 4

1. Lockhart and McClure, "Literature, the Law of Obscenity, and the Constitution," 38 *Minn. L. Rev.* 295 (1954) at 385.

2. Ibid., p. 380.

3. *Granahan Hearings, 1959,* p. 129.

4. Quoted in *Granahan Hearings, 1961,* p. 28.

5. Sheldon and Eleanor Glueck, *Unraveling Juvenile Delinquency* (Cambridge, Mass.: Harvard University Press, 1950).

6. *United States* v. *Roth,* 237 F. 2d 796 (2d Cir., 1956) at 811–12.

7. See D. H. Lawrence, "Pornography and Obscenity," *D. H. Lawrence: Sex, Literature and Censorship,* ed. Harry T. Moore.

8. Quoted in Harold C. Gardiner, S.J., *Catholic Viewpoint on Censorship,* p. 187.

9. U.S., Congress, House, Committee on Post Office and Civil Service, *Hearings on H.R. 569, A Bill to Authorize the Postmaster General to Impound Mail in Certain Cases,* 83d Cong., 2d sess., 1953, p. 22.

10. *Granahan Hearings, 1959,* p. 212.

11. *Granahan Hearings, 1961,* p. 314.

12. Ibid., p. 315.

13. *Granahan Hearings, 1959,* p. 164.

14. Ibid., p. 175.

15. *Granahan Hearings, 1961,* p. 68.

16. Ibid.

17. *Kefauver Hearings, 1956,* p. 10. Dr. Henry also observed that "a great many of these so-called adults are really still adolescents . . ." (p. 11).

18. Copyright 1953, 1954 by Frederic Wertham. All quotations from this work by permission of Holt, Rhinehart and Winston, Inc. Since this work is, in my judgment, generally underrated, I devote considerable attention to it.

19. Wertham, *Seduction of the Innocent,* p. 94.

20. Ibid., p. 117.

21. Ibid., p. 118.

22. A professor of clinical psychiatry, Dr. Lauretta Bender, writes that "comics are representative of the folklore of the times, spontaneously given to and received by children, serving at the same time as a means of helping them solve the individual and sociological problems appropriate to their lives." *A Dynamic Psychopathology of Childhood,* pp. 227, 229, 230 (1954). Quoted in *Roth Briefs,* "Brief of Morris L. Ernst, *amicus curiae,*" p. 46.

Wilbur Schramm, Jack Lyle, and Edwin Parker's study, *Television in the Lives of Our Children,* lends support to some of Wertham's conclusions. Summing up the effects of television violence, the authors conclude: "(1) A certain number of young children (and a few older ones) will inevitably confuse the rules of the fantasy world with the rules of the real world and transfer violence from television to real life. (2) Children who come to television with aggression will be more likely to remember aggressive acts and to apply them when they are aggressive in real life. (3) Children may remember (and presumably be able to use) violence, even though it is in conflict with their ethics and values. (4) Children want to be like the 'successful' characters they see in fantasy, and tend to imitate them, villainous or not" (p. 163).

But the authors are careful to qualify these conclusions: "Children who do not confuse the fantasy world with reality, who do not come to television with a great deal of aggression, . . . will be much less likely than others to pick up this violence" (p. 163). They conclude that "very little delinquency can be traced directly to television" (p. 174).

23. Pitirim A. Sorokin, *The American Sex Revolution.*

24. See Margaret Mead, "Sex and Censorship in Contemporary Society," *New World Writing;* and Ernest van den Haag, "Quia Ineptum," *"To Deprave and Corrupt . . . ,"* ed. John Chandos, pp. 109–24.

25. Lockhart and McClure, "Law of Obscenity," p. 385.

26. Marie Jahoda, *The Impact of Literature: A Psychological Discussion of Some Assumptions in the Censorship Debate.* Cited by Judge Frank, 237 F. 2d 796 (2d Cir., 1956) at 815.

27. For a summary of the Brown University report see Eberhard and Phyllis Kronhausen, *Pornography and the Law,* pp. 343–44. (All quotations from this work reprinted with permission.)

28. Richard McKeon, Robert K. Merton, and Walter Gellhorn, *The Freedom to Read,* p. 72.

29. Ibid.

30. Leo M. Alpert, "Judicial Censorship of Obscene Literature," *Harvard Law Review,* 52 (November, 1938): 73.

31. Kronhausen and Kronhausen, *Pornography and the Law,* pp. 340–42.

32. Alfred C. Kinsey, *et al., Sexual Behavior in the Human Female,* pp. 669–70.

33. Lockhart and McClure, "Law of Obscenity," p. 385.

34. Kronhausen and Kronhausen, *Pornography and the Law,* p. 337.

35. Ibid., p. 344.

36. Benjamin Karpman, *The Sexual Offender and His Offenses* (New York:

Julian Press, 1954), p. 101. Dr. Karpman has served as Chief Psychiatrist of St. Elizabeth's Hospital, Washington, D.C.

37. Louis S. London and Frank S. Caprio, *Sexual Deviations* (Washington, D.C.: Linacre Press, 1950), p. 627.

38. Walter Gellhorn, *Individual Freedom and Governmental Restraints,* p. 61.

39. This presentation of Jahoda's findings is taken from an extensive summary of them written by her to Judge Frank. The summary can be found in Judge Frank's concurring opinion in *United States* v. *Roth,* 237 F. 2d 796 (2d Cir., 1956) at 815–16. The study itself is out of print and generally unavailable.

40. Wertham, *Seduction of the Innocent,* p. 114.

41. Ibid., pp. 242–43.

42. McKeon, Merton, and Gellhorn, *The Freedom to Read,* p. 70.

43. Karpman, *The Sexual Offender and His Offenses,* p. 485.

44. Kronhausen and Kronhausen, *Pornography and the Law,* p. 338.

45. Ibid., pp. 335–36.

46. See Aristotle, *Poetics* 6. 1449^b. 20–30.

47. Mead, "Sex and Censorship," p. 23.

48. Wertham, *Seduction of the Innocent,* p. 246.

49. See *supra,* pp. 141–42.

50. Wertham, *Seduction of the Innocent,* p. 247.

51. *Commonwealth* v. *Gordon,* 66 Pa. D. & C. 101 (Philadelphia County, 1949), pp. 137–38.

52. Gellhorn, *Individual Freedom and Governmental Restraints,* pp. 61–62.

53. Kronhausen and Kronhausen, *Pornography and the Law,* pp. 327, 329.

54. van den Haag, "Quia Ineptum," p. 117.

55. Paul Gebhard, *et al., Sex Offenders: An Analysis of Types,* p. 678.

56. Ibid., p. 669.

57. One enthusiast draws this sweeping conclusion from the Institute's findings: "Those judges, regardless of their position in the obscenity law dispute, who have the intellectual honesty to accept the scientific value of the Kinsey Study on sex offenders must conclude that the old bromide about a causal relationship between sexual transgression and pornography is false." Albert B. Gerber, *Sex, Pornography and Justice,* p. 318.

58. Quoted in James Jackson Kilpatrick, *The Smut Peddlers,* p. 237. With regard to the effects of pornographic literature upon normal persons, author Terrence J. Murphy reports the results of a discussion held in 1958 with Dr. Clair E. Hubert, Associate Professor of Psychology, University of Cincinnati, who was studying the subject. Murphy says: "Specific comment was invited on the view that only the maladjusted is affected by pornography and that such a person might also be similarly influenced by decent literature. Professor Hubert expressed the opinion that obscene literature can have a pernicious effect upon the average person. While admitting that the 'susceptible' will be more influenced by pornography, he contended that the 'susceptible' person falls within the psychologist's range of the normal or average person." Terrence J. Murphy, *Censorship: Government and Obscenity,* p. 271, n. 20.

59. *Roth* v. *United States,* 354 U.S. 476 (1957) at 502.

60. D. W. Abse, "Psychodynamic Aspects of the Problem of Definiiton of Obscenity," *Law and Contemporary Problems,* 20 (Autumn, 1955): 572.

61. Ibid., p. 586.

62. Wertham, *Seduction of the Innocent,* pp. 90–91.

63. *Roth Briefs,* "Brief of Morris L. Ernst, *amicus curiae,*" pp. 44–45.

64. Douglas Waples, Bernard Berelson, and Franklyn R. Bradshaw, *What Reading Does to People,* pp. 108–09.

65. Joseph T. Klapper, *The Effects of Mass Media.*

66. Ibid., sec. 4, p. 6.

67. Ibid., sec. 4, p. 7.

68. Ibid., sec. 2, p. 3.

69. *Roth Briefs,* "Briefs for the United States," p. 60.

70. *Supra,* p. 164.

71. For an interesting discussion of the indispensability of moral sentiments see C. S. Lewis, *The Abolition of Man* (New York: Collier Books, 1947), chapter 1, "Men Without Chests."

72. Quoted in Gellhorn, *Individual Freedom and Governmental Restraints,* p. 64; and by Judge Frank, 237 F. 2d 796 (2d Cir., 1956) at 812.

73. McKeon, Merton, and Gellhorn, *The Freedom to Read,* p. 20.

74. van den Haag, "Quia Ineptum," pp. 111–12.

Chapter 5

1. *Commonwealth* v. *Gordon,* 66 Pa. D. & C. 101 (Philadelphia County, 1949) at 156.

2. Idem at 127.

3. *The Wolfenden Report: Report of the Committee on Homosexual Offenses and Prostitution,* Authorized American Edition, p. 48.

4. Louis Henkin, "Morals and the Constitution," *Columbia Law Review* 63 (March, 1963): 407.

5. For a discussion of the nonmoral rationales for such laws, see H. L. A. Hart, *Law, Liberty and Morality,* chapter 2.

6. *Wolfenden Report,* par. 62.

7. Ibid., par. 257.

8. Hart, *Law, Liberty and Morality.* The reader's attention is directed to an interesting and rather fruitful body of literature which has resulted from the debate over the principles of the *Wolfenden Report.* In 1959 Sir Patrick Devlin delivered his now famous "Maccabaean Lecture" on "The Enforcement of Morals" in which he seriously questioned the premises of the Wolfenden Committee. Justice Devlin's arguments were answered by Professor Richard Wollheim in "Crime, Sin, and Mr. Justice Devlin," *Encounter,* November, 1959, pp. 34–40; and by Professor Hart in *Law, Liberty and Morality.* Devlin replies to his critics and further develops his views in several lectures which are now published, together with the "Maccabaean Lecture," in Patrick Devlin, *The Enforcement of Morals.* See also Eugene V. Rostow, *The Sovereign Prerogative* (New Haven: Yale University Press, 1962), chapter 2, "The "Enforcement of Morals."

Notes

9. Hart, *Law, Liberty and Morality,* p. 25.

10. Ibid., p. 57.

11. Ibid., p. 25.

12. *Wolfenden Report,* par. 13.

13. *Dominus Rex* v. *Curl* (1727), 2 Strange 789.

14. Idem at 792.

15. 2 All England Law Reports, 448 (1961).

16. Idem at 452. Lord Reid, in dissent on this point, was critical of the broad, encompassing terms in which this offense was stated. He said: "I must advert to the consequences of holding that this very general offense exists. It has always been thought of primary importance that our law, and particularly our criminal law, should be certain; that a man should be able to know what conduct is and what is not criminal, particularly when heavy penalties are involved." Idem at 460–61.

17. Idem at 452.

18. *Davis* v. *Beason,* 133 U.S. 333 (1890) at 342.

19. *Trist* v. *Child,* 21 Wall. 441 at 450. Quoted in *Roth Briefs,* "Brief for the United States," p. 51.

20. *People v. Seltzer,* 122 N.Y. Misc. 329 (Supr. Ct., N.Y., 1924) at 335.

21. *Nicomachean Ethics,* 2.1.1103^b. 3–6.

22. See Aristotle, *Nicomachean Ethics,* Bks. 1–5; and Leo Strauss, *Natural Right and History,* chapters 3–4.

23. Walter Berns, *Freedom, Virtue and the First Amendment,* p. 246.

24. Ibid., p. 243.

25. Ibid., p. 253.

26. H. L. A. Hart, *The Concept of Law* (London: Oxford University Press, 1961), pp. 187–88.

27. Ernest van den Haag, "Quia Ineptum," *"To Deprave and Corrupt . . . ,"* ed. John Chandos, pp. 113–14.

28. Ibid., p .114.

29. Devlin, *The Enforcement of Morals,* p. 94.

30. Ibid., p. 90

31. Ibid., p. 104.

32. Ibid., p. 111.

33. See Jean-Jacques Rousseau, *Jean-Jacques Rosseau: Politics and the Arts —Letter to M. d'Alembert on the Theater,* translated with notes and introduction by Allan Bloom; and Baron de Montesquieu, *The Spirit of the Laws.*

34. See Alexis de Tocqueville, *Democracy in America* (New York: Vintage Books, 1945), 2: 9–11. See also Sebastian de Grazia, *The Political Community.*

35. *West Virginia State Board of Education* v. *Barnette,* 319 U.S. 624 (1943), opinion of Justice Robert Jackson at 642.

36. Weston La Barre, "Obscenity: An Anthropological Appraisal," *Law and Contemporary Problems,* 20 (Autumn, 1955): 533–43.

37. Margaret Mead, "Sex and Censorship in Contemporary Society," *New World Writing,* p. 7.

38. Ibid., p. 11.

39. *Supra,* p. 175.

40. For a substantiation of this proposition presented from a point of view quite different from that of this essay, see Harvey Cox, *The Secular Society* (New York: Macmillan Co., 1965).

41. H. L. A. Hart reports the following assertions of a nineteenth-century Royal Commission on capital punishment: "The fact that men are hanged for murder is one great reason why murder is considered so dreadful a crime." Hart is not impressed with this proposition, but he does not refute it. See *Law, Liberty and Morality,* p. 58.

42. See Albert Ellis, *The American Sexual Tragedy,* particularly pp. 293–302; and Paul Goodman, *Growing Up Absurd* (New York: Random House, 1960); idem, *Utopian Essays and Practical Proposals* (New York: Vintage Books, 1964), chapter on "Pornography and the Sexual Revolution."

43. Eberhard and Phyllis Kronhausen, *Pornography and the Law,* p. 331.

44. Mead, "Sex and Censorship," p. 17.

45. Kronhausen and Kronhausen, *Pornography and the Law,* p. 347.

46. Quoted in Norman St. John-Stevas, *Obscenity and the Law,* p. 68.

47. Quoted in Kronhausen and Kronhausen, *Pornography and the Law,* p. 388.

48. *Brown* v. *Board of Education,* 347 U.S. 483 (1954); 349 U.S. 394 (1955).

49. Benjamin Cardozo, *The Paradoxes of Legal Science,* p. 37.

50. Benjamin Cardozo, *The Nature of the Judicial Process,* pp. 108–09.

51. *Roth Briefs,* "Brief for the United States," pp. 7–8.

Chapter 6

1. Havelock Ellis, *On Life and Sex,* p. 100.

2. *Roth Briefs,* "Brief of Morris L. Ernst, *amicus curiae,*" p. 52.

3. *State* v. *Lerner,* 81 NE (2) 282 (1948) at 286.

4. *Granahan Hearings, 1959,* p. 143.

5. Harold Gardiner, S.J. *Catholic Viewpoint on Censorship,* p. 62.

6. Ibid., p. 64.

7. Ibid., p. 65.

8. Ibid.

9. Quoted in Harold Gardiner, S.J. "Moral Principles Toward a Definition of the Obscene," *Law and Contemporary Problems,* 20 (Autumn, 1955): 562.

10. John Courtney Murray, S.J. *We Hold These Truths* (New York: Sheed and Ward, 1960), pp. 173–74.

11. For an analysis of pornographic literature in these terms see W. G. Eliasberg, "Art: Immoral or Immortal," *Criminal Law* 45 (1954): 274.

12. Eberhard and Phyllis Kronhausen, *Pornography and the Law,* p. 18.

13. Ibid., p. 245.

14. Ibid., p. 253.

15. Ibid., p. 300.

16. Ibid., pp. 301–2.

17. Ibid., p. 300.

18. With regard to the pornography of the Victorian age, Steven Marcus observes: "It is, I suppose, possible to explain the kind of sexual writings we are discussing strictly according to the pleasure principle as it undergoes the usual procedures of distortion. I do not think, however, that its distinct unpleasurableness, its violence and aggressiveness, its impulse toward extinction are satisfactorily explained by that principle alone. Something darker seems to be there, something inexorable, from which there is no escape and which cannot be understood as pathology alone." Steven Marcus, *The Other Victorians*, p. 184.

19. Margaret Mead, "Sex and Censorship in Contemporary Society," pp. 18 and 19, respectively.

20. Marcus, *The Other Victorians*, p. 214.

21. Both New York and Massachusetts have adopted a hard-core pornography test for obscenity. But New York declared that Henry Miller's *Tropic of Cancer* can be censored because it is hard-core pornography, while Massachusetts declared that the book cannot be censored because it is not hard-core pornography. See *People of New York State* v. *Margaret Fritch*, 13 N.Y. 2d 119 (1963); and *Attorney General* v. *"Tropic of Cancer,"* 345 Mass. 11 (1962). In 1964 the Supreme Court decided the issue in the book's favor in a *per curiam* decision without opinion.

22. Richard M. Weaver, *Ideas Have Consequences*, p. 29.

23. George P. Elliott, "Against Pornography," *Harper's Magazine*, March, 1965, pp. 52–53.

24. Jonathan Swift, *Gulliver's Travels*, p. 61.

25. Ibid., pp. 66–67.

26. Jean-Paul Sartre, *Le Mur* (Paris: Librairie Gallimard, 1939), pp. 75–76. My translation.

27. Viewed as such, the parts of the body and of human existence are "ridiculous," or, to use the language of the author's philosophy, "absurd." See Jean-Paul Sartre, *Being and Nothingness*, trans. Hazel E. Barnes (New York: Philosophical Library, 1965), pp. 361–412.

28. Joseph Heller, *Catch 22*, pp. 347–48.

29. Ibid., p. 335.

30. Ibid., pp. 449–50.

31. Gardiner, "Moral Principles," p. 563.

32. Abraham Kaplan, "Obscenity as an Aesthetic Category," *Law and Contemporary Problems* 20 (Autumn, 1955): 548.

33. Act 5, scene 1, lines 155–210.

34. *The National Enquirer*, August 21, 1966.

35. D. H. Lawrence, *Lady Chatterley's Lover*, p. 108.

36. Perhaps something should be said here about Lawrence's occasional use of four-letter words in *Lady Chatterley*, a factor which surely accounts for some of the hostility which the book has aroused. Since the *Ulysses* case, judges have taken account of an author's purpose in using such words and their function in a particularly literary work. Lawrence thought that most of the words ordinarily employed in conventional discourse about sexual matters do not convey, but rather conceal, the human reality of those matters.

And he wanted to use words which would be appropriate to Mellors—the character he sought to create. It was apparently his hope and intention to redeem those words from the degrading connotations which ordinarily attach to them and to make them serviceable for literary purposes. In this *Lady Chatterley's Lover* does not quite succeed. But at least it can be said that Mellors does not employ these words in their degrading sense, and the reader is not intended to experience their obscene connotation. See D. H. Lawrence, "A Propos of *Lady Chatterley's Lover," Sex, Literature and Censorship,* pp. 84–85.

37. John Cleland, *Fanny Hill: Memoirs of a Woman of Pleasure,* pp. 88–89.

38. With regard to the book's "redeeming literary importance," George Elliott has this to say: "The one literary quality which has made the book celebrated is a certain elegance of style; compared to most simple pornography it reads like a masterpiece, but to anyone familiar with eighteenth-century prose it reads like several other third-rate novels. Surely the world is not in such need of third-rate eighteenth-century English fictional prose as to allow this consideration alone to justify the public sale of a work of sheer pornography." George Elliott, "Against Pornography," p. 56. It is sometimes asserted that *Fanny Hill* is a picaresque novel—a novel of roguish adventure and discovery in the same genre as that of Fielding's *Tom Jones.* It is true that the structure of the book—the organization of its events—has certain features in common with works of this type. But this is not a very important fact with regard to judgment about a book's obscenity. What is most important is the dominant effect which the book is designed to have and which it does have. Today one can easily find pornographic novels which are organized in imitation of the plot or structure of serious novels like *Lady Chatterley* and *The Well of Loneliness.* They do not thereby become serious works.

39. Marcus, *The Other Victorians,* p. 216. My citation of Marcus' observations here does not mean that I subscribe wholly to his rather Freudian interpretation of these phenomena, and I do not intend to suggest that Marcus would necessarily agree with the definition of obscenity developed in this chapter.

40. Ibid., pp. 216–17. Those familiar with the ideas of Martin Buber will recognize here a particularly virulent form of the "I-it" relationship.

41. *Supra,* p. 34.

42. *Supra,* p. 33.

Chapter 7

1. *Roth* v. *United States,* 354 U.S. 476 (1957) at 512.

2. Henry Miller, *Henry Miller on Writing,* ed. Thomas H. Moore, p. 180.

3. *People* v. *Friede,* 133 N.Y. Misc. 329 at 615.

4. *United States* v. *One Book Entitled "Ulysses,"* 72 F. 2d 705 at 711.

5. 354 U.S. 476 (1957) at 509–10.

6. Lockhart and McClure, "Literature, the Law of Obscenity, and the Constitution," 38 *Minn. L. Rev.* 295 (March, 1954) at 369.

7. Ibid., p. 370.

8. Ibid., p. 371.

9. George Santayana, *The Life of Reason—Reason in Art* (New York: Charles Scribner's Sons, 1905, 1948), p. 171.

10. With regard to his literary objective, Lawrence said: "I want men and women to be able to think sex, fully, completely, honestly and cleanly. . . . Even if we can't act sexually to our complete satisfaction, let us at least think sexually, complete and clear." D. H. Lawrence, "A Propos of *Lady Chatterley's Lover*," *Sex, Literature and Censorship*, p. 85.

11. Alexis de Tocqueville, *Democracy in America* (New York: Random House, Vintage Books, 1945), 2: 136–41, 152–56.

12. Henry Miller, *Tropic of Cancer*, pp. 1–2.

13. Miller, *Henry Miller on Writing*, p. 194.

14. George Elliott, "Against Pornography," *Harper's Magazine*, March, 1965, p. 59.

15. Miller, *Henry Miller on Writing*, p. 142.

16. Jefferson spoke of the progress of the arts and sciences "softening and correcting the manners and morals of men," Thomas Jefferson, *The Living Thoughts of Thomas Jefferson*, ed. John Dewey, p. 182.

17. *Supra*, pp. 77–78, and footnotes p. 78.

18. *Supra*, pp. 188–90.

19. See Leo Strauss, *The City and Men* (Chicago: Rand McNally & Co., 1964), chapter 2; and Reinhold Neibuhr, *Moral Man and Immoral Society* (New York: Charles Scribner's Sons, 1932).

20. See H. L. A. Hart, *Law, Liberty and Morality*, pp. 50–52, 71–72. Hart appears to believe that if a society's moral code is destroyed that society will inevitably replace it with another (and equally valuable) moral code. At any rate, whether he would avow this belief or not, his argument does not take seriously the possibility that important standards could be lost and not replaced with equally valuable ones.

21. Eberhard and Phyllis Kronhausen, *Pornography and the Law*, p. 193.

22. Alexander Hamilton, James Madison, and John Jay, *The Federalist Papers*, p. 432.

23. Benjamin Cardozo, *The Paradoxes of Legal Science*, p. 37.

24. In Cardozo's thought, the "social mind," which is the source of the law's moral guidance, sometimes appears to be identified with an *underlying* popular conviction or aspiration reflecting an historic trend or "spirit of the times." See generally *The Paradoxes of Legal Science*. Sometimes he speaks of the "mores" of the community or the "considerate judgment of the community." See Cardozo, *The Nature of the Judicial Process*, pp. 108–09.

25. Patrick Devlin, *The Enforcement of Morals*, Preface, p. x.

26. Ibid., p. 90.

27. Ibid., p. 95.

28. Madison said that in a republic the legislative process is designed to "refine and enlarge the public views by passing them through the medium of a chosen body of citizens, whose wisdom may best discern the true interest of their country and whose patriotism and love of justice will be least likely to sacrifice it to temporary or partial considerations." *The Federalist Papers*, no. 10, p. 82.

29. It is doubtful that jurors who have to interpret the community's morality

generally proceed to do so on the basis of a sharp separation between "fact" and "value."

Chapter 8

1. *Politics* 5.9. 1310ᵃ. 20–23.

2. *Supra,* p. 245.

3. The British system, established under the Obscene Publications Act of 1959, provides for two separate findings. Section 1 of the Act defines "obscene" as follows: "The book is to be deemed to be obscene if its effect . . . if taken as a whole, [is] such as to tend to deprave and corrupt persons who are likely, having regard to all revelant circumstances, to read . . . the matter contained . . . in it." But section 4 of the Act provides a special defense: "A person shall not be convicted of an offense . . . if it is proved that publication of the article in question is justified as being for the public good on the ground that it is in the interests of science, literature, art or learning, or of other objects of general concern." See *The Trial of Lady Chatterley,* ed. C. H. Rolph, pp. 10–11. Thus, the initial determination of obscenity is made on the basis of the statutory definition of the term, which does not explicitly include competing considerations of merit. But, after obscenity has been determined, a separate judgment may be rendered on the literary or other merits of the work, and it can be shown that, in spite of its obscenity, publication is justified. In certain cases this procedure might help to simplify problems of judgment confronting a jury. But in all difficult cases the judgment about justification would have to turn upon some weighing of a work's obscenity against its redeeming values.

4. See the discussion of motion pictures in chapter 2.

5. *Supra,* pp. 83–85.

6. Richard Kuh hopes, by means of precise statutes and exact definitions, to abolish many of these difficulties. See my footnote on p. 274. He seeks to ensure that "applying the obscenity laws will become almost as clear-cut as applying the laws against robbery, or rape, or assault" (*Foolish Figleaves?* p. 231). Hence, his model statutes specify, as exactly as words can specify, what constitutes the "nudity," "sexual conduct," and other activities which may not be shown under certain stipulated conditions. For instance, " 'nudity' means uncovered, or less than opaquely covered, post-pubertal human male or female genitals, pubic areas or buttocks, or the female breast below a point immediately above the top of the nipple (or the breast with the nipple and immediately adjacent area only covered), or the covered human male genitals in a discernibly turgid state" (p. 253). Judges, juries, and prosecutors who have to apply these provisions would not be making those determinations about prurient appeal or aesthetic values which introduce vagueness and personal judgment into the law of obscenity. There would be no weighing and balancing and, hence, no subjectivity (or very little) in the interpretation of such provisions. As a result, "the reliance upon personal judgment that is at the nub of the resentment toward censorship, the idea that many of us may be barred access to items because of the censor's *personal* distastes, would evaporate" (p. 229). It may be doubted that "the reliance upon personal judgment . . . is at the nub" of the libertarian's resentment toward censorship. He resents the restraint of expression as distinguished from conduct, and he often resents restraints based on moral

considerations as such. Precise statutes, such as those offered by Kuh, would surely render the task of law enforcement officials and judges less difficult. But the task of weighing and balancing diverse and subtle considerations (of which the prosecutors and judges would be relieved) must be performed somewhere. The legislature, in the formulation of its precise statutes, would have to weigh the evils of obscenity, the values of art, and contemporary public opinion (presumably Kuh has done so in the formulation of his recommended legislation) and arrive at some balance of the relevant public interests. This would involve judgments about what is obscene and what is valuable art. Someone must make the delicate judgments and arrange for the accommodation of the various elements of the common good. And, wherever or however this is done, there will always be plenty of room for dissatisfaction and for charges that personal opinions or dislikes have influenced judgment. The task of *deciding* what is obscene and ought to be prohibited can never be as clear-cut as the task of deciding what is robbery or rape and ought to be prohibited. As for specificity and detail in the description of what obscenity statutes forbid, this poses difficulties with regard to certain kinds of materials, and, in some respects, it could be a mixed blessing. Definitions like that of "nudity" cited above are obviously more serviceable for determinations about visual or pictorial material than for determinations about written material. It is more difficult to specify what, exactly, may not be done or said in a novel. (Kuh's proposals, therefore, do not include any restrictions upon reading materials for adults. Further, it is not possible to list, exhaustively and in detail, all that might constitute an unredeemed obscene picture, film, or novel. A statute undertaking to do so might fail to serve the purposes for which obscenity is regulated, since the film maker or author could often find ways to achieve his prurient or indecent aim while avoiding the precise terms of such a statute. I do not mean to imply by these remarks that precision is undesirable, but only that there is a price to be paid for the degree of precision advocated by Kuh.

7. Aristotle *Politics* 5.9.1309[b]. 20–23.

8. Ibid., 5.9.1309[b]. 35–37.

Selected Bibliography

Public Documents

U.S. Code. *18 U.S. Code, Section 1461, Mailing Obscene or Crime-Inciting Matter.*

U.S. Congress, House. *Report to the Committee on Post Office and Civil Service by the Subcommittee on Postal Operations.* 86th Congress, 1st Session, 1959. (Subtitled: *Obscene Matter Sent Through The Mail.*)

U.S. Supreme Court. *U.S. Supreme Court Records and Briefs: 354 U.S. 476–514, Vol. 1*

Books and Collected Works

Aristotle. *Politics.* Translated and Edited by Ernest Barker. New York: Oxford University Press, 1946.

————. *The Basic Works of Aristotle.* Edited and with an Introduction by Richard McKeon. New York: Randon House, 1941.

Berns, Walter. *Freedom, Virtue and the First Amendment.* Chicago: Henry Regnery Co., Gateway Edition, 1965.

Cardozo, Benjamin. *The Nature of the Judicial Process.* New Haven: Yale University Press, 1921.

————. *The Paradoxes of Legal Science.* New York: Columbia University Press, 1928.

Chandos, John, ed. *"To Deprave and Corrupt . . .": Original Studies in the Nature and Definition of "Obscenity."* New York: Association Press, 1962.

Cleland, John. *Memoirs of a Woman of Pleasure: Fanny Hill.* New York: G. P. Putnam's Sons, First Paperback Edition, 1963.

Devlin, Patrick. *The Enforcement of Morals.* London: Oxford University Press, 1965.

Ellis, Albert. *The American Sexual Tragedy.* New York: Grove Press, Inc., 1962.

Ellis, Havelock. *On Life and Sex: Essays of Love and Virtue.* Garden City, New York: Garden City Publishing Co., 1937.

Ernst, Morris L., and Lindey, Alexander. *The Censor Marches On: Recent*

Selected Bibliography

Milestones in the Administration of the Obscenity Law in the United States. New York: Doubleday, Doran & Co., 1940.

Ernst, Morris L., and Schwartz, Alan U. *Censorship: The Search for the Obscene.* New York: Macmillan Co., 1964.

Ernst, Morris L., and Seagle, William. *To the Pure: A Study of Obscenity and the Censor.* New York: Viking Press, 1928.

Freud, Sigmund. *Civilization and Its Discontents.* Translated and edited by James Strachey. New York: W. W. Norton & Co., 1962.

Gardiner, Harold C., S.J. *Catholic Viewpoint on Censorship.* Garden City, New York: Doubleday & Co., Image Books, 1961.

Gebhard, Paul, *et al. Sex Offenders: An Analysis of Types.* New York: Harper & Row, 1965.

Gellhorn, Walter. *Individual Freedom and Governmental Restraints.* Baton Rouge: Louisiana State University Press, 1956.

Gerber, Albert B. *Sex, Pornography and Justice.* New York: Lyle Stuart, Inc., 1965.

Grazia, Sebastian de. *The Political Community: A Study of Anomie.* Chicago: University of Chicago Press, 1948.

Hamilton, Alexander; Madison, James; and Jay, John. *The Federalist Papers.* New York: The New American Library of World Literature, Mentor, 1961.

Hart, H. L. A. *Law, Liberty and Morality.* New York: Vintage Books, 1966.

Heller, Joseph. *Catch-22.* New York: Dell Publishing Co., 1961.

Jahoda, Marie. *The Impact of Literature: A Psychological Discussion of Some Assumptions in the Censorship Debate.* New York: Research Center for Human Relations, New York University, 1954.

Jefferson, Thomas. *The Living Thoughts of Thomas Jefferson.* Edited by John Dewey. Greenwich, Conn.: Fawcett Publications, Premier Books, 1963.

Kilpatrick, James Jackson. *The Smut Peddlers.* Garden City, New York: Doubleday & Co., 1960.

Kinsey, Alfred C., *et al. Sexual Behavior in the Human Female.* Philadelphia: W. B. Saunders Co., 1953.

Klapper, Joseph T. *The Effects of Mass Media.* New York: Bureau of Applied Social Research, Columbia University, 1949.

Kronhausen, Eberhard, and Kronhausen, Phyllis. *Pornography and the Law.* Rev. ed. New York: Balantine Books, 1964.

Kuh, Richard H. *Foolish Figleaves? Pornography in and out of Court.* New York: Macmillan Co., 1967.

Lawrence, D. H. *Lady Chatterley's Lover.* New York: The New American Library of World Literature, Signet Books, 1959.

————. *Sex, Literature and Censorship.* Edited by B. Harry T. Moore. New York: The Viking Press, Compass Books Edition, 1959.

Levy, Leonard. *Legacy of Suppression: Freedom of Speech and Press in Early American History.* Cambridge, Mass.: Harvard University Press, 1960.

Marcus, Steven. *The Other Victorians: A Study of Sexuality and Pornography in Mid-Nineteenth-Century England.* New York: Bantam Books, 1967.

McKeon, Richard; Merton, Robert K.; and Gellhorn, Walter. *The Freedom to Read: Perspective and Program.* New York: R. R. Bowker Co., 1959.

Meiklejohn, Alexander. *Political Freedom: The Constitutional Powers of the People.* New York: Oxford University Press, Galaxy, 1965.

Selected Bibliography

Mill, John Stuart. "On Liberty." *The English Philosophers from Bacon to Mill.* Edited by Edwin A. Burtt. New York: The Modern Library, 1939.

Miller, Henry. *Henry Miller on Writing.* Selected by Thomas H. Moore from the published and unpublished works of Henry Miller. Norfolk, Conn.: New Directions, Paperbook, 1957.

———. *Tropic of Cancer.* New York: Grove Press, Inc., First Black Cat Edition, 1961.

Milton, John. "Areopagitica." *Areopagitica and Of Education.* Edited by George H. Sabine. New York: Appleton-Century-Crofts, Inc., 1951.

Murphy, Terrence J. *Censorship: Government and Obscenity.* Baltimore: Helicon Press, 1963.

Paul, James C. N., and Schwartz, Murray L. *Federal Censorship: Obscenity in the Mail.* Glencoe, Ill.: Free Press of Glencoe, Inc., 1961.

Rolph, C. H., ed. *Does Pornography Matter?* London: Routledge & Kegan Paul, 1961.

———. *The Trial of Lady Chatterley.* Baltimore: Penguin Books, 1961.

Rousseau, Jean-Jacques. "Letter to M. d'Alembert on the Theatre." *Jean-Jacques Rousseau: Politics and the Arts—Letter to M. d'Alembert on the Theater.* Translated with notes and an introduction by Allan Bloom. Glencoe, Ill.: Free Press of Glencoe, 1960.

St. John-Stevas, Norman. *Obscenity and the Law.* London: Secker & Warburg, 1956.

Schram, Wilbur; Lyle, Jack; and Parker, Edwin B. *Television in the Lives of Our Children.* Stanford, Cal.: Stanford University Press, 1961.

Sorokin, Pitirim A. *The American Sex Revolution.* Boston: P. Sargeant, 1956.

Strauss, Leo. *Natural Right and History.* Chicago: University of Chicago Press, 1953.

Swift, Jonathan. *Gulliver's Travels. Gulliver's Travels and Other Writings by Jonathan Swift.* Edited by Ricardo Quintana. New York: Modern Library, College Editions, 1958.

Waples, Douglas; Berelson, Bernard; and Bradshaw, Franklyn. *What Reading Does to People.* Chicago: University of Chicago Press, 1940.

Weaver, Richard M. *Ideas Have Consequences.* Chicago: University of Chicago Press, Phoenix Books, 1948.

Wertham, Fredric. *Seduction of the Innocent.* New York: Rinehart & Co., 1953.

Wolfenden Report: *Report of the Committee on Homosexual Offenses and Prostitution.* Authorized American Edition. New York: Stein and Day, 1963.

Articles and Journals

Black, Hugo L. "The Bill of Rights." *New York University Law Review* 35 (1960): 865–81.

Cairns, Robert B.; Paul, James C. N.; and Wishner, Julius. "Sex Censorship; The Assumptions of Anti-Obscenity Laws and the Empirical Evidence." *Minnesota Law Review* 46 (May, 1962): 1009–41.

Elliott, George. "Against Pornography." *Harper's Magazine,* March, 1965: 51–60.

Henkin, Louis. "Morals and the Constitution." *Columbia Law Review* 63 (March, 1963): 391–414.

Selected Bibliography

Kalven, Harry, Jr. "The Metaphysics of the Law of Obscenity." *1960 Supreme Court Review*. Edited by Philip B. Kurland. Chicago: University of Chicago Press, 1960, 1–45.

Law and Contemporary Problems, vol. 20 (Autumn, 1955), *Obscenity and the Arts.*

Lockhart, William B., and McClure, Robert C. "Literature, the Law of Obscenity, and the Constitution." *Minnesota Law Review* 38 (March, 1954): 295–395.

―――. "Censorship of Obscenity: The Developing Constitutional Standards." *Minnesota Law Review* 45 (1960).

Magrath, C. Peter. "The Obscenity Cases: Grapes of Roth." *1966 Supreme Court Review*. Edited by Philip B. Kurland. Chicago: University of Chicago Press, 1966, 7–77.

Mead, Margaret. "Sex and Censorship in Contemporary Society." *New World Writing*. New York: The New American Library of World Literature, Third Mentor Selection, 1953, 7–24.

Meiklejohn, Alexander. "The First Amendment Is an Absolute." *1961 Supreme Court Review*. Edited by Philip B. Kurland. Chicago: University of Chicago Press, 1961, 245–66.

Schwartz, Louis B. "Morals Offenses and the Model Penal Code." *Columbia Law Review* 63 (April, 1963): 669–86.

Other Sources

American Law Institute, *Model Penal Code on Obscenity, No. 207.10* (tent. draft No. 6, 1957).

Acknowledgments

For whatever may be valid or useful in this study a great deal is owed to my former teachers and counsellors—Professors Herbert Storing, C. Herman Pritchett, and Joseph Cropsey. As my doctoral dissertation advisors, and then as colleagues, they have provided that vital combination of encouragement and searching criticism. Professor Cropsey's advice and guidance has been invaluable. Professor Storing's contribution is not confined to his detailed analysis and critique of the original manuscript. His teaching, by illuminating the ethical and theoretical dimensions of legal issues, has inspired this inquiry in more ways than he is probably aware of.

I am particularly appreciative for the generous Relm Foundation grant which enabled me to devote time to completion of the manuscript. To my friend Paul Eidelberg I am greatly indebted for a penetrating exploration of the text which resulted in some necessary changes. Valuable assistance has also been rendered by Professor Robert Horwitz and by Erica Aronson. And to my wife, Margaret, I am most grateful for so many hours of hard work, so many helpful comments and corrections, and so much indispensable patience and encouragement.

306

Index of Cases

United States

Great Britain

Index

309

Index

Index

Index

230

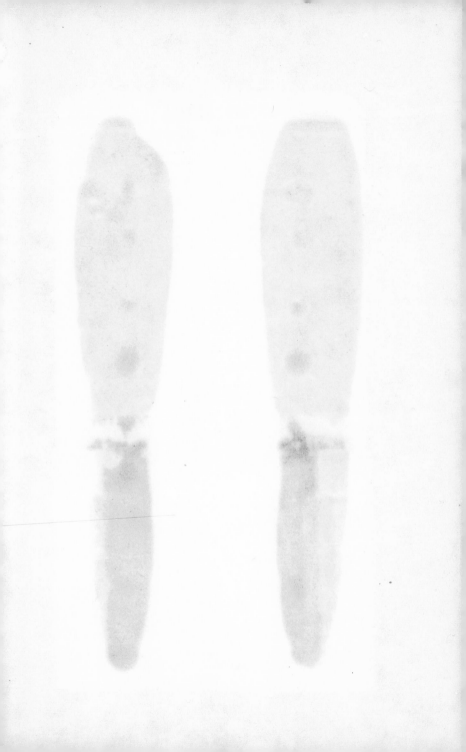